SACRED VOICES

SACRED VOICES

STORIES FROM THE CARAVAN OF WOMEN

Mariam Baker

Illustrated by Cynthia Dollard

SECRET ONE PUBLISHING
Fairfax, California

Secret One Publishing

*"Dedicated to the unfolding of personal
and planetary Peace"*

© 2018 Mariam Baker and Cynthia Dollard
All Rights Reserved.
No part of this publication may be reproduced, stored in a retrieval system, or transmitted, in any form or by any means, electronic, mechanical, photocopying, recording, or otherwise, without the written permission of the author.

Produced by Secret One Publishing, Fairfax, California

First published by Dog Ear Publishing, 4011 Vincennes Road
Indianapolis, IN 46268 www.dogearpublishing.net

ISBN: 978-145755-483-4

This book is printed on acid free paper.
Printed in the United States of America

SACRED VOICES

TABLE OF CONTENTS

Chapter 1 — **The Journey Begins**: *Overview of Islam*   1
      Creating Heart Space: *Embodied Prayer*   17

Chapter 2 — **Nomads in the Desert**: *The Path of Surrender*   25
      Creating Heart Space: *Purification*   49

Chapter 3 — **Love Human and Divine**: *Faith in the Friend*   53
      Creating Heart Space: *Divine Generosity*   77

Chapter 4 — **Gift of the Silk Route**: *Women in Early Islam*   83
      Creating Heart Space: *The Three Gifts*   113

Chapter 5 — **Prayer**: *Concentrated Conversation*   117
      Creating Heart Space: *Deep Listening*   135

Chapter 6 — **Being Human**: *Into the Twenty-First Century*   137
      Creating Heart Space: *Divine Guidance*   163

Chapter 7 — **Nourishing Body and Soul**: *Recipes*   164
      Recipe for Peace   182

Bibliography and Glossary   188

Foreword

In the true style of the feminine, this book is an invitation to an experience on many levels. You are about to embark on an adventure in sight, smell, touch, taste, movement, dreams and visions. It is not a book "about" a topic, although you will learn things about the *Sacred Voices* of women in Islam and Sufism. Those already familiar with this path are offered expansion through hearing women's voices. Others unfamiliar with the path of Islam and Sufism have the wonderful opportunity to enter this mystical path through these *Sacred Voices*.

Sacred Voices author, Mariam Baker, and illustrator, Cynthia Dollard, are both dervishes, practicing the turn as a deep and primary spiritual practice. As dervishes, they exemplify the meaning of the word as "one who stands in the doorway between the worlds." They have stood in this doorway, and have moved and whirled in and out of the worlds, for many years of their lives. They have shared the beauty of turning, not only through their whirling bodies, but also through words, art and story. They know what it means to be a woman, to hear the voice of Unity, to express the exquisite beauty of life in both worlds. They invite us to enter.

From the beginning of time, women's voices have offered us wisdom to live by, songs to lift our spirits or carry our sorrows, recipes for delicious nurturing food for body and soul, healing arts handed down from mother to daughter, though often passed in secret for fear of punishment or even execution. *Sacred Voices; Stories from the Caravan of Women* invites us to hear the voices from those who have been the "invisible ones," historically, culturally and spiritually.

Women's voices have influenced our world in significant and profound ways. Although invisible in history books, the voices of women have influenced history as they influenced the lives of husbands, friends, brothers and lovers who listened to them. And though publicly invisible, never seen to be recognized in face and body, or known by name, the voices of women have been heard through the men in their lives who listened to them, men whose faces and names were, and are, still recognized. And women's voices have been heard across the ages through the day-to-day lives of men and women living in small villages, towns and pueblos across the globe. Women's voices have primarily been heard at the gathering places for women, in ancient times around the fire, at wells drawing water, at rivers washing clothes, and modern day equivalents across backyard fences, in grocery lines, at hairdressers, over tea, and throughout all times, whispered in hidden places.

We have heard the adage, "Behind every great man there is a woman." It is beyond time that the greatness of women's wisdom is spoken and heard directly from women themselves. It is time for names and faces that were, and are, carriers of some of the wisdom that has guided the world to be known. We are grateful that authors such as Mariam Baker continue to unveil information, truths, and wisdom acknowledging their true origins in the *Sacred Voices* of women. This recovery strengthens the role of women and heightens our sensitivity to women's voices directly in our modern world today.

"The time is now." You will hear these words often through Mariam Baker. She carries this alert, this call to action, this call to integration and to balance, wherever you find her. The earth is crying for stronger efforts to heal her body from the destruction perpetually wrought by corporate greed, which feeds upon the greed of its populations. We long for these *Sacred Voices* in this day, where the consequences of division, hierarchy, and oppression are violence, aggression, war, hunger and homelessness. We long for them and search for answers and hope to quiet the anguished cries of humanity at home and abroad.

Sacred Voices. We hear them and long to hear them louder and stronger; in this day, where across this planet we experience deep yearning to manifest "a consciousness of Oneness"; in this time, where, from UN speeches, to unknown voices on social media platforms, people repetitively call out, cry out, invite, demand and also celebrate expressions and actions toward "Unity."

This unity is sought across many of the distinctions and differences that are part of the universe expressing itself, in and through the beauty of diversity. However, where these "distinctions and differences divide" us (in the words of Sufi teacher, Hazrat Inayat Khan), we seek to uncover the underlying Unity. This means that all expressions of the diversity, which includes diversity of sex and sexuality, must be brought to awareness and offered respect. All the *Sacred Voices* come to the table to be heard. First comes the possibility for large-scale healing, then the possibility for the boundless creativity of co-creation.

Elizabeth A. Reed, Ph.D.
Executive Director, Shalem Center
Columbus, OH

May 1, 2018

Dedication

This book is dedicated to personal and planetary Peace. The author and illusrator wish for this work to widen understanding and tolerance of both the commonality of our humanity, and the great diversity of experience which allows for the variety of human expression. May all who open this volume find some benefit and may that benefit spread to all of humanity.

Acknowledgements

The co-creators gratefully thank The Shalem Center and all the many people who have helped to bring this work to completion. We would especially like to thank Marlowe Rafelle, whose expert editing has been an integral part of the process.

We are extremely grateful to the women who agreed to share their stories in the interviews included in this book, and to our families and friends who believed in this vision and gave steady support throughout its germination and completion.

May each person who has supported the unfolding of *Sacred Voices* feel the profound gratitude of its creators, including all of those who supported us in the Infinite realm, as well as that Mysterious One who gave us this assignment.

Notes to the Reader

You are invited to settle into the world of *Sacred Voices*. The text includes eleven interviews with women representing various aspects of experience. Some of the women interviewed have chosen to use a pseudonym in order to remain anonymous.

The Prophet Muhammad is referred to throughout the text. Traditionally, the phrase, "Salla Allahu alayhi wa sallam" (May God's peace and blessings be upon him, often abbreviated as PBUH), usually follows the Prophet Muhammad's name in formal works. The author has abstained from placing this phrase within the text in order to address a wider audience. The Muslim reader is invited to personally formulate this prayer as he or she reads.

Any errors found within this volume are solely the responsibility of the author.

Eyes are at rest. The stars are setting.
Hushed are the stirrings of birds in their nests,
Even the Life in the Ocean has stilled.

You are the Just, who knows no change,
The Balance that can never swerve,
The Eternal, which never passes away.

The doors of Kings are bolted now and guarded by soliders.
Your Door is open to all who call upon You.

Each love is now alone with his Beloved
And I am alone with You.

—Rabia of Basra

Introduction

SACRED VOICES is a story of profound beauty and generosity as evoked through poetry, oral tradition and recipes for the soul and the body. *Sacred Voices* speaks first to the Heart of our human existence, from the experience of women in the great circle of time, past, present and future. The foundation of the sacred psychology of SoulWork supports the weaving of the threads of many voices, unique, individual, and united in one resonating voice for Peace within and without.

Sacred Voices calls upon the inner and outer voices and reality of women from multicultural, multigenerational, multi-temporal existence to the organic unfolding story of human life. The art, poetry, recipes for body and soul, and stories from the oral tradition invite the reader into a world of experience accessing ancestors and women of today.

Sacred Voices affirms that it is time, now, in the twenty-first century, to move beyond and through internalized oppression and degradation of the last many millennia to claim the inherent beauty, power and wisdom that is our human birthright.

In the poignant unfolding of *Sacred Voices*, the human echo of pain and joy, love and suffering, giving and receiving, this women's wisdom is brilliantly alive. *Sacred Voices* lives below the superficiality of the mundane world and above the icing on the cake.

This book is an exploration of the sacred feminine within Islam, a belief system that has dominated the Middle East for over thirteen centuries. These pages present the lives of Muslim and Sufi women in both a historic and contemporary context. The intention is to create a journey into understanding through the direct, widely varying experiences of these women. This is an intimate story of lover and Beloved, a reflection of relationship with Allah, who is known as the One and Only Being.

This work contains dreams, narratives, recipes, scriptural passages, interviews, and poetry, grounded with suggestions for spiritual practices and meditation. Dreams throughout our recorded history have always been valued within the mystical journey. Within Sufism there is a well-developed science of dream interpretation. Within each chapter are the personal dreams experienced by the author while working on *Sacred Voices*.

Sacred Voices seeks to illuminate the essential nature of Islam, rather than provide an analysis or critique of the Muslim way of life and the practice of the Muslim faith, especially as it relates to women. This human approach uses the research methodology of "Organic Inquiry," rather than a scholarly or political reflection. Our primary resources for consideration are the life experiences and stories of the women presented. This is not a scholarly investigation into Islam. This is a book that is easily accessible to anyone wanting to know more about Islam.

Sacred Voices reflects experiences common to all women. The act of carefully listening to and respecting another's story is a direct action toward peace. Transmitting these stories to the wider audience opens the possibility of peace through understanding of the commonality of our human experience. This collection of women's wisdom and tradition has been gifted to me by teachers and friends in the exploration of the deep peace inherent in the sacred tradition of Prophet Muhammad. This is a book born of grace.

Sacred Voices is an exploration of female Muslim perceptions during a time of global struggle and violence: tribal warfare, religion-driven wars, post-colonialism; a global economy that is power-, sex-, wealth-, and commodity-driven.

We live in a time of consuming images of women in veils; the veil outlawed in certain countries, and punishable as crime if one does not follow the proscriptions of country and culture. It is a time of secularization and modernization for women, a time of exploitation and empowerment. The backlash and war against women and children, the war against tenderness and mercy, escalates. There is violence in the home, in the field and in the marketplace. We learn of the warring Caliphates, ISIL and Boko Haram.

Have you ever been afraid to speak your truth? We are trained to fit within the parameters of dominant leadership and authority when we speak, or we are told, "Don't talk! Shut up!" Brutal family domestic violence can arise around the attempt to exercise the freedom to speak or choose not to. "Who are you to speak?" "Back down and sit quietly."

There is a strident and driving emotion on the planet manifesting in militaristic attacks on women and girls. Without the opportunity to speak and articulate one's truth, we never achieve masterful communication and confidence in our Voice. This is true of not only of women but also of those who have a generational or racial inheritance of enslavement, unworthiness and internalized oppression.

WHOSE VOICE?

In deconstructing the patriarchal paradigm, within the spiritual and religious community, the honoring of the voice of women is imperative. The ones with no voice are diminished and discounted, ineffectual in the political and everyday world.

The intention of this book is to be a reflection of beauty, wisdom, strength and generosity. The cyclical and spiral nature of experience allows for the inclusion of complexity and paradox, mystery and diversity.

The psychological and physical binding of women through the ages, in some places continues, in others, is exploding with questions and action, as women become free in their bodies and minds; as women increase self-esteem and release the imprint of abject servitude. In some global areas, women are gaining greater education and equal status economically.

Women have been viewed through the lenses of prophecy, sainthood, mastery, virginity, mother, daughter, mystery sexual object, siren and spirit. Do these idealizations lead us toward Peace, Unity, Wholeness, and the ability to honor and respect our true nature as sons and daughters of God? We are fortunate to be discovering many of the lost stories and identities of women heroes of this time.

WHAT IS SACRED?

The approach of this book is that every member of our human family is sacred; every rock, plant, animal is sacred; the stars and sun and moon are sacred. Why are we sacred? We can begin with the premise that we are the sons and daughters of the One and Only Being, who is called by many names. In this text we honor the sacred name of Allah.

We are sacred, holy, blessed. When we speak our story, we give the gift of our life. Each story is of value and important, just as each cell of our body is of value and important. Respect and deep listening and hearing as we read the interviews within *Sacred Voices* is an approach that will deepen our understanding of what it is to be a Muslim woman in this time.

The Caravan of Women is a caravan traveling through time and space moving ever toward Unity with all beings; at times, within recorded history, this caravan has been respected, and at times, the target of hatred, bias, prejudice, abuse and violence.

In this context we focus on the voices of a few Muslim and Sufi women, and we enter into a history/herstory of Islam to familiarize ourselves with the manifest reality of these women, the story of their lives, and how they have chosen to be sacred.

We honor the reality that exists within the maleness and femaleness of every living being. In concentrating on the feminine principle, we do not divorce from the male community, rather we hold the intention that through this focus on *Sacred Voices,* we may actively and consciously move toward gender reconciliation and Peace.

The intention of *Sacred Voices* is to reflect some of the beauty and wisdom of this small sample of women who walk the Sufi and Muslim paths. May this be fulfilled in our increased understanding of human nature. May respect for Life, the Earth and all Beings be enhanced. May our active responsibility towards our bodies, our minds, as well as our families and jobs, be enhanced. May our generosity to all beings within and without be enhanced. May it be so.

Voice is a potent blessing. Let us expand this blessing within ourselves as we stretch to inclusivity for those who are different, for those whom we do not understand. Let us expand this blessing within ourselves, opening to those parts that we may abhor or that cause discomfort, opening to hearing all our voices. We observe judgment; we release judgment; inhaling, exhaling centered in the Heart, breathing, hearing the Sacred.

Let us listen, relax and allow all our sacred voices.

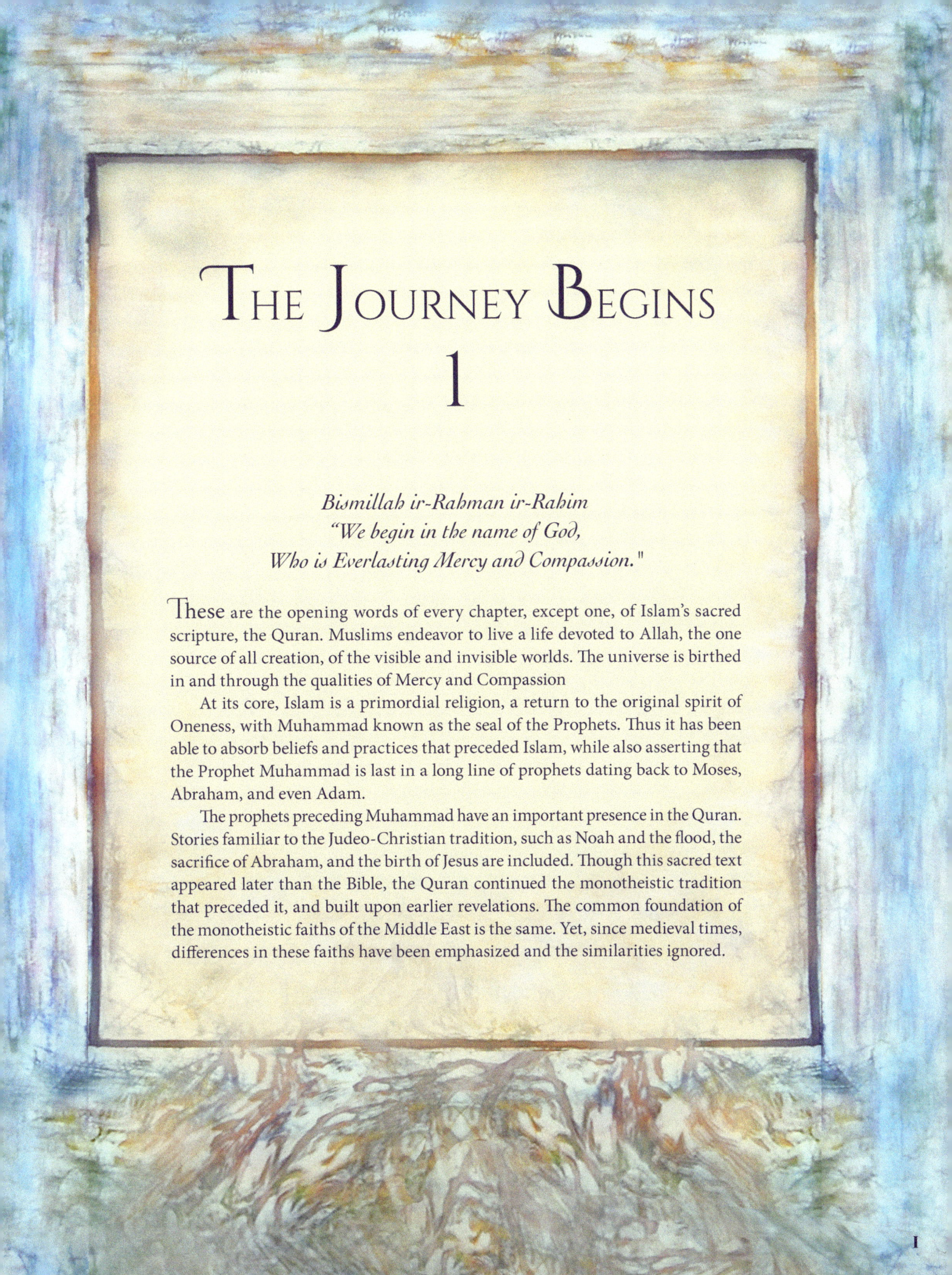

THE JOURNEY BEGINS
1

Bismillah ir-Rahman ir-Rahim
"We begin in the name of God,
Who is Everlasting Mercy and Compassion."

These are the opening words of every chapter, except one, of Islam's sacred scripture, the Quran. Muslims endeavor to live a life devoted to Allah, the one source of all creation, of the visible and invisible worlds. The universe is birthed in and through the qualities of Mercy and Compassion

At its core, Islam is a primordial religion, a return to the original spirit of Oneness, with Muhammad known as the seal of the Prophets. Thus it has been able to absorb beliefs and practices that preceded Islam, while also asserting that the Prophet Muhammad is last in a long line of prophets dating back to Moses, Abraham, and even Adam.

The prophets preceding Muhammad have an important presence in the Quran. Stories familiar to the Judeo-Christian tradition, such as Noah and the flood, the sacrifice of Abraham, and the birth of Jesus are included. Though this sacred text appeared later than the Bible, the Quran continued the monotheistic tradition that preceded it, and built upon earlier revelations. The common foundation of the monotheistic faiths of the Middle East is the same. Yet, since medieval times, differences in these faiths have been emphasized and the similarities ignored.

DREAM SEQUENCE

I remove my shoes quickly, replacing them with a pair of house slippers from the shelf by the door. The intoxicating aroma of baking bread draws me down a dark hallway into the arms of Abla, my Turkish older sister. Women are bustling around the kitchen, busy with pots and pans in preparation for a feast. I remain in the warmth of Abla's arms for a moment before being greeted and embraced by the others. We are preparing for the wedding of Gulshan, one of the beautiful young daughters. Esin is stirring the large vat of fresh milk heating on the stove to pasteurize. She turns to me and says,

"Welcome, we have been waiting for you!"

MYSTICAL TRADITION

Although Sufism has origins in Islam, as a mystical tradition, it draws on the wisdom of all the prophets, emphasizing the similarities at the root of their message to humanity. Sufi ceremonies often begin by invoking the sacred phrase, *Bismillah ir-Rahman ir-Rahim*, evoking the mercy and compassion of the realization of the God ideal.

In Islam and in Sufism, one strives to become fully human in a multidimensional sense. The individual strives to be an emissary for the compassion and mercy of the Beloved, fully participating in the divine plan of God, and in the unique destiny that is the divine inheritance of every person.

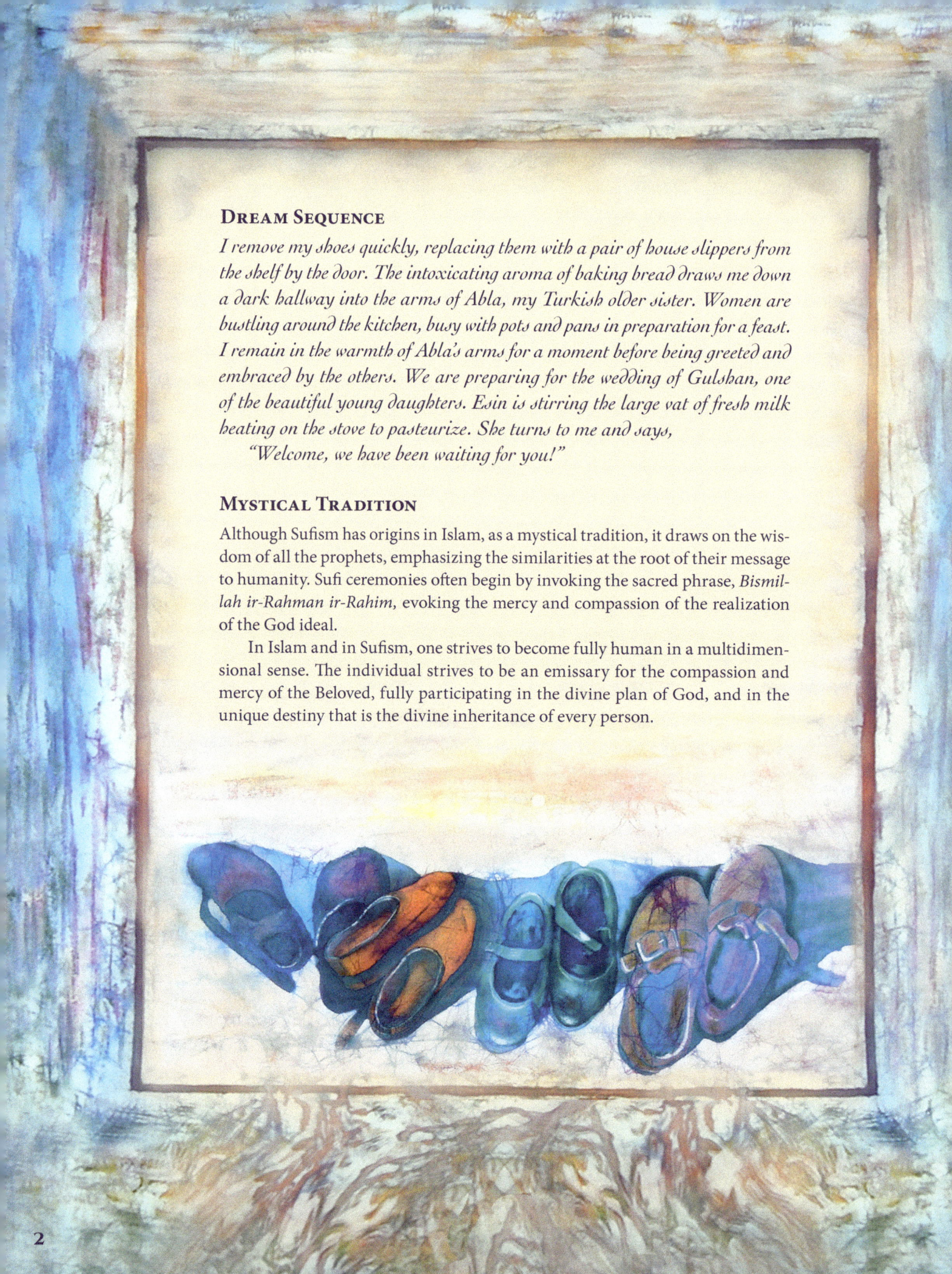

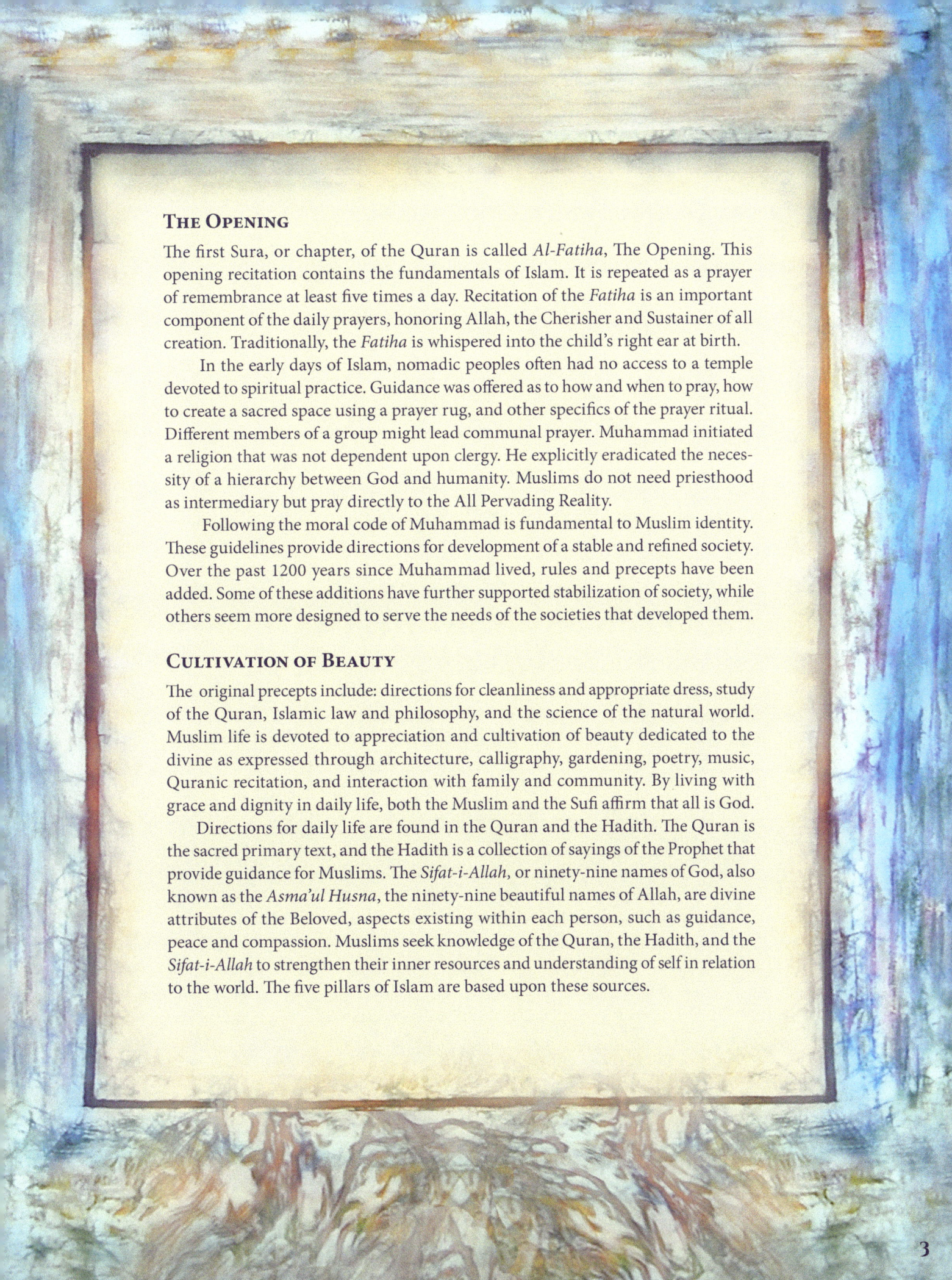

The Opening

The first Sura, or chapter, of the Quran is called *Al-Fatiha*, The Opening. This opening recitation contains the fundamentals of Islam. It is repeated as a prayer of remembrance at least five times a day. Recitation of the *Fatiha* is an important component of the daily prayers, honoring Allah, the Cherisher and Sustainer of all creation. Traditionally, the *Fatiha* is whispered into the child's right ear at birth.

In the early days of Islam, nomadic peoples often had no access to a temple devoted to spiritual practice. Guidance was offered as to how and when to pray, how to create a sacred space using a prayer rug, and other specifics of the prayer ritual. Different members of a group might lead communal prayer. Muhammad initiated a religion that was not dependent upon clergy. He explicitly eradicated the necessity of a hierarchy between God and humanity. Muslims do not need priesthood as intermediary but pray directly to the All Pervading Reality.

Following the moral code of Muhammad is fundamental to Muslim identity. These guidelines provide directions for development of a stable and refined society. Over the past 1200 years since Muhammad lived, rules and precepts have been added. Some of these additions have further supported stabilization of society, while others seem more designed to serve the needs of the societies that developed them.

Cultivation of Beauty

The original precepts include: directions for cleanliness and appropriate dress, study of the Quran, Islamic law and philosophy, and the science of the natural world. Muslim life is devoted to appreciation and cultivation of beauty dedicated to the divine as expressed through architecture, calligraphy, gardening, poetry, music, Quranic recitation, and interaction with family and community. By living with grace and dignity in daily life, both the Muslim and the Sufi affirm that all is God.

Directions for daily life are found in the Quran and the Hadith. The Quran is the sacred primary text, and the Hadith is a collection of sayings of the Prophet that provide guidance for Muslims. The *Sifat-i-Allah*, or ninety-nine names of God, also known as the *Asma'ul Husna*, the ninety-nine beautiful names of Allah, are divine attributes of the Beloved, aspects existing within each person, such as guidance, peace and compassion. Muslims seek knowledge of the Quran, the Hadith, and the *Sifat-i-Allah* to strengthen their inner resources and understanding of self in relation to the world. The five pillars of Islam are based upon these sources.

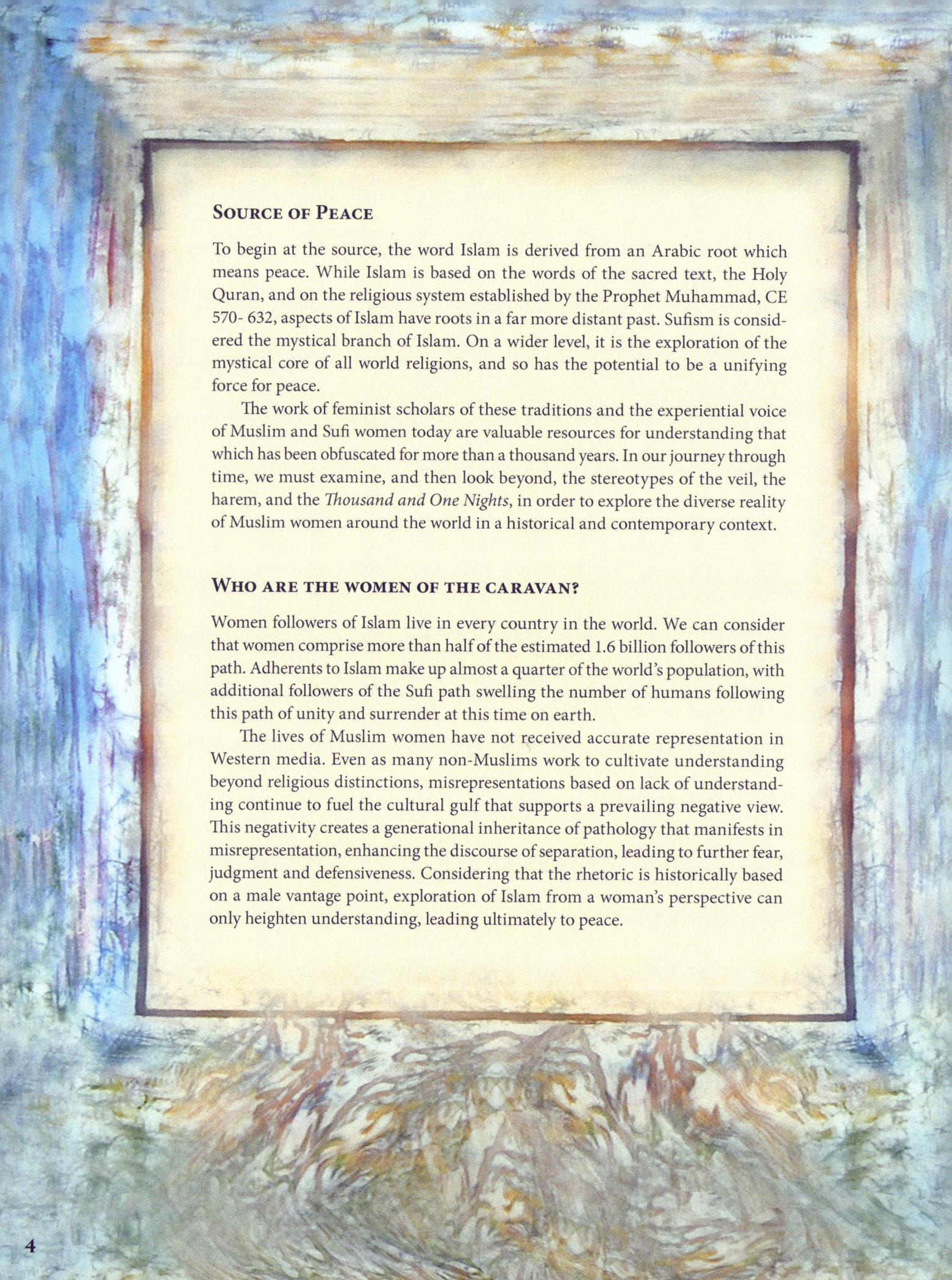

SOURCE OF PEACE

To begin at the source, the word Islam is derived from an Arabic root which means peace. While Islam is based on the words of the sacred text, the Holy Quran, and on the religious system established by the Prophet Muhammad, CE 570- 632, aspects of Islam have roots in a far more distant past. Sufism is considered the mystical branch of Islam. On a wider level, it is the exploration of the mystical core of all world religions, and so has the potential to be a unifying force for peace.

The work of feminist scholars of these traditions and the experiential voice of Muslim and Sufi women today are valuable resources for understanding that which has been obfuscated for more than a thousand years. In our journey through time, we must examine, and then look beyond, the stereotypes of the veil, the harem, and the *Thousand and One Nights*, in order to explore the diverse reality of Muslim women around the world in a historical and contemporary context.

WHO ARE THE WOMEN OF THE CARAVAN?

Women followers of Islam live in every country in the world. We can consider that women comprise more than half of the estimated 1.6 billion followers of this path. Adherents to Islam make up almost a quarter of the world's population, with additional followers of the Sufi path swelling the number of humans following this path of unity and surrender at this time on earth.

The lives of Muslim women have not received accurate representation in Western media. Even as many non-Muslims work to cultivate understanding beyond religious distinctions, misrepresentations based on lack of understanding continue to fuel the cultural gulf that supports a prevailing negative view. This negativity creates a generational inheritance of pathology that manifests in misrepresentation, enhancing the discourse of separation, leading to further fear, judgment and defensiveness. Considering that the rhetoric is historically based on a male vantage point, exploration of Islam from a woman's perspective can only heighten understanding, leading ultimately to peace.

The Fatiha

In the name of Allah, the most Gracious,
The most Merciful Praise be to Allah,
The Cherisher and Sustainer of the Worlds;
Most Gracious, Most Merciful,
Master of the Day of Judgment,
Thee do we worship,
And Thine aid do we seek.
Show us the straight way,
The way of those on whom Thou hast bestowed
Thy Grace, those whose portion is not wrath,
And who go not astray.
—Amen

Holy Water

No one lives outside the walls of this
    Sacred place called existence.
The holy water that I need upon my eyes is
    You, dear, you
        Each form of you.

You cannot wander anywhere that will not aid you.
    Anything you can touch,
        God brought it into the classroom of your mind.
        Differences exist, but not in the city of love.

Thus my vows and yours, I know they are the same.
    No one lives outside the walls of this
    Sacred place called existence.
The holy water my soul's brow needs is unity.
    Love opened my eye and I was cleansed by the
    Purity of each unique form.

—Rabia al Basri

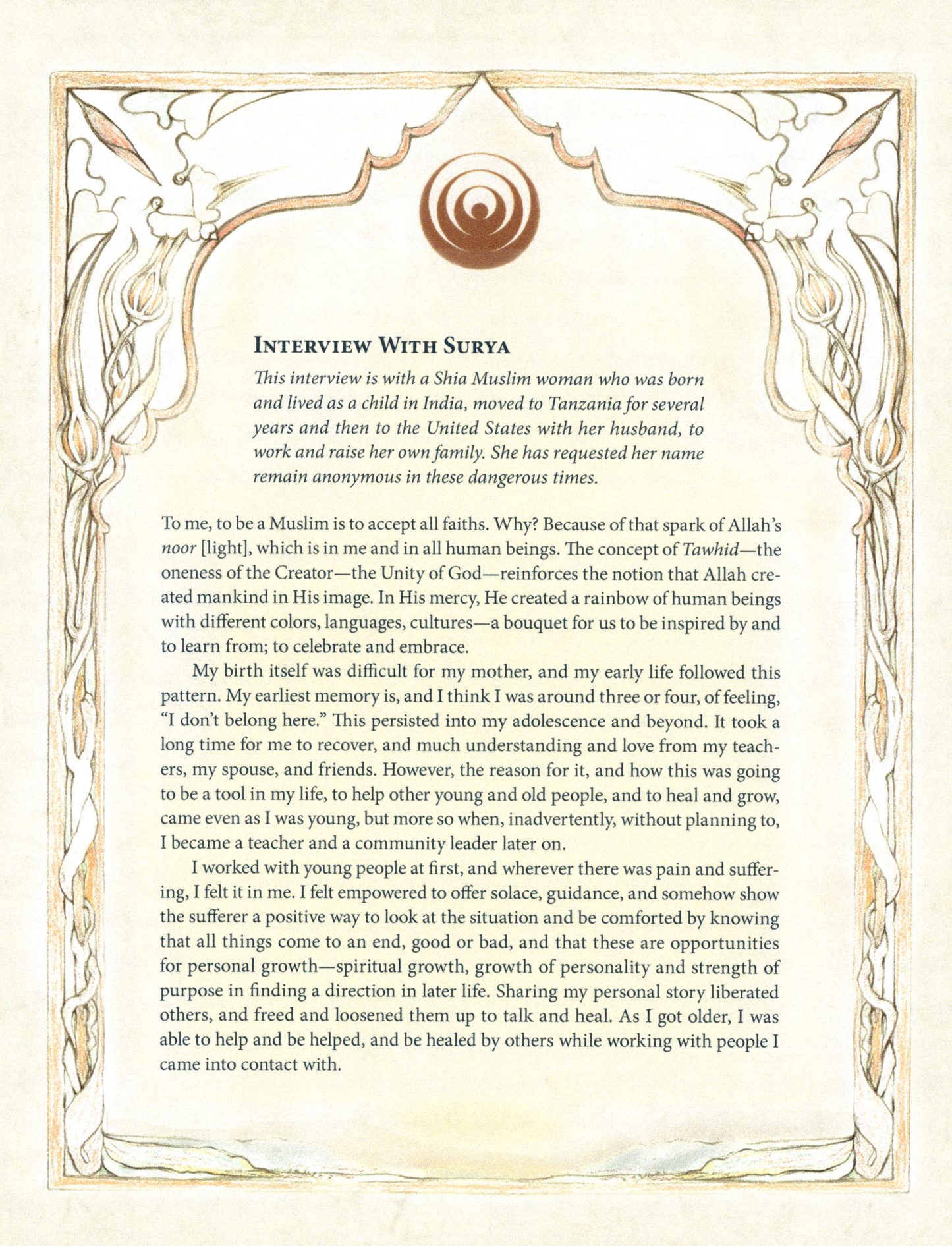

Interview With Surya

This interview is with a Shia Muslim woman who was born and lived as a child in India, moved to Tanzania for several years and then to the United States with her husband, to work and raise her own family. She has requested her name remain anonymous in these dangerous times.

To me, to be a Muslim is to accept all faiths. Why? Because of that spark of Allah's *noor* [light], which is in me and in all human beings. The concept of *Tawhid*—the oneness of the Creator—the Unity of God—reinforces the notion that Allah created mankind in His image. In His mercy, He created a rainbow of human beings with different colors, languages, cultures—a bouquet for us to be inspired by and to learn from; to celebrate and embrace.

My birth itself was difficult for my mother, and my early life followed this pattern. My earliest memory is, and I think I was around three or four, of feeling, "I don't belong here." This persisted into my adolescence and beyond. It took a long time for me to recover, and much understanding and love from my teachers, my spouse, and friends. However, the reason for it, and how this was going to be a tool in my life, to help other young and old people, and to heal and grow, came even as I was young, but more so when, inadvertently, without planning to, I became a teacher and a community leader later on.

I worked with young people at first, and wherever there was pain and suffering, I felt it in me. I felt empowered to offer solace, guidance, and somehow show the sufferer a positive way to look at the situation and be comforted by knowing that all things come to an end, good or bad, and that these are opportunities for personal growth—spiritual growth, growth of personality and strength of purpose in finding a direction in later life. Sharing my personal story liberated others, and freed and loosened them up to talk and heal. As I got older, I was able to help and be helped, and be healed by others while working with people I came into contact with.

To be religious is to belong to humanity, and know that I was created to leave this world a better place, by being who I am, living the ethics of Islam, of compassion and sharing—charity is not just sharing of one's material wealth, but of one's physical, intellectual and spiritual wherewithal. The ethic of voluntarism is therefore a cornerstone of Muslim tradition, celebrated in the *Ansar* [helpers]—the people of Medina who gave refuge to Prophet Muhammad and his followers when he emigrated to Mecca to escape persecution.

The unfortunate, and those at the margins of existence, have a moral right to society's compassion, to be empowered to make good their life and become self-reliant. "Man shall have only that for which he labors," says the Quran. Self-help is encouraged in the Prophetic traditions: "Man cannot exist without constant effort." "The effort is from me; its fulfillment comes from God." The greater effort of the charitable has therefore been to help the needy to become self-reliant. Care of the sick and disabled, too, is articulated in the Quran. The ethic of respect for life and health care is emphasized in the Holy Book; the saving of one life is equated to the saving of the entire humanity.

The ethic of sound mind—any substance that interferes with normal functioning of the mind is a violation of the ethical code, as it impairs one's judgment and it amounts to self-inflicted loss of dignity and of the ability to fulfill one's responsibility to oneself, the family, and the society.

With the gift of intellect given to us, we have the not always easy task of using moral reasoning to make right choices to live life ethically. The way we live our lives encompasses the rules of Islam. "There are many ways to kneel and kiss the ground." Religious traditions and cultures have common values. Islam is a way of life. It provides a road map and gives us a moral compass. ❧

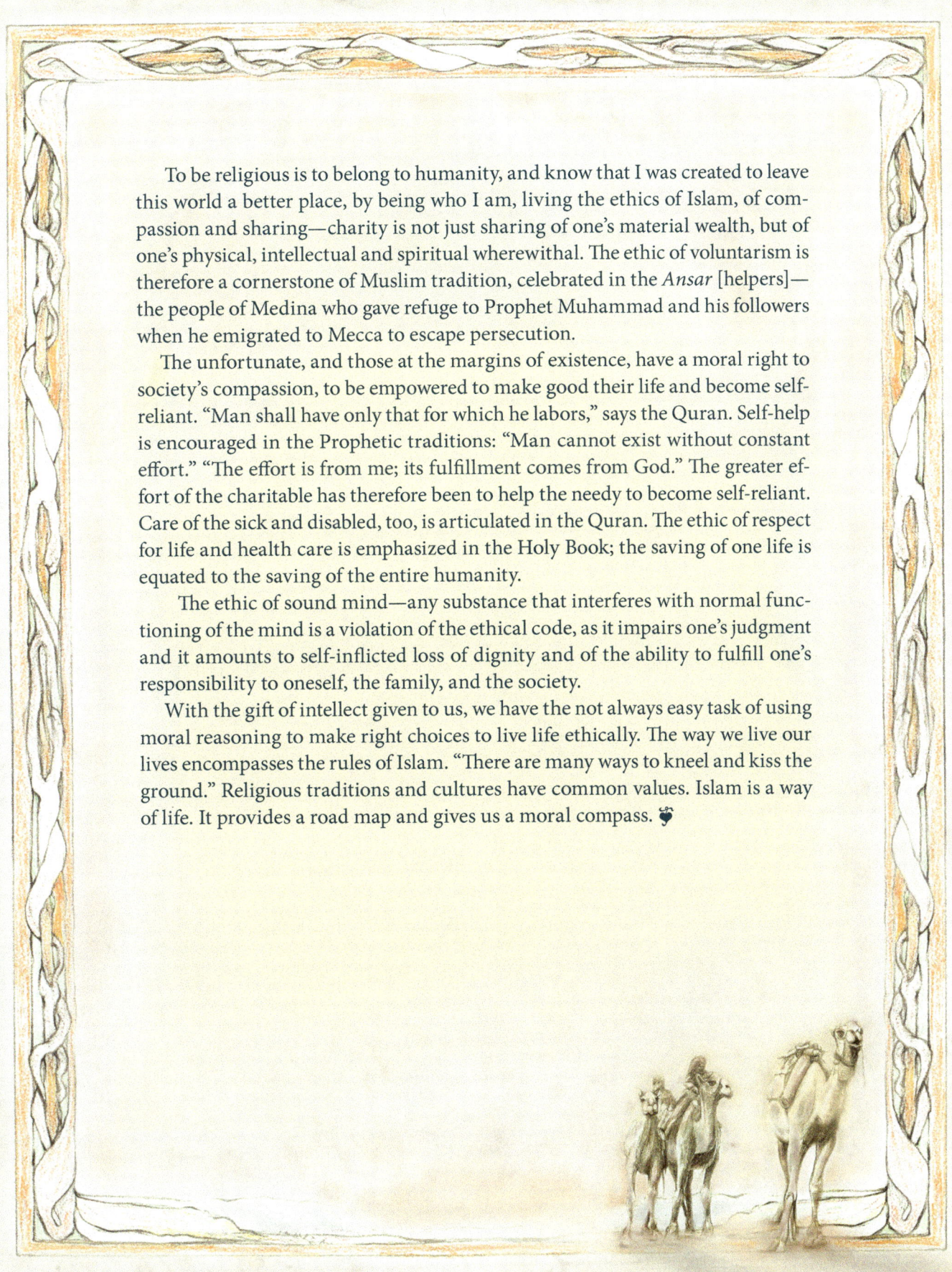

The Tale that Needs Retelling

Biased stories resulting in misconceptions about Muslims date back to the birth of Islam. This dichotomy was strengthened in Western society by the Christian Crusades, the "Holy Wars" carried out between the eleventh to fifteenth centuries throughout the Middle East and Asia Minor. In more recent times, the actions of Islamic extremists have strengthened societal prejudice. Yet, in reality, the Islamic faith is rooted in a commitment to remembrance of God, reflected in a life of compassion and mercy towards fellow humans. Throughout history, Islamic women have lived their lives in expression of this foundational tenet of the faith.

Like histories of other civilizations throughout the world, Muslim history includes stories of greed and oppression—of misrepresentations of faith. Many devout Christians are appalled by interpretations of the Bible that inspire followers to stray from the way of Jesus' message of love and forgiveness. This is also true of many Muslims who are deeply disturbed by interpretations of their sacred text, the Quran, which vacillate from the way of the Prophet Muhammad as understood by the majority of followers.

The small minority of extremists who use the sacred text to justify unholy violence have colored the view of non-Muslims toward this profound book of peace. The Quran remains a place of comfort and peace for the vast majority of devout Muslims. The Prophet Muhammad's way of gentleness and acceptance is reflected within the sacred text. While language of the Quran reflects the tribal culture of Muhammad's time, the guidelines for life and spiritual practice bring great comfort to the devout in modern times.

Global Responsibility

We live in a time when the human race is catapulted into a new arena of personal and communal responsibility, as we face problems that threaten our survival as a species. Within the intricate web of cultures that comprises our diversity as human beings, we must explore the common nature of this shared humanity while embracing the refuge of traditions and practices that form the structural foundation upon which life is built and enriched. We will explore how the tenets of Islam address the responsibilities inherent in a civilized society, in a very specific and direct way, in relationship to self, to one another, and to God.

Throughout history, humans have depended upon one another for their survival. The focus on individual expression is very recent in the trajectory of human societal development.

As Western cultures embrace the doctrine of individualism, there is a natural weakening of the web that holds a society together. Our interdependence as a species will be nurtured through our shared compassion, strengthened by the feminine asset of empathic listening. We live globally, to a lesser or greater degree, in a culture both patriarchal and hierarchical, a place where women are often excluded from teaching roles and positions of power. This is the direct result of thousands of years of human history in which women were not viewed as being equal to men, but as sexual objects, workers, or delicate creatures unfit for responsibility, or, at best, suited to domestic servitude in the home. The remnants of this ancient prejudice and maltreatment of women are part of the complexity of understanding the lives of women, and understanding is key to transformation and empowerment. As humanity faces unprecedented challenges, the intuitive approach and more hidden strength of feminine compassion provides a remedy with far-reaching implications

The Muslim standard of human justice, as given in the Quran, and exemplified in the life of Prophet Muhammad, provides a blueprint for improving conditions for women and for all of humanity. Muhammad delivered an inspired message that reversed the existing cultural status quo of tribal life. In direct opposition to common tribal practices of the time, the Quran specifically addresses the issues of abuse and discrimination. Abusive and animalistic treatment of women is not the way of Muhammad or true Islam.

The protection for women that Islam offers can be very attractive to western women who have been harassed as sexual objects within a materialistic, promiscuous, and sexually driven society, dominated by film and electronic media. Those who have a negative view of Islam can have difficulty comprehending this trend towards the simplicity of purification and refinement inherent in its practice. We will investigate the original teachings of the Prophet Muhammad and the Quran relating to the role of women, with the intention of opening the doors of wider perceptions as we move towards illumination and understanding.

No frivolity will they hear therein, nor any taint of ill, only the saying, "Peace, Peace, Peace."

—Quran, Sura 56: 25-26

INTERVIEW WITH ZARINA

Zarina, born in Tanzania to a large extended family of Shia Imami Ismaili Muslims, is an intelligent, elegant and modestly dressed woman. The Shia Imami Ismaili Muslims are a branch within Islam that follows the Imamat of Hazrat Ali, through Ismail [Ishmael, son of the biblical Abraham/Ibrahim] and continuing lineage through H.H. Prince Aga Khan III.

Within this sect of Islam, the instruction is to harmonize with the culture in which one lives. Zarina does not wear Hijab in her everyday life. Culturally and historically, this community traces routes from the loss of the Fatimid Caliphate in Egypt to the highlands of Syria, Lebanon, and the mountains of Iran. Today this group is found throughout the Islamic world.

Zarina's father, to the dismay of his father, journeyed to Tanzania from India in the early 1900s to make his own way. Successful in all his business ventures, he eventually brought his parents, siblings, and their families to East Africa. Zarina's youth and education was in Tanzania. After marriage, she worked in both the French and American Embassies. Concerned for the education and future of her two young children, she left with her son, daughter, and husband for the United States in 1970. This was a volatile time in Africa, the time of Idi Amin and great political upheaval, which has continued into the present time.

We meet for lunch and to share sohbet (spiritual discussion) relative to the subject of women and Islam. She is a mother and grandmother, professionally employed in the United States. Both her children follow the Muslim faith. She is devout and practices, in a quiet and simple way, the five pillars of Islam. Following are her comments on the spiritual reality of Islam in her every day life.

I never question my life, as I surrender to the will of Allah. Allah is the river; we are raindrops. The living guide tells us how to live in the corporal, temporal, and spiritual world. I am so lucky to have this guidance. Unity—*Tawhid*, is the essence.

I have not made *Hajj* [pilgrimage] yet. *Hajj* is not about proving I did it. The western media tells us nothing about Islam. They have no knowledge of the Quran. The terrorists have distorted Islam.

My religious guidance says: Educate your daughters more than you would your sons. When one educates a daughter, one educates a community. In the *Jamatkhana*, the Ismaili mosque, the men and women are separated, but side-by-side across an aisle. There are equal rights through the Prophet Muhammad. Our philosophy is that the body has two hands, two lungs, and two eyes—why not use and respect both? Prophet Muhammad and the Quran say we are equal spiritually and complimentary physically.

Prostration and prayer are important as well as constant *Fikr* [silent remembrance of Allah on the breath]. The true *Mu'min* [faithful one] does not seek *Jannah* [heaven]. The true *Mu'min* seeks to become One with Allah. Without service, *abd'Allah*, we are nothing.

Zakat, or the tithe, is a purification of all lawfully earned income. *Zakat* assures that whatever is consumed is pure by following the path of God and the Prophets, which is to give.

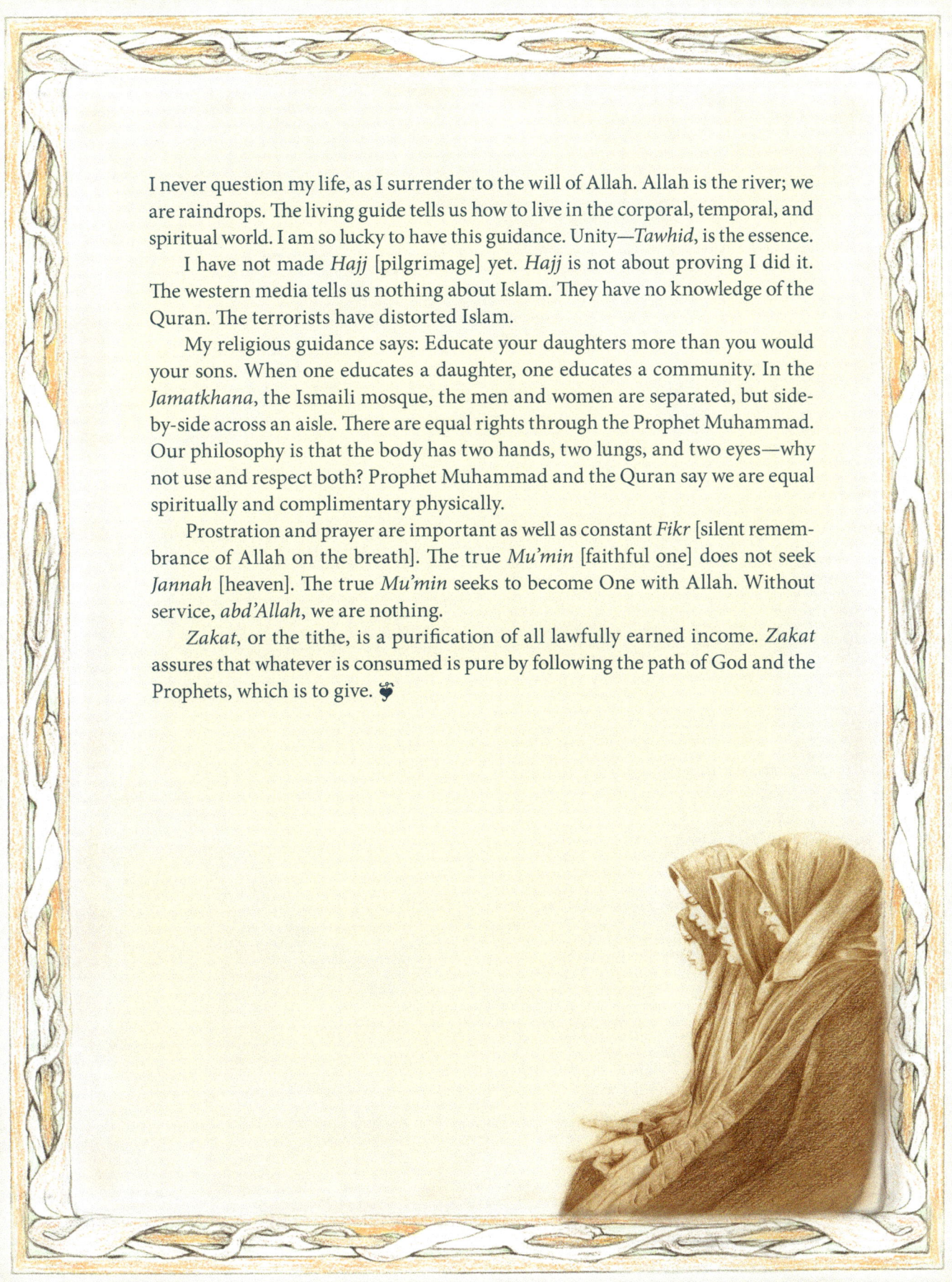

THE FIVE PILLARS OF ISLAM

Shahada—The first of the five pillars is an affirmation known as the *Shahada: la ilaha ilAllah hu—Muhammad Rasul Allah*. There is no reality except God and Muhammad is the Messenger of God. This phrase, spoken throughout the Muslim world, can also be understood as: There is no reality except the one Reality; or: God is everywhere, in all—no aspect of life is apart from Unity.

Salaat—The second pillar is *Salaat*, daily prayer. The practice of structuring the rhythm of life around cyclical prayer allows Muslims to take time out of the day, to leave worldly worries behind, and come into the remembrance of Allah, the Merciful, the Compassionate, and to connect with practitioners throughout the world as all turn in the direction of Mecca and put attention on God. The majority of Muslims follow the Sunni tradition, by praying five times a day, while the Shia branch of Islam calls for three daily prayers, and the Sufi endeavors to maintain a state of constant prayer.

Fasting—The third pillar is fasting. All Muslims are directed to fast during the lunar month of Ramadan. The purpose is to deepen spiritual focus and to develop discipline and empathy with those who lack sustenance. This practice also serves to commemorate the time when the holy Quran was revealed. Muslims strive to follow this directive unless ill, pregnant, nursing or traveling.

Zakat—The fourth pillar is *Zakat*, or charity, to those less fortunate. This is an annual requirement of all Muslims, and is a way to give back of all that has been received from Allah. As the generosity of the Beloved is celebrated through giving to others, the spiritual life of the practitioner is strengthened.

Hajj—The fifth pillar is *Hajj*, or pilgrimage, to the *Kaaba*, the most sacred site in Islam, birthplace of Muhammad, located in Mecca, Saudi Arabia. Every Muslim aspires to make this pilgrimage at least once in their lifetime. The site at Mecca was a holy site before Muhammad, and so has ancient roots as a center of spiritual pilgrimage and renewal.

> *The Compassionate has taught the Koran, created humans, taught speech.*
> *The sun and the moon are in harmony; and the plants*
> *And the trees prostrate, and the sky He has raised aloft,*
> *And He has established the measure of all things,*
> *So that you do not violate this measure but uphold it with justice,*
> *Without falling short.*
>
> —Quran, Sura 55: 1-9

CREATING HEART SPACE
RECIPES FOR PRACTICE OF THE SACRED

The beloved is as close as your jugular vein and as
Wide as the vast Universe beyond the realm of the stars into Infinity.
—Quran, Sura 50: 16

By moving beyond written words into integration of body, mind and heart—through practices of breath, spoken word, movement and deep stillness, we open ourselves to the vast mystery of the Infinite.

Sufis, often referred to as the mystics of Islam, say that Allah lives within the chambers of the heart. Therefore, to awaken our consciousness of the Divine, we cultivate the heart and the breath. Prophet Muhammad reminds us that God is closer than our jugular vein. The practices of Heart Space are directions for experiencing the beauty of the sacred in all aspects of life.

When one perceives the human race as one family, and this family as living in the reality of God, notions of "yourself" and "myself" begin to dissolve. There is then the opportunity to transcend the dichotomy of "self and other" through humility, respect and the experience of empathy.

These practices are not in any way a prescription for how to be a Muslim or Sufi, or even a description of what a Muslim does. They are signposts that provide directions to move toward understanding of another, deeper and more refined, aspect of the self.

THE PRACTICE OF EMBODIMENT

Body prayer has a long tradition in the Middle East and is also expressed in spiritual practices of all faiths. To enter the realm of embodied spirituality, make the intention to allow your entire being to participate in the prayer and meditation. The natural wanderings of the mind are part of the meditation process. Gentle, nonjudgmental observation is a key to unlocking the body's surrender to embodied prayer.

Divine Intention—Niyah

Niyah means to decide or determine to do something. It is the soul's willingness to perform some act after conceiving of it, and then acknowledging its advantage and judging its necessity. *Niyah* involves setting an intention and then bringing as much attention as possible to that intention. Bringing that approach into the practices presented in these pages will increase their benefit.

Intention is an essential part of every spiritual act. The intent with which one undertakes purification, prayer, fasting, pilgrimage, and acts of charity are important at every phase of a practice; from original inspiration, to commencement, to completion. Cultivation of this willingness of the soul, or *niyah,* can greatly enhance the consciousness around enactment.

Pause now, explore and consider your intention at this place in time and space relative to the possibility of living an awakened life. What is your intention relative to the understanding of the religion of Islam? The possibility exists for the essential peace of these practices to permeate the reader, whether one is a committed practitioner of Islam, Sufism, of another belief system, or an inquisitive seeker with no clearly defined faith structure.

Suggestions for Creating Sacred Space

Work with the Cycle of the Moon. The rhythm of creating sacred space and listening to the sacred voice within is based on the lunar calendar, which flows in twenty-eight day cycles. This rhythm rules the seas as well as the heaven, rules a woman's cycles, and the rise and fall of creative and receptive energies.

As you enter these practices, cultivate awareness of the rhythm of the waxing and waning of the moon. Within this meter of luminosity and shadow is the symbol of death and resurrection. The natural spiral of time is in harmony with the natural pulse of the galaxies, the oceans of the earth, and the lunar cycles of women's bodies. As we open, honoring and celebrating these rhythms in our lives, our endeavors gain energetic assistance from the Infinite.

Keep a Journal. Find a way that is natural for you to write of your experiences. Some suggestions are provided, although each person's guidance will direct how this will work best for her. For some, writing can be a cathartic means to access and develop inner wisdom.

Dream Record. For one lunar month, record your dreams, your feelings about the dreams, and lessons gained from this exploration.

Rhythm of Spiritual Practice. Keep a written record of your practices, experiences that result from these practices, and how the practices evolve.

Nourishment, Cravings and Desire. Cultivate awareness of conscious and unconscious patterns of how you nourish your body or eat from emotional need. Set the intention to record and notice rather than to judge. Explore how watching the pattern of craving can lead to the deepest root of that desire.

Create or Enhance a Space for Prayer and Meditation. Begin with emptiness. In traditional Islam, symbols or icons for God are avoided because God is beyond any human representation. Any rendering of God, Muhammad or the Prophets is seen as limiting. However, many find inspiration in images or objects that remind them of the inexpressible infinite by creating an altar, while others prefer simplicity to evoke emptiness and receptivity.

Altars traditionally face the east. In Islam, the orientation of prayer is toward Mecca, located in Saudi Arabia. Ultimately, the creation of a sacred space for prayer is personal, and will evolve with use. Consider the addition of a special rug or pillow to sit on, a candle, incense, a vase for flowers, or whatever evokes the infinite for you. This physical space is apart from the rest of life's distractions, and so helps to set the inner tone for deepening meditation and contemplation.

> *Into the veiled village of intention,*
> *Your love guides my way,*
> *Polishing the rust that clouds*
> *My heart's looking glass.*
>
> *A desperate lifetime spent*
> *At the tavern's door,*
> *That I might finally raise the goblet*
> *In which the vision of all worlds is revealed.*
>
> —Bibi Hayati

DIVINE ATTRIBUTES

The *Sifat-i-Allah,* or Ninety-Nine Divine Qualities of Allah, are attributes of God reflected in humans. Each chapter of this book includes one or more of these sacred phrases for concentration and contemplation. The term, *wazifa,* refers to these sacred phrases, or divine archetypes.

In Sufism, as in many mystical traditions, sacred phrases are used as remembrance, mantras for concentration and contemplation, and to keep the mind focused on divine attributes. Since the mind can only focus on one thing at a time, continuing to return to the sacred phrase and breath throughout the day can help to move past cycling thoughts and bring quiet to the mind.

Breathe: *Ya Rahman Ya Rahim,* Inhale Mercy; Exhale Compassion
Body prayer has along tradition in the Middle East. To activate this tradition in your own being, begin with the breath. This is the practice of allowing oneself to enter the realm of embodied spirituality and allowing the entire being to participate in the prayer and meditation. Throughout the meditation, allow the breath to be equally balanced between the inhalation and exhalation. Inhale for a count of four; exhale for a count of four.

Sitting Meditation

Place yourself in a comfortable sitting position, spine erect yet relaxed. Practice the following spoken prayer, using the opening line of the Quran:

Bismillah ir-Rahman ir-Rahim

In the name of God, who is Mercy and Compassion. This also translates as, "In the name of God, all Merciful, All Compassionate," or, "In the name of the One; In the name of the Beloved."

Speak the word, *"Bismillah,"* in the name of God, into the heart center in the middle of the breast. Speak *"ir-Rahman"* to the right, invoking the divine quality of Mercy, and *"ir-Rahim,"* to the left, invoking the divine quality of Compassion.

Envision all reality beginning as the sound moves into the heart chakra; envision mercy and compassion radiating from horizon to horizon as the head travels from right to left to right. Repeat eleven times. Allow free association to arise in the mind. Contemplate the reality of mercy and compassion in your life. Breathe mercy and compassion.

Focus on yourself; focus on the world. Know you are meditating on this reality of compassion and mercy with others in the seen and unseen world. Let each inhaled breath radiate mercy, each exhalation, compassion. Imagine these qualities dripping like life-giving rain from the fingertips into our lives and for all beings.

Ya Rahman, Ya Rahim

Mercy, Compassion, flowing into and through the DNA of our humanity.

Standing Meditation

The body is in an erect standing position radiating compassion from the heart center. Focusing on *ir-Rahman* (Mercy) and *ir-Rahim* (Compassion), balance tension and relaxation within the body. Allow the energy to radiate outward from the heart, eyes, hands, voice, and the entire energy field of the body.

 Begin to open and extend the arms outward from the heart center, as energetic rays permeating the space, with the remembrance of the quality of *ir-Rahman* (Mercy), palms extended outward. Let the palms turn upward and allow the energy to travel from the heart through the arms and upturned palms, flowing like water down into the atmosphere, again infusing the space with the quality of *ir-Rahim* (Compassion). Repeat the entire cycle eleven times.

Walking Meditation

Now, add the movement of walking in a counter-clockwise circle. Fold your arms and cross them over the heart. Take a step with the right foot. Bring your feet together. Take a step with the left foot. Bring your feet together. Continue with the words, *Bismillah, ir-Rahman, ir-Rahim,* on one note. Allow the air to flow fully into the belly and lungs to sustain the sound. With each breath and each step is the remembrance and affirmation that all creation is Mercy and Compassion. Continue walking. Extend the arms and palms outward from the heart center, palms slightly downward as you breathe in *ir-Rahman*, Mercy. Keep the arms extended, lower slowly towards the earth and gently open the palms into a receiving gesture as you breathe out *ir-Rahim*, Compassion. Each footstep, plant Mercy, *Rahman;* each footstep plant Compassion, *Rahim.*

Let this concentration be simple and practical in daily life.
Rahman Rahim on the breath through our daily tasks and relaxation.

Love's Instruction

In the study of love, this heart is your
    devoted apprentice.
    As the night grabs the light at dusk,
    This love is clasping the daylight's feet.
    Wherever I wander,
This face of love is in front of me like oil,
    Forever in search of a lamp
    To fulfill its purpose.

Repetition of the name of God illuminates
    the full moon.
    This repetition returns the lost ones to the
    Path of truth.
Every morning and each evening
    Make this your word,
The saying of the sacred phrase
    "There is no God but God."

        —Rumi

For Palestine

Some people place their whole bodies
    Inside a dream
A woman steps out of a dream
    With fresh almonds wrapped in a towel
Holding them out
    To any open mouth.

—Naomi Shihab Nye

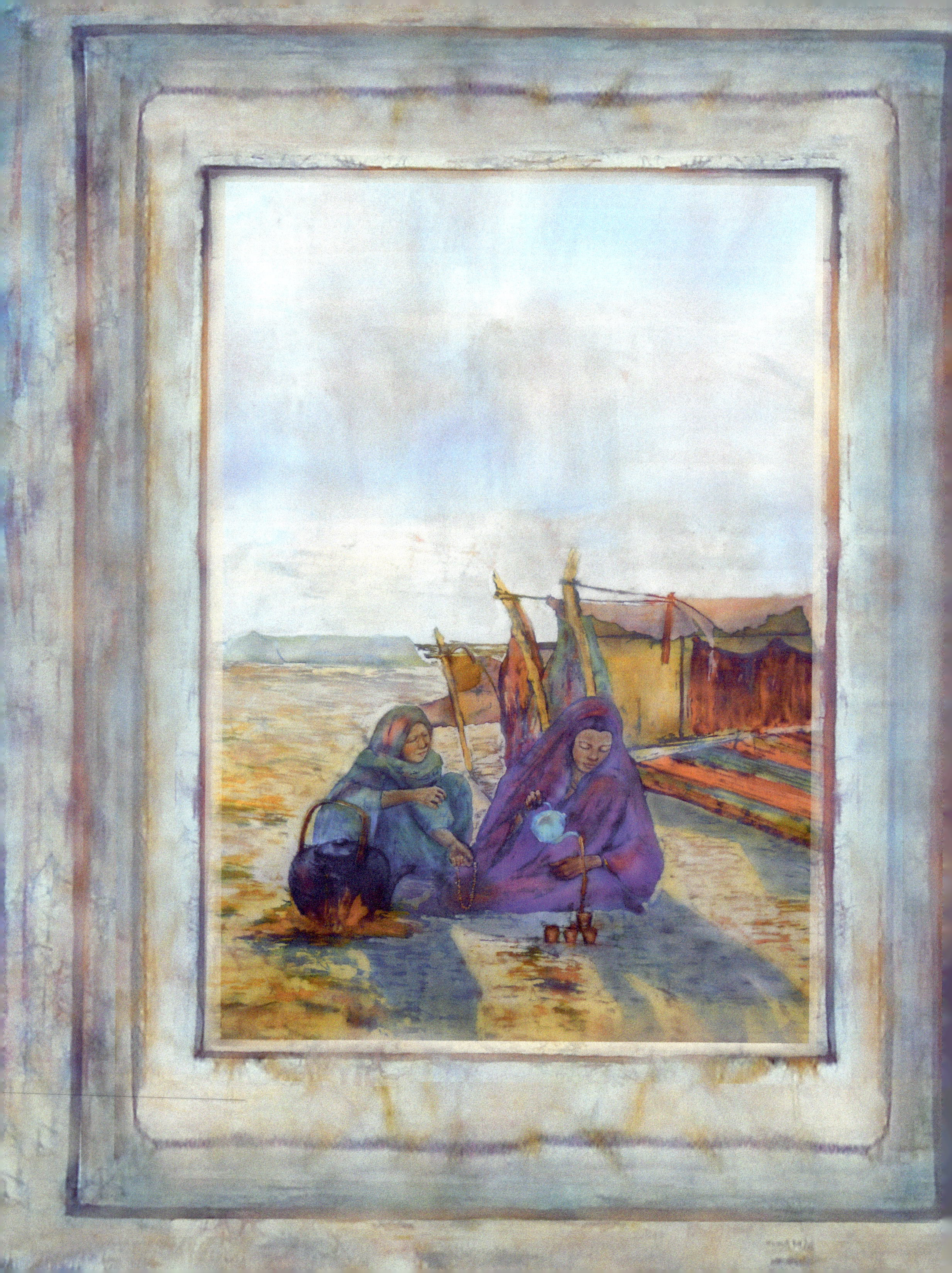

Nomads in the Desert 2

The Path of Surrender

The basic principle of Islam is absolute and complete submission to Allah, Unity, the One God. This God is beyond any name and form, beyond sexuality and gender, neither He nor She, but existing beyond our conceptions and comprehension, yet permeating all our being. This experience of God is both extremely personal and all encompassing, an experience cultivated by each individual in her own way and strengthened for many people by shared spiritual practice. For over one and a half billion humans on the earth at this time, this shared spiritual experience takes the face of the practice of Islam

Implicit within Islam is surrender to the will of God and the peace that ensues when one surrenders to the guidance of God, relinquishing the anxiety and anguish of the limited individual self. This concept of God is truly beyond definition, both universal and individual. The reader is invited to explore her relationship to this divine animating force, and to bring that Being to the reading of this work.

In the practice of Sufism, God is often referred to as "The Beloved," and it is said that through the act of breath and surrender, the Sufi swims in a vast ocean of love that permeates all things. This all-pervasive energy is always available as profound presence. One need only to remember. A primary practice of Sufism is *zikr*, "remembrance of God," through the repetition of sacred phrases.

DREAM SEQUENCE

I am running on a path in a cypress forest, which climbs a small hill. The old trees create a canopy of light and shade, and the delicious odor of fresh cypress is invigorating. The path ends in a courtyard. I recognize that it is part of the compound at the chapel of Mary in Ephesus, Turkey. There are many people; pregnant women, mothers with infants and toddlers, families with picnic baskets and blankets. Old men relax in the sun, chatting and playing backgammon. Behind a rock wall, I see only women, dressed in blue and white, by a bubbling spring. They are filling bottles with water, and performing ablutions; nearby is a table with jars of blue honey. I am greeted: "As-salaam Alaikum"—Peace be with you.

In the far corner, under an olive tree at the base of stone steps, there is a woman who is praying on a rosary, or tasbih *(prayer beads). She beckons me with her eyes and a slight nod of the head to come closer. I walk in her direction, and see that she is crying as she prays. I feel myself magnetically attracted to this woman even as I am embarrassed by my curiosity. Her soft and sorrow-filled voice intones; "Ya Raqib, Allah, Ya Rahman, Ya Rahim" – Oh Lord God, Oh Mercy, Oh Compassion. As I come closer, she lifts her face and opens her cloak. Inside the folds are the children of the world.*

Daily Life

The ideal of followers of Islam and Sufism is to become fully human; to become emissaries for the compassion and mercy of Allah, or Divine Unity. According to this ideal, the unique destiny and divine inheritance of every person is to fully participate in the divine plan of God. Spiritual practices can greatly aid this journey to a fuller humanity.

Muhammad explicitly eradicated the necessity of a hierarchy between God and humanity. He envisioned a religion with no need for an intermediary. The role of clerics and imams was originally a function of organization and a means to call worshipers to prayer. In some cases these positions of leadership have lead to misuse of power, but these actions do not accurately reflect the message of the Prophet. Early Islam was not a religion of segregated clergy. One prays directly to the all-pervading reality with no interpreter or counsel. This divine presence can be seen in the mirror of the heart and in the vastness of the starry, infinite reality.

Directions for daily life are found in the Quran and in the *hadith* (sayings) of Muhammad. *Sunna*, or proper behavior, includes following the rhythm of daily prayers, fasting, remembrance of the qualities of Allah, development of deep generosity of heart, and affirming the primary statement, *"La Ilaha Il Allah Hu, Muhammadur Rasulullah,"* or, "Nothing exists except God [God is within all things] and Muhammad is the Prophet of God." Muhammad's life is an example of the highest human ideal for both men and women. Muslims endeavor to live a life that embodies these qualities.

While Shia Muslims have different prayer cycles, and others in the world practice a range of ceremonies around the unity of Allah, the five-times-daily prayer remains the practice for the majority of Muslims. This marking of the day with periodic breaks for purification and deep remembrance adds a rhythm and peace to the bustle of life. Whatever a person's individual belief system, integration of a rhythm of prayer and practice into life can bring a fundamental peace and strengthen compassion for the common experience of humanity.

Oh, traveler on this caravan of love,
Leave worldly worries behind.
Come into the remembrance of Allah,
Who is All Mercy and Compassion.

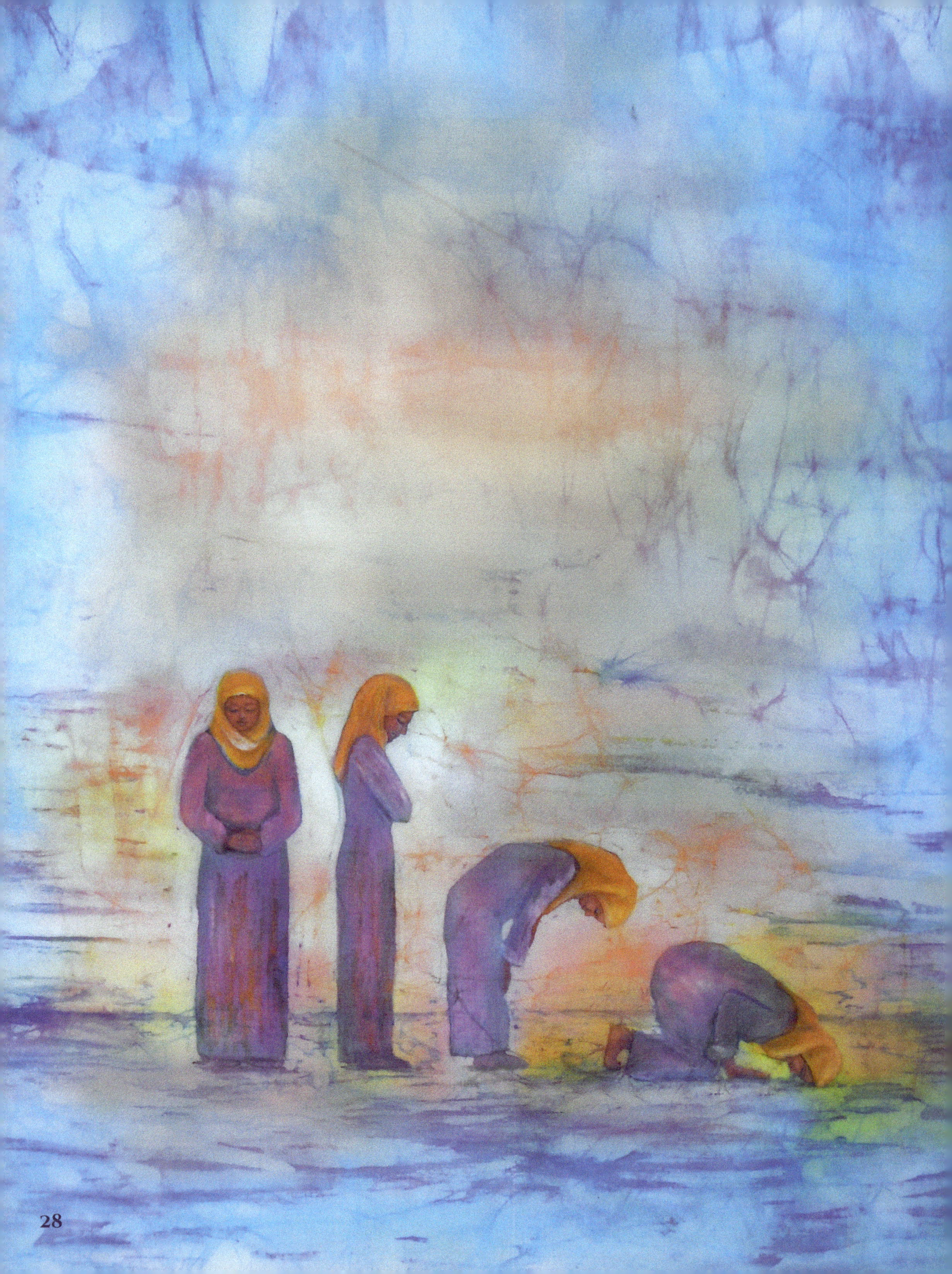

THE CUSTOM OF VEILING

Muslims reside throughout the world within a diversity of cultures. The message of Islam manifests in unique customs relative to the culture and climate of each country in which it is planted. Education is crucially important in discerning the difference between pre-Islamic cultural practice and what is considered to be proper behavior for a Muslim.

Customs associated with Islam include veiling and separation of women, a practice that often elicits a strong reaction from non-Muslims. The Quran calls for modesty in dress for both sexes, and this has been open to interpretation by various societies. The exact dictate of the Prophet Muhammad concerning veiling is a subject of debate.

There are places in the Middle East where use of the veil is compulsory, and others where it is prohibited. Interviews in the following pages will explore the attitudes held by Muslim and Sufi women on this practice. Generalizations about veiling can be a distraction that diverts attention from discovering the great variety of stories and wisdom that comprise the reality of Muslim women's lives.

Many Muslim women only cover their heads during times of prayer and when entering a mosque, holy site, or sacred gathering, although in some societies, Islamic dress has reached a high point of controversy. The veil and headscarf have become symbols of Islam, and, at times, the symbolism seems to have become more important than the inner dimensions of the faith.

Celebrate with praises, and do this often.
Glorify God morning and evening.
Praise the One who sends blessings to you,
As do the angels,
That you may be brought from darkness to light.
And be as one who invites God's grace,
As a lamp illuminates the darkness with its light.

—Quran, Sura 33: 42-46

HISTORIC WOMEN ROLE MODELS

Throughout the history of Islam, women have played primary roles, but many of their stories are lost to time. The Quran includes the stories of Adam and Eve, Noah and Lot, and their wives and daughters, as well as Jesus, Joseph, Jacob and Moses, patriarchs familiar to those of Judeo Christian background from stories in the Christian Bible.

While Eve is not mentioned by name in the Quran, the story of Adam and his wife eating the forbidden fruit is included in the text. In the Islamic version, the forbidden fruit is offered by the tempter demon Satan, known as *Iblis*, or *Shaitan*, in Arabic. This Quranic story is very similar to the story of Genesis and the Garden of Eden, Paradise.

The Quranic version holds that when the fruit was picked from the Tree of Knowledge, the tree bled. The ramifications of following the destiny of temptation biologically imprint Eve and her daughters with bleeding each month.

When viewed as a natural aspect of life, menstruation allows a woman to tune into her body in relation to the cycles of the moon, of the tides, and to the rhythm of other women. Traditionally, this is a woman's time to rest, turn inward, and honor the intuitive, hidden aspect of her being. The idea of this being an unclean time originated from a male perspective and is perhaps simply a matter of misunderstanding of the inner workings of women's reproduction.

Some theologians of the Jewish, Christian, and Islamic religions interpret Eve as the tool of Satan, representing the perceived inferior character of all women. This limited view holds that all women are susceptible to temptation in the realm of moral and religious action. In such an interpretation, Eve, her daughters, and all women are worthy of blame. Perhaps the origin of this point of view lies within a fear of the power inherent in the mysterious, intuitive shadow side of the feminine realm, as interpreted by a highly rational, logical, typically male aspect of human nature.

Throughout history, women living within societies where such belief systems were prevalent have cultivated the means to maintain the strength of the intuitive feminine nature, while living within cultures based on rational thought. Ultimately, the union of the intuitive, emotional aspect and the logical, rational aspect will lead to a well-rounded society and widening understanding. This begins with opening perceptions in the inner world.

الرَّزَّاقُ

HAGAR THE HANDMAIDEN

To tell the story of Hagar (*Hajar* in Arabic), mother of Ishmael (*Ismail*), one must begin with the story of Abraham, or Ibrahim, beloved patriarch and prophet of three religions: Judaism, Christianity, and Islam.

Abraham is considered to be the father of monotheism. According to the story, he suffered a trial by fire when he challenged the omnipotence of an earthly king, Nimrod, and was cast into prison. Nimrod commanded that he be burned to death. Abraham sank into the heart of the fire, where the angel *Jabril* (Gabriel) appeared, and asked him what he wanted. He replied that God already knew his unspoken desires. Abraham then emerged untouched by the flames.

He departed with his family and a band of people who followed the teachings of monotheism. They journeyed to Syria, Palestine and Egypt. In Egypt, the Pharaoh lusted after Abraham's beautiful wife, Sarah. As he reached out to touch her breast the Pharaoh's hand was paralyzed and withered. Sarah implored God to return his hand to its normal condition and, after much begging by the Pharaoh, his hand was returned to normal. Afterward, the Pharaoh freed Sarah, and offered her the gift of the Egyptian slave/princess, Hagar, as her handmaiden.

Sarah had not been successful in giving her husband his greatest desire: children. So, as a gift to her husband, she offered him her handmaiden Hagar, who became pregnant and gave birth to Ishmael. Sarah, honored in the position of first wife, became increasingly jealous of the handmaiden, who had replaced her in the role of mother to Abraham's first son, Ishmael.

Sarah was finally blessed with a son of her own, Isaac, which brought her great joy. After the birth of Isaac, Sarah insisted to Abraham that Hagar and Ishmael must be banished. In some versions of this tale, she also demands that Hagar must receive three cuts, believed by some to refer to female circumcision, or clitorectomy, and piercing of the earlobes.

Abraham took Hagar and Ishmael into the wasteland of the Arabian Desert, a place with harsh rocky terrain and no water. He was instructed by God to leave Hagar and Ishmael in this barren land. As Abraham prepared to leave, he gave Hagar a bag of dates and a skin container of water. Devastated, Hagar cried out that she and her child were too weak to survive the vast desert wilderness. She implored Abraham, "Did God tell you to do this?" Abraham affirmed that God had a plan for them and would protect them, allowing Hagar to then embrace her destiny with faith.

Struggling to survive and protect her son in this land of burning winds and sands that parched her mouth and skin, Hagar desperately sought a safe place for herself and Ishmael. She journeyed in anguish until eventually she came to Mount Safa, but saw neither water nor signs of human life. She continued on to Mount Marwah, and saw nothing but black rocks. Hagar traveled between these two mountains seven times, in an urgent effort to save herself and her child. In some versions of this story, Hagar's deep prayer and escalated need for water for her child turns the earth inside out as she runs back and forth between Mount Safa and Mount Marwah.

After her seventh attempt, as she stood anguished atop Mount Marwah, Hagar heard a voice and ran to her child, Ishmael. A radiant angel had appeared near him. The angel struck its wing upon the ground, and life-giving water gushed forth. Hagar and Ishmael drank deeply of this water as it bubbled forth from the earth. The water relieved their parched skin, and both were revived in heart and body. After they were rejuvenated from the life-giving water, Hagar protected the spring with earth and stone.

Soon after the appearance of the angel and the miracle of the spring, named *Zamzam*, a caravan of tribal Amalekites appeared on the distant horizon. They spotted birds circling on the horizon, and sent two men in advance to look for water. They questioned Hagar as to who she was and who owned the spring. Hagar explained how God brought forth the spring for them. They then asked her permission to bring their caravan to the spring, and she happily agreed. Tents were pitched, and there was wonder at the brightness and abundance of the water from the spring, and the radiant countenance of Hagar and Ishmael. Hagar remains an inspiring symbol of faith and Islamic identity, a symbol of blessing and success for the one who trusts in Divine Guidance.

Did the curls of those scattered locks learn from the hyacinth?
Or did the hyacinth learn its curls from those locks?
Did I learn to cry and weep from the songbird?
Or did the songbird learn its singing from me?

—Sahinah Shirazi

Should I weep for lack of provision
Or for the duration of the sojourn?
How shall I ever attain the Real Aim?
My provisions fall short.

Shall you punish me by fire,
Oh, Ultimate Aim of all desire?
In this lies both my fear's origin
And the source of all my hope.

—Rabi'a of Syria

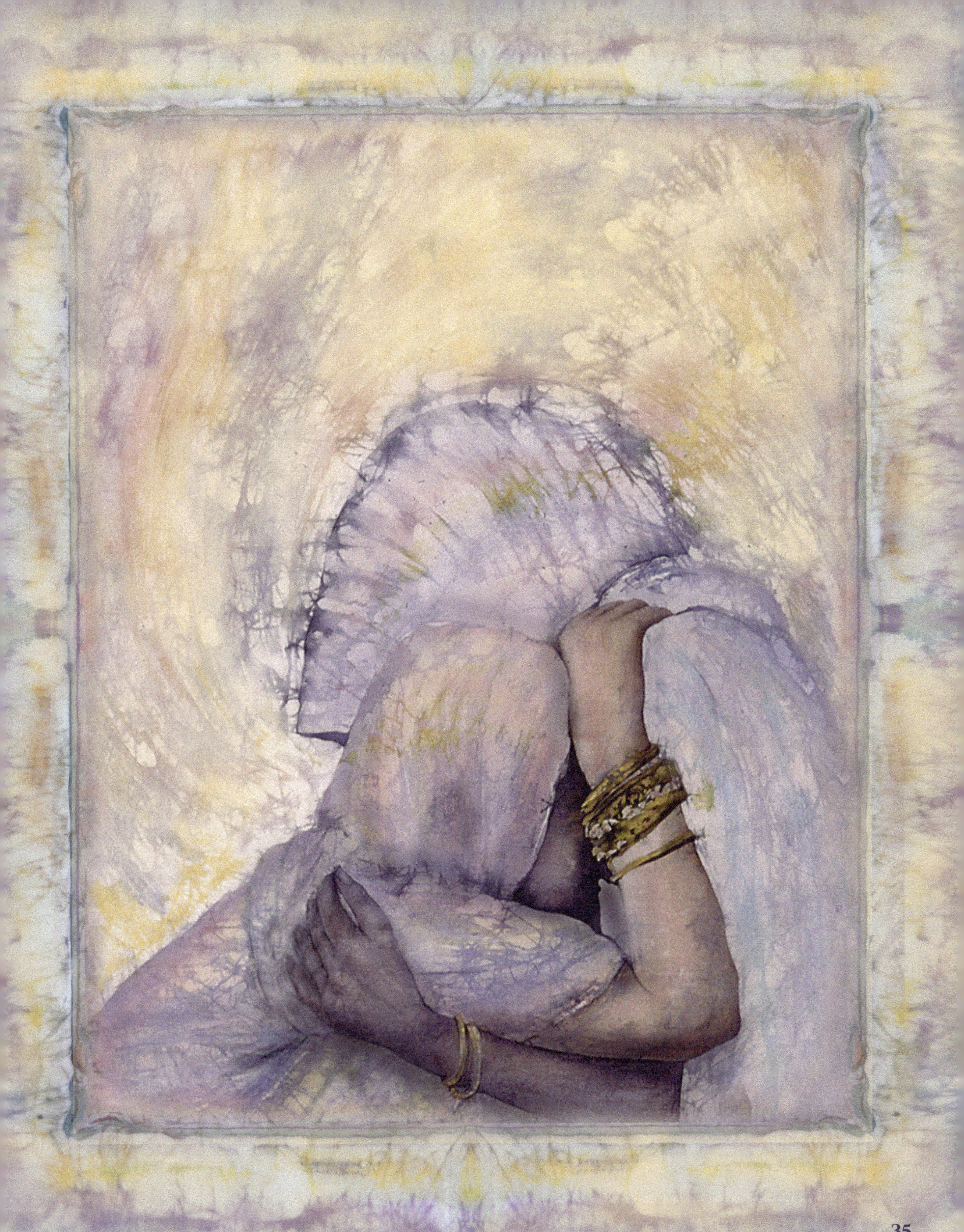

Jewels of Konya

With thanks to Aysel, Mufide, Mine, Ebru, Rahime, Derya, Esra, Esma and Sukrye who shared their thoughts over tea in a gathering that spanned three generations.

On Beauty

Physical beauty is not important. The heart's beauty is important.
It's important that your heart is good. A pure heart makes your face more beautiful.

On the Wisdom of God

The most important thing is that the soul must be pure to receive.
Clean the eyes, the ears, and the heart.
The world tests all the mystics. The world is a university. Our diploma is the work that we do here, and our respect, gratitude and service.
The new generation of women is awake, conscious.

On Holy Quran and following Islam

The Quran has revealed everything about the world.
We learn Islam from our family. Terror never includes religion.
We are Turkish Muslim women who pray.
The sky and the earth pray for healing all women victims.
In the early days of Islam, life was simple, not difficult.
Prophet Muhammad created a road and everyone followed.
In the past, *Hijab* was by parental decision.
Today Turkish Muslim women protest to wear *Hijab* in the university.
Islam today is difficult, like carrying fire in your hand. This is because of globalization, which makes the world small. There is little understanding of Islam outside of Islamic countries.
Now, optional actions are replacing good deeds.
    Pornography is spoiling new generations.

Zakat: Generosity

Hadith—Who goes to bed when his neighbor is hungry is not a Muslim.
A smile is *Zakat*.
In the Mevlevi Order, Islam is understanding, forgiveness (*Estagfurullah*), and unconditional love.
Don't compare my journey to God.
    Each of us is unique.
        Don't compare your journey.

Bringing the Past to the Present

During the ritual of the pilgrimage to Mecca, or the *hajj*, the pilgrim runs seven times between Mount Safa and Mount Marwah, as Hagar did when abandoned in the desert by Abraham. Pilgrims then drink water from Zamzam, the same water that, according to the story, arose under the angel's wing to nourish Hagar and Ishmael. It is a great gift to be offered this water from the *hajji* who has made the journey and drunk from the sacred spring. Bringing the sacred water home, as a gift to loved ones, is often done by those making the pilgrimage to Mecca.

While on a pilgrimage in Turkey with a group of Mevlevi dervishes, we were offered water from the well of *Zamzam* by the kind caretaker of the tomb and museum of *Haji Bektash*, a Sufi saint. Throughout the Islamic world, receiving the sacred water from Mecca is considered a great blessing.

This story exemplifies the aspect of compassion and mercy that gives strength in difficult times. While it is easy to feel the Beloved's loving grace in times of ease, the compassion and mercy of Allah become one's own when all else is gone, and all that remains is surrendering to a love beyond human understanding. The unlimited, life-giving water of *Zamzam* was offered to Hagar when she had nothing left, when she arrived at the point of complete surrender.

The discord between Muslim and Jew represents an ancient clash of cultures that begins before Isaac and Ishmael, with the story of Hagar and Sarah. Early political and economic components are evident in this story. Sarah is entitled and privileged as the favored wife. Hagar is a princess slave, daughter of Pharaoh, given to Sarah, given by Sarah to her husband, and eventually betrayed and abandoned by him. With no personal wealth and no rights, Hagar is completely dependent upon God's mercy.

And what will explain to you what the steep path is?
   It is the freeing of a slave from bondage;
     Or the giving of food in a day of famine to an orphan relative,
        Or to a needy person in distress.
  Then will He be of those who believe,
    Enjoying fortitude and encourage kindness and compassion.

—Quran, Sura 90: 12-17

Interview with Shahinaz el Hennawi

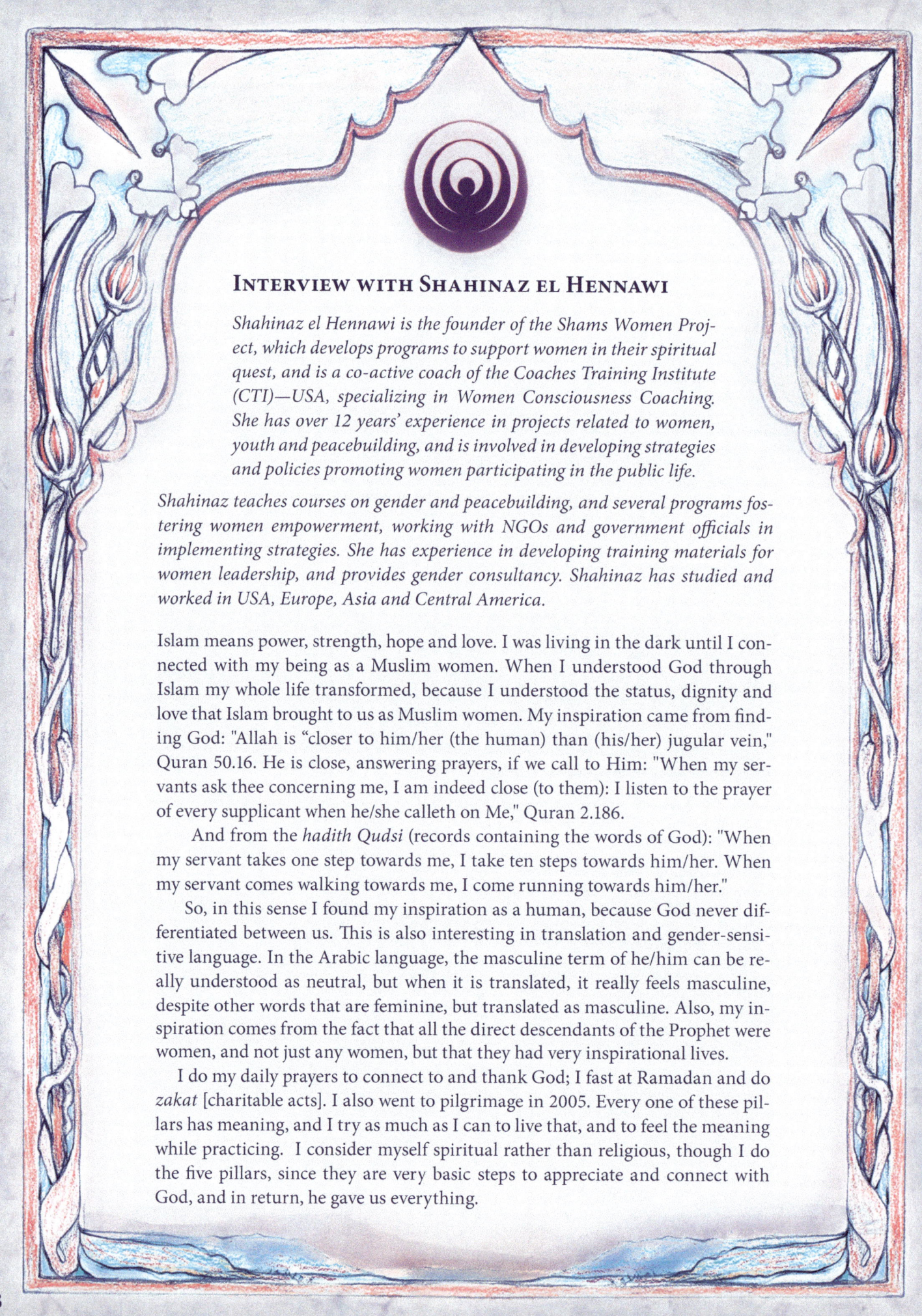

Shahinaz el Hennawi is the founder of the Shams Women Project, which develops programs to support women in their spiritual quest, and is a co-active coach of the Coaches Training Institute (CTI)—USA, specializing in Women Consciousness Coaching. She has over 12 years' experience in projects related to women, youth and peacebuilding, and is involved in developing strategies and policies promoting women participating in the public life.

Shahinaz teaches courses on gender and peacebuilding, and several programs fostering women empowerment, working with NGOs and government officials in implementing strategies. She has experience in developing training materials for women leadership, and provides gender consultancy. Shahinaz has studied and worked in USA, Europe, Asia and Central America.

Islam means power, strength, hope and love. I was living in the dark until I connected with my being as a Muslim women. When I understood God through Islam my whole life transformed, because I understood the status, dignity and love that Islam brought to us as Muslim women. My inspiration came from finding God: "Allah is "closer to him/her (the human) than (his/her) jugular vein," Quran 50.16. He is close, answering prayers, if we call to Him: "When my servants ask thee concerning me, I am indeed close (to them): I listen to the prayer of every supplicant when he/she calleth on Me," Quran 2.186.

And from the *hadith Qudsi* (records containing the words of God): "When my servant takes one step towards me, I take ten steps towards him/her. When my servant comes walking towards me, I come running towards him/her."

So, in this sense I found my inspiration as a human, because God never differentiated between us. This is also interesting in translation and gender-sensitive language. In the Arabic language, the masculine term of he/him can be really understood as neutral, but when it is translated, it really feels masculine, despite other words that are feminine, but translated as masculine. Also, my inspiration comes from the fact that all the direct descendants of the Prophet were women, and not just any women, but that they had very inspirational lives.

I do my daily prayers to connect to and thank God; I fast at Ramadan and do *zakat* [charitable acts]. I also went to pilgrimage in 2005. Every one of these pillars has meaning, and I try as much as I can to live that, and to feel the meaning while practicing. I consider myself spiritual rather than religious, though I do the five pillars, since they are very basic steps to appreciate and connect with God, and in return, he gave us everything.

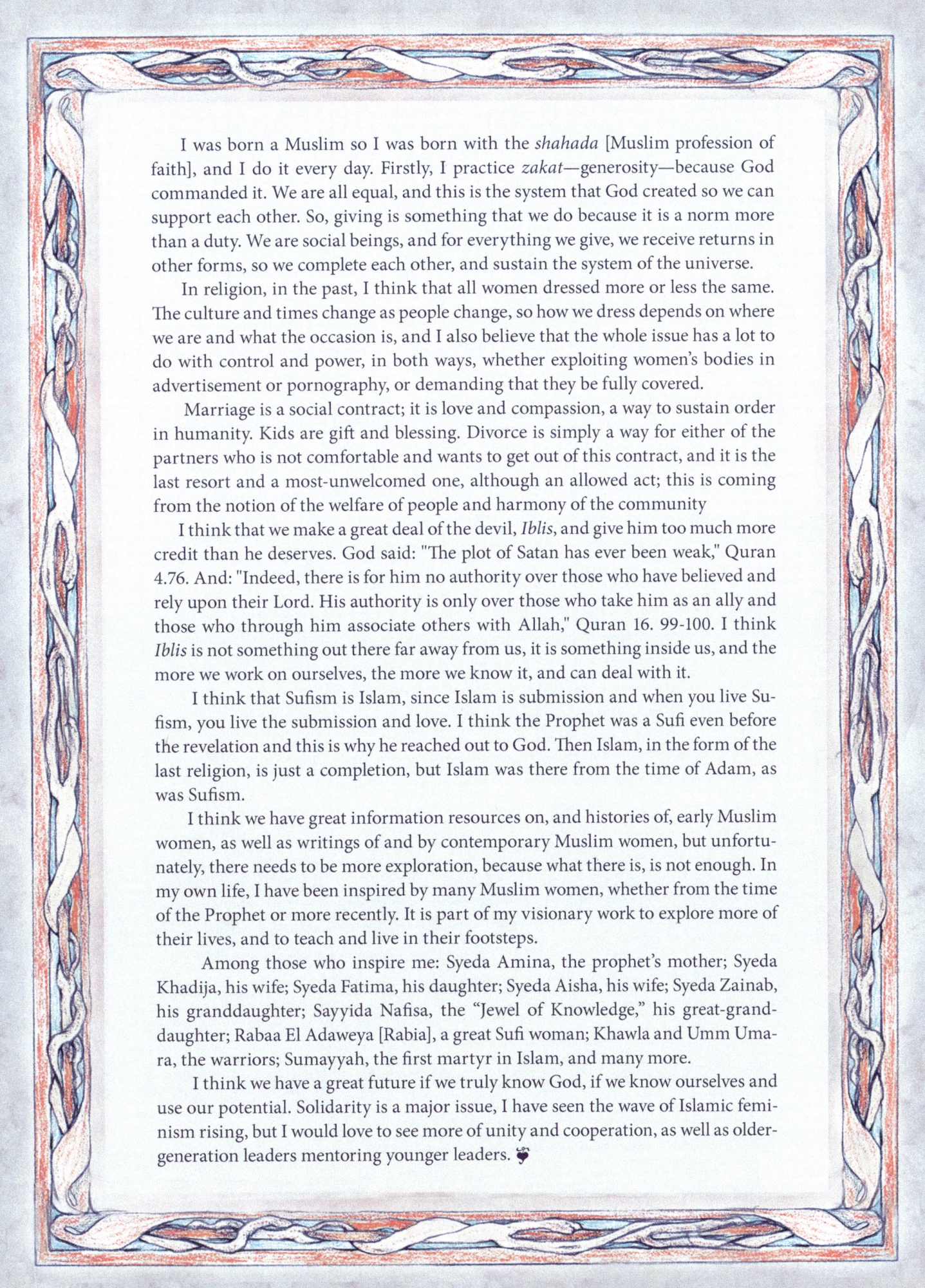

I was born a Muslim so I was born with the *shahada* [Muslim profession of faith], and I do it every day. Firstly, I practice *zakat*—generosity—because God commanded it. We are all equal, and this is the system that God created so we can support each other. So, giving is something that we do because it is a norm more than a duty. We are social beings, and for everything we give, we receive returns in other forms, so we complete each other, and sustain the system of the universe.

In religion, in the past, I think that all women dressed more or less the same. The culture and times change as people change, so how we dress depends on where we are and what the occasion is, and I also believe that the whole issue has a lot to do with control and power, in both ways, whether exploiting women's bodies in advertisement or pornography, or demanding that they be fully covered.

Marriage is a social contract; it is love and compassion, a way to sustain order in humanity. Kids are gift and blessing. Divorce is simply a way for either of the partners who is not comfortable and wants to get out of this contract, and it is the last resort and a most-unwelcomed one, although an allowed act; this is coming from the notion of the welfare of people and harmony of the community

I think that we make a great deal of the devil, *Iblis*, and give him too much more credit than he deserves. God said: "The plot of Satan has ever been weak," Quran 4.76. And: "Indeed, there is for him no authority over those who have believed and rely upon their Lord. His authority is only over those who take him as an ally and those who through him associate others with Allah," Quran 16. 99-100. I think *Iblis* is not something out there far away from us, it is something inside us, and the more we work on ourselves, the more we know it, and can deal with it.

I think that Sufism is Islam, since Islam is submission and when you live Sufism, you live the submission and love. I think the Prophet was a Sufi even before the revelation and this is why he reached out to God. Then Islam, in the form of the last religion, is just a completion, but Islam was there from the time of Adam, as was Sufism.

I think we have great information resources on, and histories of, early Muslim women, as well as writings of and by contemporary Muslim women, but unfortunately, there needs to be more exploration, because what there is, is not enough. In my own life, I have been inspired by many Muslim women, whether from the time of the Prophet or more recently. It is part of my visionary work to explore more of their lives, and to teach and live in their footsteps.

Among those who inspire me: Syeda Amina, the prophet's mother; Syeda Khadija, his wife; Syeda Fatima, his daughter; Syeda Aisha, his wife; Syeda Zainab, his granddaughter; Sayyida Nafisa, the "Jewel of Knowledge," his great-granddaughter; Rabaa El Adaweya [Rabia], a great Sufi woman; Khawla and Umm Umara, the warriors; Sumayyah, the first martyr in Islam, and many more.

I think we have a great future if we truly know God, if we know ourselves and use our potential. Solidarity is a major issue, I have seen the wave of Islamic feminism rising, but I would love to see more of unity and cooperation, as well as older-generation leaders mentoring younger leaders.

TREE OF WOMEN—SILSILA OF SISTERHOOD

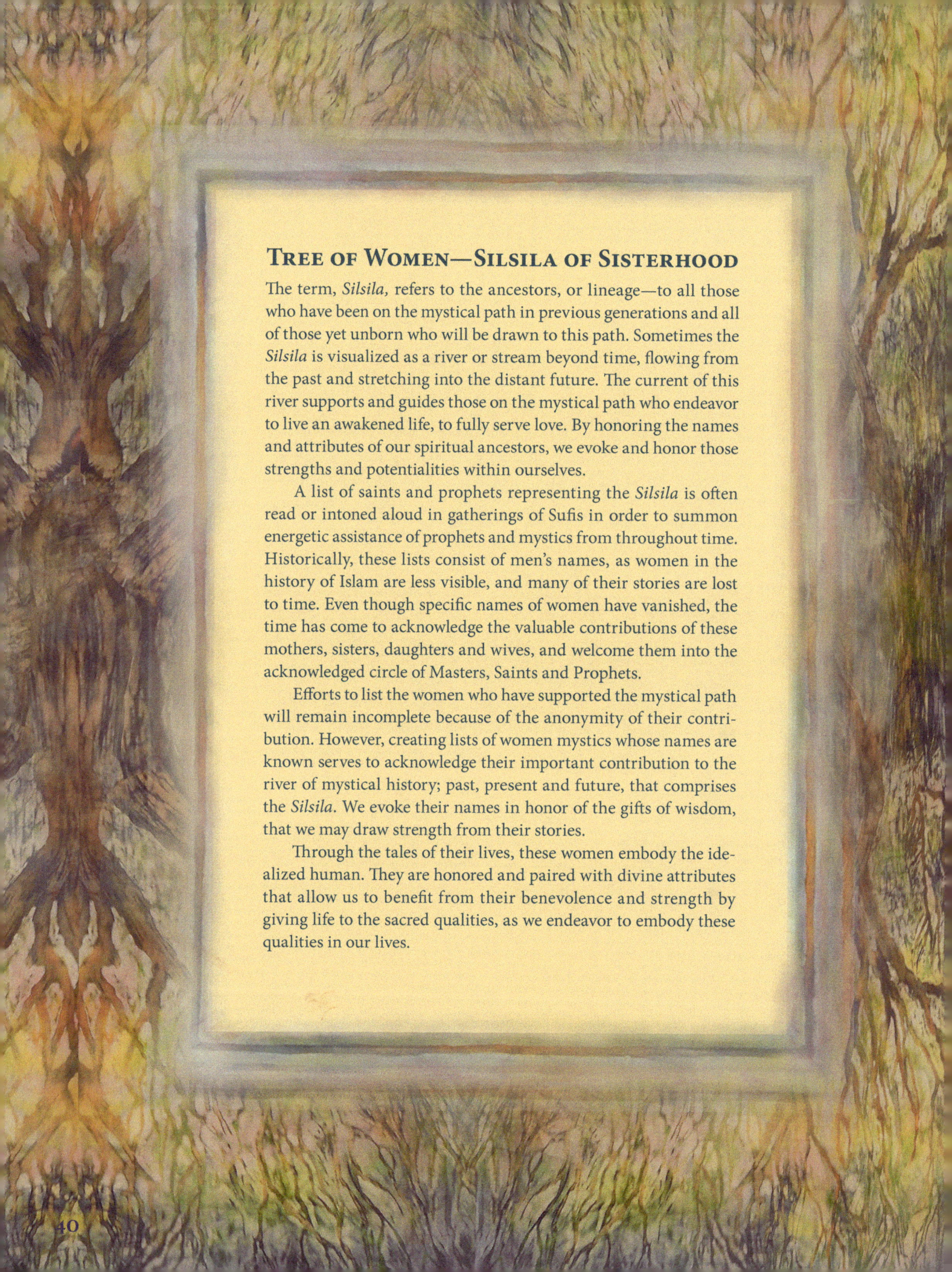

The term, *Silsila*, refers to the ancestors, or lineage—to all those who have been on the mystical path in previous generations and all of those yet unborn who will be drawn to this path. Sometimes the *Silsila* is visualized as a river or stream beyond time, flowing from the past and stretching into the distant future. The current of this river supports and guides those on the mystical path who endeavor to live an awakened life, to fully serve love. By honoring the names and attributes of our spiritual ancestors, we evoke and honor those strengths and potentialities within ourselves.

A list of saints and prophets representing the *Silsila* is often read or intoned aloud in gatherings of Sufis in order to summon energetic assistance of prophets and mystics from throughout time. Historically, these lists consist of men's names, as women in the history of Islam are less visible, and many of their stories are lost to time. Even though specific names of women have vanished, the time has come to acknowledge the valuable contributions of these mothers, sisters, daughters and wives, and welcome them into the acknowledged circle of Masters, Saints and Prophets.

Efforts to list the women who have supported the mystical path will remain incomplete because of the anonymity of their contribution. However, creating lists of women mystics whose names are known serves to acknowledge their important contribution to the river of mystical history; past, present and future, that comprises the *Silsila*. We evoke their names in honor of the gifts of wisdom, that we may draw strength from their stories.

Through the tales of their lives, these women embody the idealized human. They are honored and paired with divine attributes that allow us to benefit from their benevolence and strength by giving life to the sacred qualities, as we endeavor to embody these qualities in our lives.

*From the initial instant of time's breath
Your love lay within our soul
Treasure of the heart's secret chest.
In your meadows our soul's lark soared aloft,
Homebound on your way
Even before the sprouting of a flower from
Possibility's rose bed.*

—Bibi Hayati

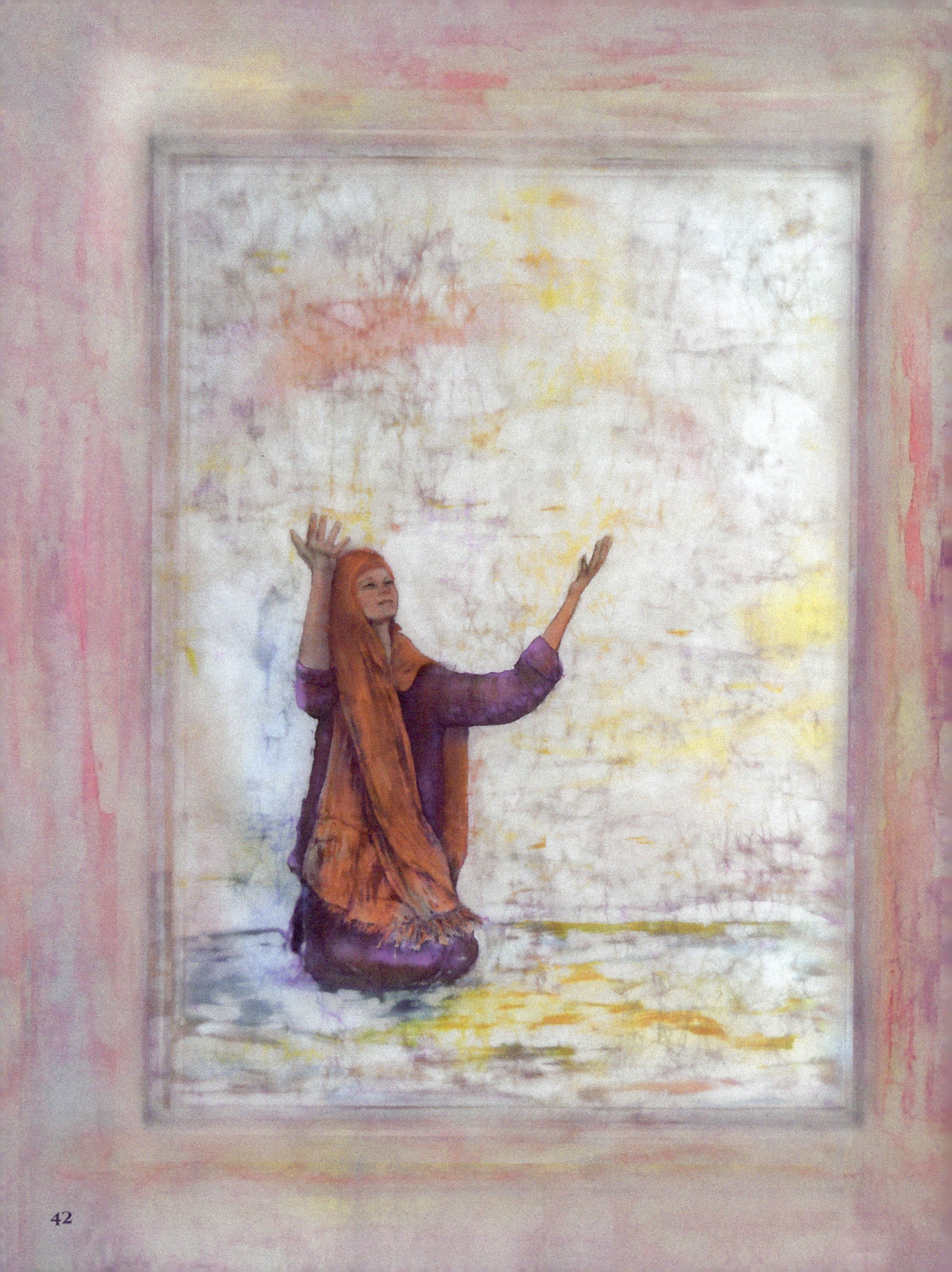

Purification

I Am A Child Of Allah, I Am Womb I Am,
My Body Is Holy, My Blood Is Sacred.

The act of purification is foundational to Islamic life. This includes *tahara*, ritual cleansing prior to prayer, and *tazkiah*, purification of the heart and soul.

The act of completing *wudhu*, ritual cleansing with water, brings the mind and heart to the act of prayer, and allows negativity to be released. The water used for *wudhu* can be linked with luminosity, so that the spirit is cleansed with light as the body is cleansed of impurities prior to repetition of the prayers, bringing focus to the intention.

Purification of the heart and soul brings the seeker closer to the unity of the Beloved. Through the repetition of sacred phrases and focus on Allah, the heart becomes more radiant, and the spirit gains health and finds a true morality and nobility through development of the inner compass. This leads quite naturally to holding another's well being above one's own, to generosity, trustworthiness, and a natural sense of honor.

Respect in speech and action towards another is the natural reflection of the purified heart. If one speaks well of another, that kindness brings great blessings back upon the speaker. The same is true when one speaks ill of another. Harboring unkind thoughts and resentments towards others strengthens that quality at its origin.

In traditional texts, sending compassion to another person, regardless of what is reciprocated, is equated with gazing upon a beautiful, fragrant garden; while harboring ill will toward another is equated with laying in a briar patch full of snakes and scorpions. Continuing to purify the heart and surrender to the Beloved is the remedy to the natural difficulties that arise in life. Living with a peaceful heart is a natural consequence of choosing the path of kindness.

By the Soul—and the proportion and order given to it;
And its enlightenment as to its wrong and its right;
Truly she succeeds who purifies it.

—Quran, Sura 91: 79

INTERVIEW WITH FATIMA

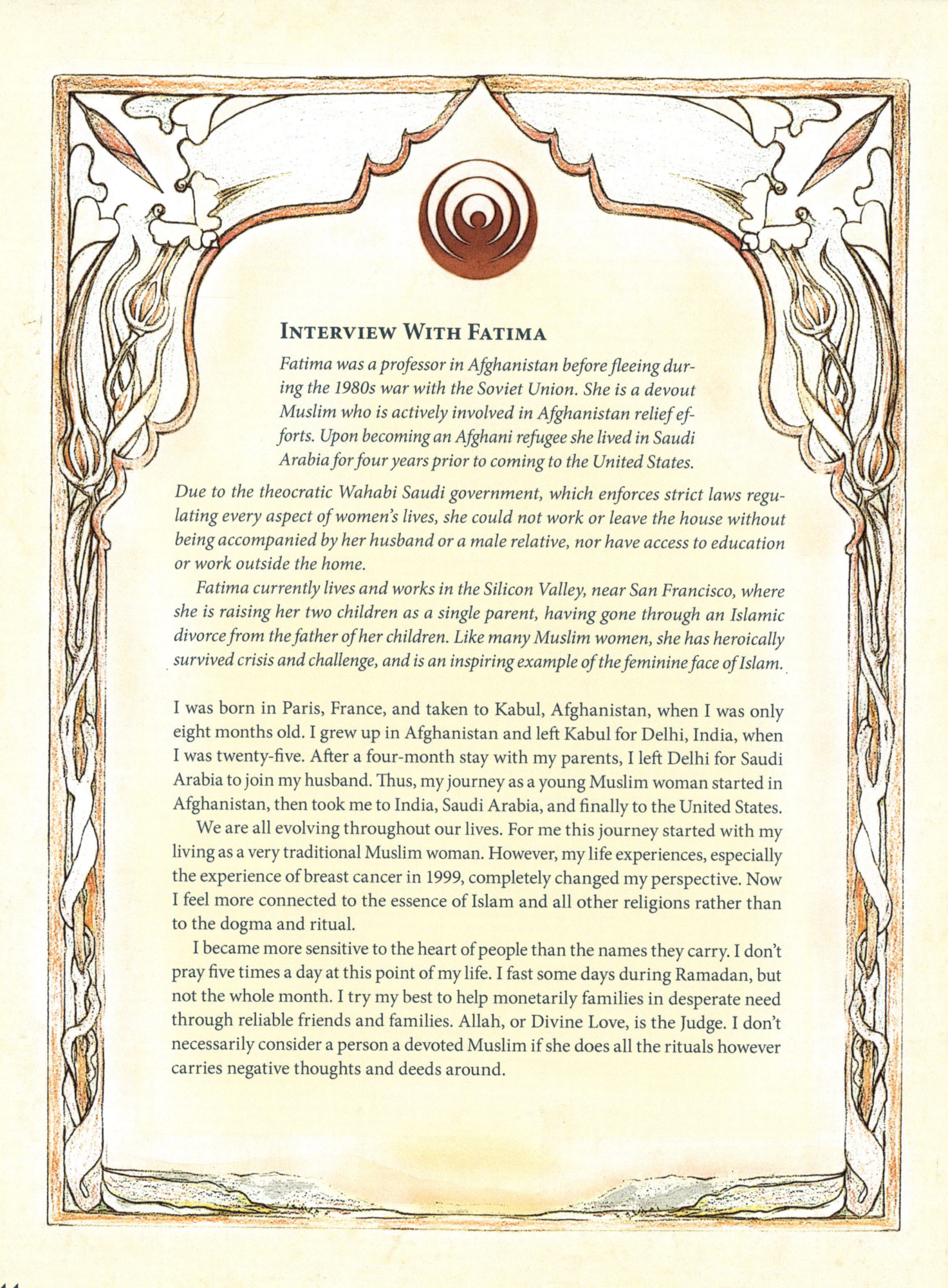

Fatima was a professor in Afghanistan before fleeing during the 1980s war with the Soviet Union. She is a devout Muslim who is actively involved in Afghanistan relief efforts. Upon becoming an Afghani refugee she lived in Saudi Arabia for four years prior to coming to the United States.

Due to the theocratic Wahabi Saudi government, which enforces strict laws regulating every aspect of women's lives, she could not work or leave the house without being accompanied by her husband or a male relative, nor have access to education or work outside the home.

Fatima currently lives and works in the Silicon Valley, near San Francisco, where she is raising her two children as a single parent, having gone through an Islamic divorce from the father of her children. Like many Muslim women, she has heroically survived crisis and challenge, and is an inspiring example of the feminine face of Islam.

I was born in Paris, France, and taken to Kabul, Afghanistan, when I was only eight months old. I grew up in Afghanistan and left Kabul for Delhi, India, when I was twenty-five. After a four-month stay with my parents, I left Delhi for Saudi Arabia to join my husband. Thus, my journey as a young Muslim woman started in Afghanistan, then took me to India, Saudi Arabia, and finally to the United States.

We are all evolving throughout our lives. For me this journey started with my living as a very traditional Muslim woman. However, my life experiences, especially the experience of breast cancer in 1999, completely changed my perspective. Now I feel more connected to the essence of Islam and all other religions rather than to the dogma and ritual.

I became more sensitive to the heart of people than the names they carry. I don't pray five times a day at this point of my life. I fast some days during Ramadan, but not the whole month. I try my best to help monetarily families in desperate need through reliable friends and families. Allah, or Divine Love, is the Judge. I don't necessarily consider a person a devoted Muslim if she does all the rituals however carries negative thoughts and deeds around.

I believe a devoted Muslim is one who performs all rituals, but also works with her conscience, *nafs*, or ego, to keep her mind and heart clear so that the purity of Divine Love can reside there at all times. That person will be a clear example of peace within and without, which is the essence of Islam.

Hijab—Veiling

I believe Hijab, or veiling, originated to save the women from disrespect and violence. Unfortunately, this original pure objective was twisted so badly by men in power, that at present it has become a way to suppress women and keep them out of sight. So, we can see extremists like the Taliban and the Saudi Arabian government twisting Islam so badly that only now are women allowed to drive. Women and girls aren't allowed to attend all the schools, and on and on.

I believe humanity as a whole is evolving and eventually we will get to the point of respecting women equally to men all around the globe. At that time, the actions of the Taliban version of Islam, as well as the actions of the entertainment and the cosmetic industry, and other businesses that use women—their faces, hair and body beauty used as a means of making more profit—this also will be obsolete. And woman will be raised again as an equal partner to man, no longer considered a lesser being, with equal rights and opportunities and with more respect for her unique position as mother and nurturer of humanity.

Hajj—Pilgrimage to the Kaaba at Mecca

I was blessed to perform *Hajj* twice while I was in Saudi Arabia. Also, every month I was there, I was able to go for prayer at the Kaaba (sacred site of the *Hajj*). Although I was very young at that time and I was not involved with the mystical side of Islam and other faiths, I still was touched by the amazing experience of *Hajj*. I remember the special time that *Hajis* (those who perform the *Hajj*) put on *Ihram* (a special white covering around the body) and set out in the buses to go to different sacred sites, and all recite in together "*Labik Allahumma Labik, Labik laka labbaik,*" meaning, "O Lord of mercy, I obeyed your call and I come to You to worship."

All the mountains and deserts look white because of the *Ihram* worn by *Hajis* on Mount Arafat who ask for forgiveness while on the mountain. Men and women intermingle around the Kaaba and pray together, and become unaware of their gender and the requirement of separation. It is all beautiful and amazing. I am looking forward to reading a special book written by a modern Persian mystic, poet, and author, Ali Shariati, about *Hajj*. Then I will go on *Hajj* again. I am sure we will fill the jar of our soul more fully if we become aware of this amazing experience as a mystical journey. May we all have the opportunity to experience these blessings in this lifetime.

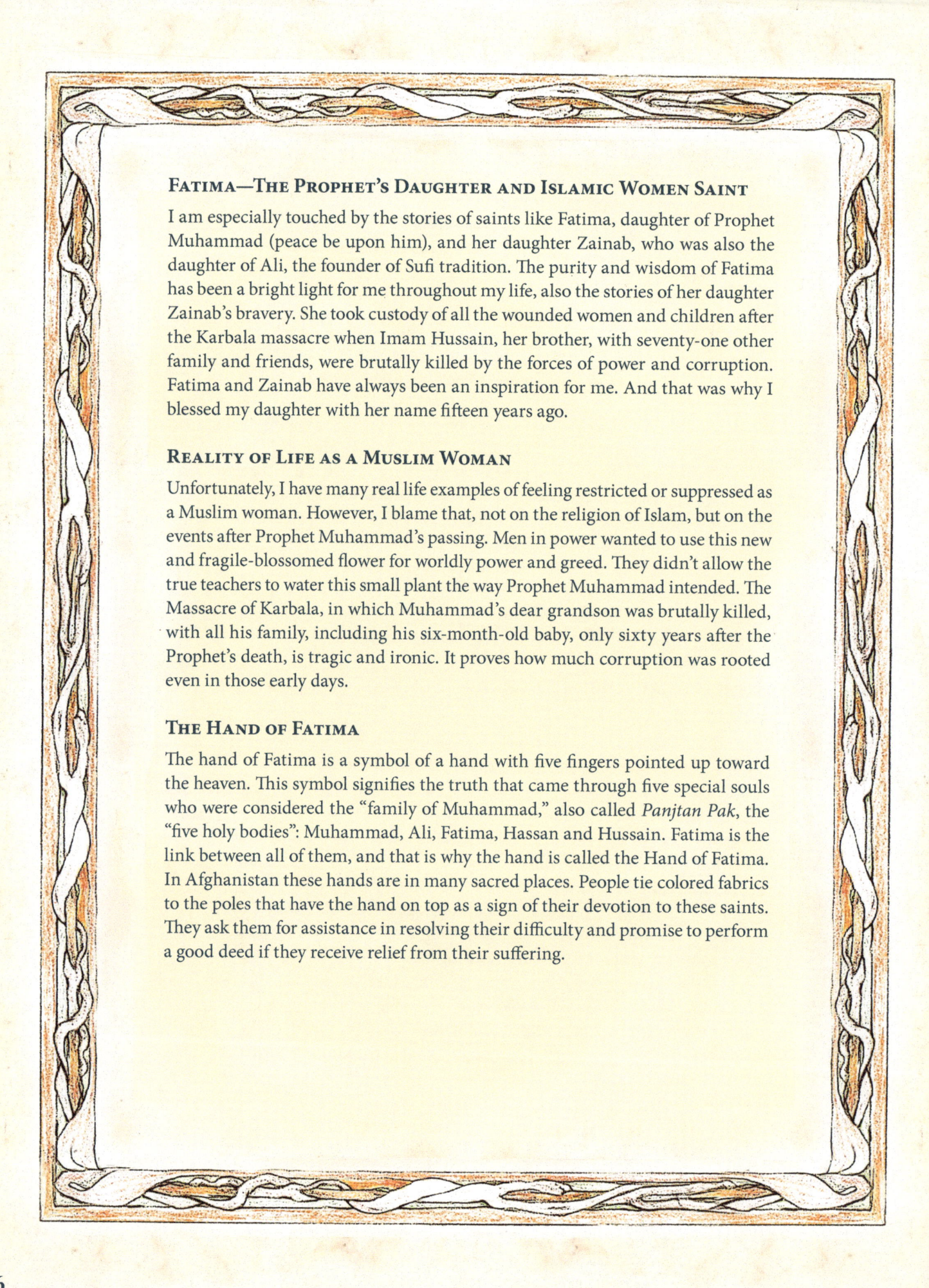

Fatima—The Prophet's Daughter and Islamic Women Saint

I am especially touched by the stories of saints like Fatima, daughter of Prophet Muhammad (peace be upon him), and her daughter Zainab, who was also the daughter of Ali, the founder of Sufi tradition. The purity and wisdom of Fatima has been a bright light for me throughout my life, also the stories of her daughter Zainab's bravery. She took custody of all the wounded women and children after the Karbala massacre when Imam Hussain, her brother, with seventy-one other family and friends, were brutally killed by the forces of power and corruption. Fatima and Zainab have always been an inspiration for me. And that was why I blessed my daughter with her name fifteen years ago.

Reality of Life as a Muslim Woman

Unfortunately, I have many real life examples of feeling restricted or suppressed as a Muslim woman. However, I blame that, not on the religion of Islam, but on the events after Prophet Muhammad's passing. Men in power wanted to use this new and fragile-blossomed flower for worldly power and greed. They didn't allow the true teachers to water this small plant the way Prophet Muhammad intended. The Massacre of Karbala, in which Muhammad's dear grandson was brutally killed, with all his family, including his six-month-old baby, only sixty years after the Prophet's death, is tragic and ironic. It proves how much corruption was rooted even in those early days.

The Hand of Fatima

The hand of Fatima is a symbol of a hand with five fingers pointed up toward the heaven. This symbol signifies the truth that came through five special souls who were considered the "family of Muhammad," also called *Panjtan Pak*, the "five holy bodies": Muhammad, Ali, Fatima, Hassan and Hussain. Fatima is the link between all of them, and that is why the hand is called the Hand of Fatima. In Afghanistan these hands are in many sacred places. People tie colored fabrics to the poles that have the hand on top as a sign of their devotion to these saints. They ask them for assistance in resolving their difficulty and promise to perform a good deed if they receive relief from their suffering.

The Essence of Islam

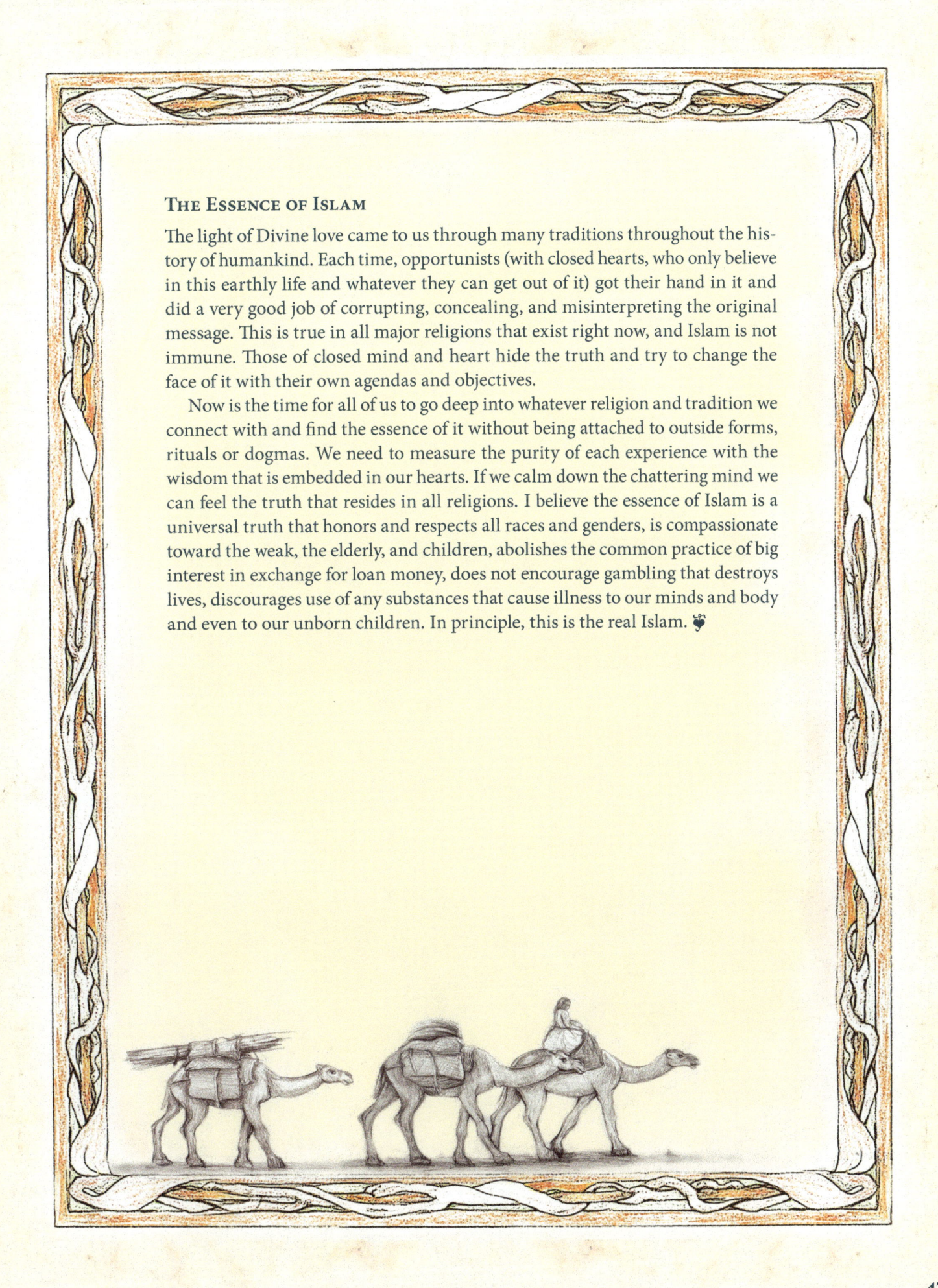

The light of Divine love came to us through many traditions throughout the history of humankind. Each time, opportunists (with closed hearts, who only believe in this earthly life and whatever they can get out of it) got their hand in it and did a very good job of corrupting, concealing, and misinterpreting the original message. This is true in all major religions that exist right now, and Islam is not immune. Those of closed mind and heart hide the truth and try to change the face of it with their own agendas and objectives.

Now is the time for all of us to go deep into whatever religion and tradition we connect with and find the essence of it without being attached to outside forms, rituals or dogmas. We need to measure the purity of each experience with the wisdom that is embedded in our hearts. If we calm down the chattering mind we can feel the truth that resides in all religions. I believe the essence of Islam is a universal truth that honors and respects all races and genders, is compassionate toward the weak, the elderly, and children, abolishes the common practice of big interest in exchange for loan money, does not encourage gambling that destroys lives, discourages use of any substances that cause illness to our minds and body and even to our unborn children. In principle, this is the real Islam.

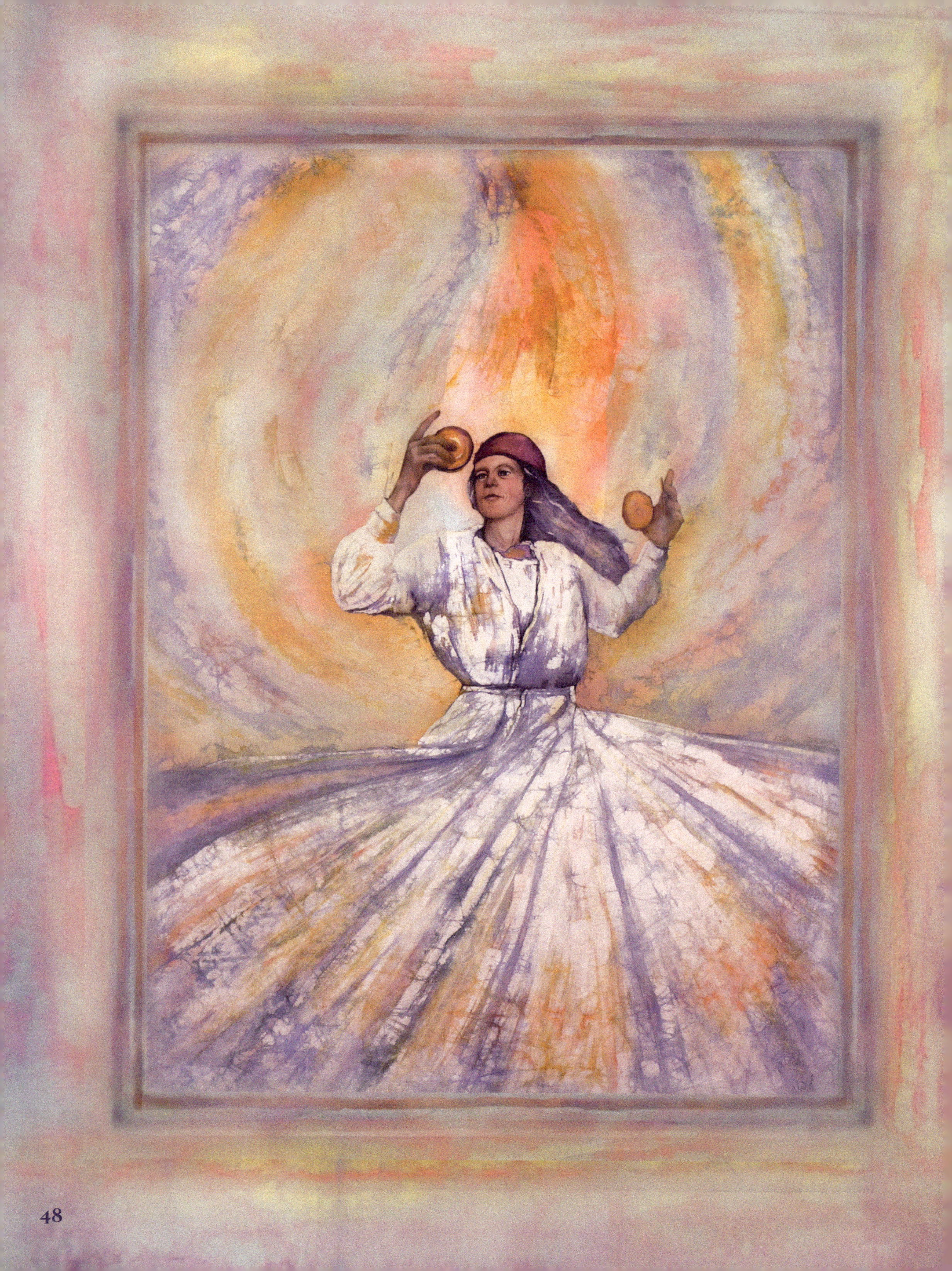

CREATING HEART SPACE

O you who have believed, do not approach prayer while you are intoxicated, until you know what you are saying, or in a state of impurity…until you have washed [your whole body].

—Quran, Sura 4: 43

WUDHU AND SALAT—ABLUTION AND PRAYER

Before prayer, ablutions are essential and are a daily part of Muslim life. When purifying the body, attention is also given to cleansing the heart and consciousness. Using clean water in the cupped hands, each area is washed three times. Begin with the top of the hands, right hand first, then left hand above the wrist. Cupping water in the palms, rinse the mouth three times. Gently inhale water into the nostrils three times. Then, cleanse the face and eyes three times. Lightly bring the water over the top of the head three times, using the tips of the fingers to gently cleanse the inside and outside of the ear. Conclude with the feet, right foot first, to the ankles.

Ghusl—*Ghusl* is a full and complete washing of the entire body, suggested weekly or more often if possible. It is an obligatory purification in specific cases of sexual activity, menstruation, *nifass* (post-natal bleeding), and for the body at death.

Purifying Heart with water and light
    We receive Peace in all humility
Purifying Mind with water and light
    We receive Forgiveness that is Beauty
Purifying the Body with water and light
    We receive patience and endurance
      Love washes
        Releasing us from bondage
We surrender into Unity.
    This skin of Light, now brightness woven.

—Mariam Baker

Purification With Light

Oh God! Grant me Light in my heart,
Light in my grave,
Light in front of me, Light behind me,
Light to my right, Light to my left,
Light above me, Light below me,
Light in my ears, Light in my eyes, Light on my skin,
Light in my hair,
Light within my flesh, Light in my Blood,
Light in my bones
Oh God! Increase my Light everywhere.

Oh God! Grant me Light in my heart,
Light in my grave,
Light on my tongue, Light in my eyes,
Light in my ears, Light to my right,
Light to my left,
Light above me, Light below me,
Light in front of me,
Light behind me, And Light within myself.
Oh God, Grant me Light in my heart.

—Prophet Muhammad

After saying this luminous purification in preparation for prayer, begin intoning the sacred sound, *Allah Nur,* Divine Light, in one note. Use the palms of the hands, to wash the body in light. Start at the heart. With open palms, gently dip into the energy field in front of the heart, as if dipping into a chalice of light, and bring the palms to the heart center. From the heart, repeat this motion, moving to wash the crown of the head with light, then proceed to the hair, the face the forehead, ears, eyes, nose, and mouth, washing all in light—luminosity. Continue intoning the sacred name, *Allah Nur,* while using the palms to continue to wash the body, moving down the center of the body through the chakra centers, throat, heart, solar plexus, hara, root chakra, and down past the knees to the feet. Return the palms to the heart. Close the eyes and breathe, listening to the silence and observing feelings and inner vision.

51

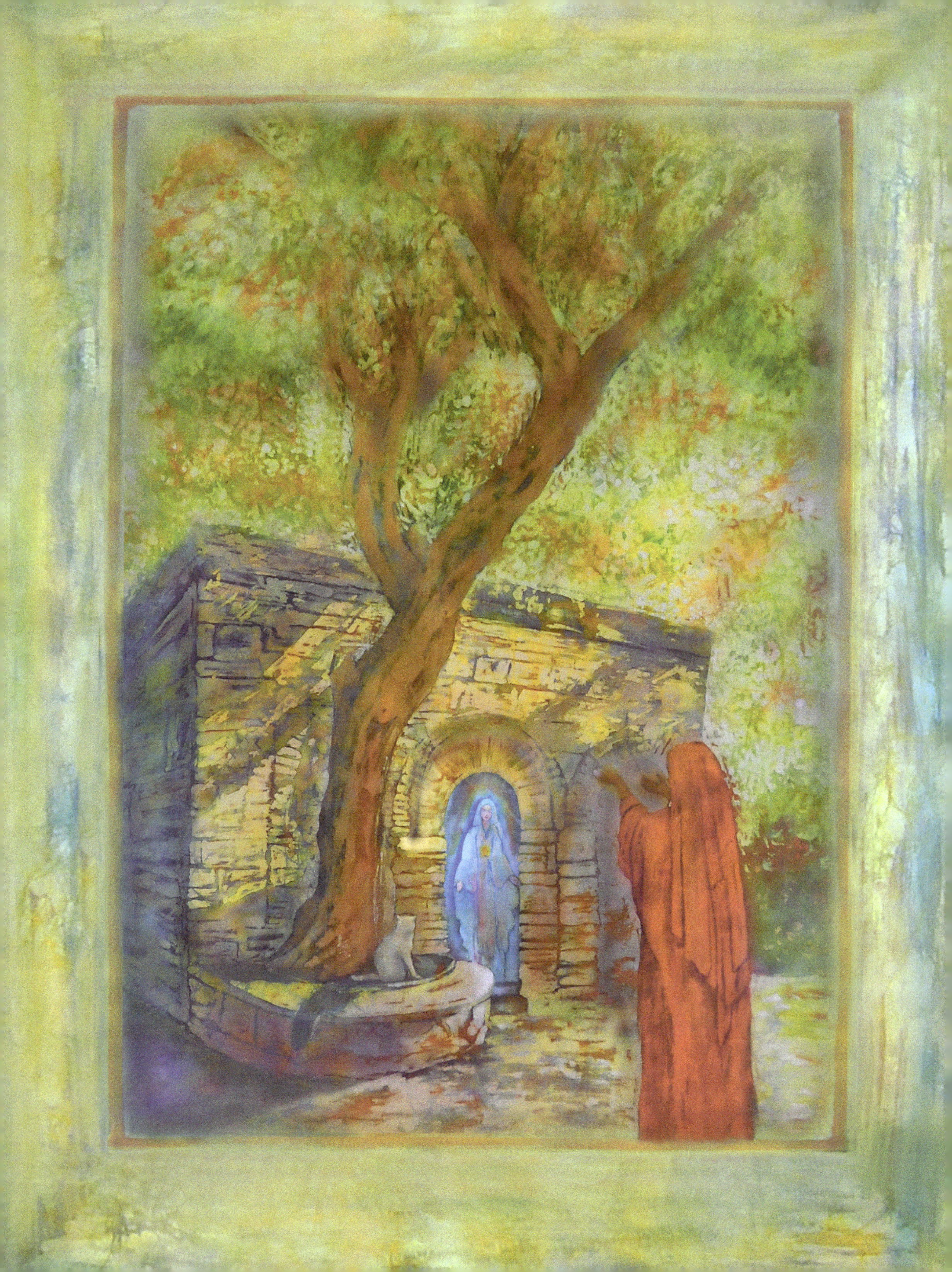

Love Human & Divine

3

The Power of Love—Faith in the Friend

Above the ancient city of Ephesus, on a wooded hill, sits the chapel of Mariam, Mary, mother of *Isa*—Jesus. Mary is a bridge builder between religions, particularly Islam and Christianity. She transcends the culture of individuals. This is experienced today at her shrine in Ephesus, Turkey.

The shrine is believed to be built upon the ruins of the house that John the Evangelist and Mariam (Mary) retired to upon leaving Palestine. Ephesus was the capital of the Roman provinces of Asia when Christianity was at its earliest beginnings. The belief that Mariam died there has made it a site of pilgrimage. Christian and Muslim women in great numbers pray side by side at this shrine. One woman kneeling recites the rosary and the Hail Mary. Another woman with *tasbih* (prayer beads) and prayer rug recites the *Fatiha* (opening Sura of the Quran) and Muslim prayers. They are united in their allegiance to the qualities embodied by Mariam.

Pilgrims from around the world come to pray and offer respect to this "woman of truth," who is an example of one immersed in the life of Allah, and surrendered to her destiny.

Prayers, on small pieces of paper and cloth, are tied to trees and stuffed between rocks all over the shrine. A multitude of languages are spoken at the site, yet the language of dedication to the divine nature is spoken by all. There are pregnant women, mothers praying for their children, women praying to conceive, and women grieving who have miscarried or aborted children, or lost beloveds to war. All are united in attuning to this Mother who remained true to herself through trial and tribulation. She is the woman clothed with the sun. The Christian gospel advises, "Put on the armor of light." Mariam was clothed in the light of Allah, or *Allah Nuri*.

DREAM SEQUENCE

It is dusk. A woman stands alone in the distance, amidst the dunes. The wind swirls the unusual white chador (head covering) around her noble form. She faces the sun. Light and shadow dance around her in waves of shimmering beauty. Brightness radiates from her body and face. She turns and smiles, extending a yellow rose.

"And Allah will pour you a glass of love from glory and generosity."

THE STORY OF MARY, MOTHER OF JESUS, IN THE HOLY QURAN

Mary, mother of Jesus, is the only woman with a chapter in the Quran or Sura named after her. Some Muslims believe she is the only recognized woman prophet, and that status has been debated amongst religious scholars since the earliest days of Islam. In any event, she is a most important figure in Islam, as in Christianity. In both religions, she is a symbol of purity and devotion to God.

Sura Mariam, number 19 in the Quran, gives a beautifully poetic account of her life. It tells of the coming birth of Isa (Jesus), the actual birth, and of the baby speaking while still in the cradle. There are parallels with the Christian gospel account of her life, but also some radical differences. Similar to the Christian account, Mariam is pure, physically and spiritually virginal, untouched by any man.

Blue is the color associated with Mariam. This includes all the various and subtle shades of blue, particularly lapis lazuli and turquoise. It is the color of the awakened mind united with the illuminated heart, attributes of Mariam as united with the will of Allah.

Behold! The angels said: O Mariam! Allah has chosen thee and made you pure and chosen thee above all the women of the nations.

O Mary! Worship Thy Lord devoutly: Prostrate thyself, and bow down in prayer with those who bow down.

—Quran, Sura 3: 42-43

During the Crusades, the Christian Holy Wars, Pope Bernard (1090-1153) had the image of Mother Mary placed on banners before the knights as they went to battle. Evident in his portrayal of Mary, as their spiritual leader in opposition to Islam, was a lack of understanding of the Muslim faith.

In the Quran, Mariam leaves her community and is alone with her infant in a "distant place." After crying out in desperation, she is led to an area where there is a date palm and instructed to shake the trunk of the tree, causing ripe dates to fall and relieve her hunger. A river would flow for her, and she and her child would be at peace.

This story is reminiscent of the story of Hagar, whose expulsion from the community left her seemingly destitute in the desert, but whose cry was heard. She and her young son, Ishmael, experienced the Mercy and compassion of Allah when the spring of *Zamzam* appeared out of nowhere to refresh their bodies and souls. In the tradition of Ibrahim (Abraham) and Musa (Moses), Hagar and Mariam found spiritual nourishment in the desert.

According to the Quran, Mariam gave birth to a prophet, not to the Son of God, as Allah is only One.

Mary is symbolic of the true Muslim, that one who surrenders to the will of Allah, to be used as a servant for humanity. The reflection of humility and obedience within the life of one chosen by Allah is profound in Mary's life. She is awake to the fulfillment of her destiny; unsurprised that Allah can create a human being from *Ruh*—breath. All Muslims look to her as an example of one who is a follower of Islam. Some interpreters of Biblical and Quran exegetics (the critical study of holy texts) also equate Mary's obedience with exonerating the sin of Eve.

The *Niyya,* or intention, of Mary was complete surrender and service to God. This was her religious training. Considered a symbol of receptivity to divine inspiration, she becomes pregnant with divine light. She is an example of one who is in active submission to the will of God. Her orientation is towards emptiness and total receptivity to the Divine Essence. In so doing, her heart and body create the accommodation to receive, from the angel Gabriel, the words and breath of God: "Be," and Jesus is conceived.

There is potent symbolism of Mary as Womb for the *Ruh Allah*, or Breath of God, to be born as Prophet Jesus. The divine names of Allah, *Rahman*, and *Rahim,* are derived from the Arabic word for womb. The soul is feminine, womblike, a receptive vessel, ideally in active submission to Allah.

It is said by the classical Sufis, especially Ibn ʿArabi, that, "The body is like Mary, and each of us has a Jesus within. If the pain appears, our Jesus will be born. But if no pain comes, Jesus will return to his origin on that same hidden road by which he came. We will be deprived of him and reap no benefit." The body is like Mariam. When the labor pains of love are strong enough within the Womb of the Heart, Jesus will be born.

Some theologians consider Muhammad parallel to Mariam. She surrenders to the will of God as a young virgin similar to the Prophet who was in an unlettered—illiterate— or in a virginal state, receiving the Quran. In receiving the sacred scripture of Islam, Muhammad delivers the essence of God, Allah, to the people. Muhammad is given the miracle of the Quran, and, after much labor and challenge, delivers this wisdom to the people. Mariam, through her submission to the will of God, is chosen in a virginal state to birth the prophet Jesus into physical form.

Mary said, "In the days I was pregnant with Jesus,
 Whenever there was someone in my house speaking with me,
  I would hear Jesus praising God inside me.
 Whenever I was alone and there was no one with me,
  I would converse with him and he with me,
 While he was still in my womb."

—Abu al-Qasim Ibn ʿAsakir

The relationship between Mary and Fatima, daughter of prophet Muhammad, is another religious parallel. Both are revered as two figures who from birth were identified and immersed in service to God. Both are visited by angels and receive food from these heavenly visitors, as children and during pregnancy. "Miraculous" midwives assisted Khadija during the birth of Fatima, Asiya (wife of the Pharaoh), Sarah, Miriam, sister of Moses, and Mary.

Mary and Fatima both birth sons, who leave them in the depth of sorrows, and are identified with the archetype of Mater Dolorosa, the sorrowing mother. Within some branches of Shia Islam, Jesus, son of Mary, and Husain, son of Fatima, are both persecuted, and Husain, is martyred. As in the Christian account of Mary and Jesus, Fatima, mother of Husain, has prescience of his death. Mary and Fatima are both exalted in heaven as true Muslims.

57

INTERVIEW WITH AMINA

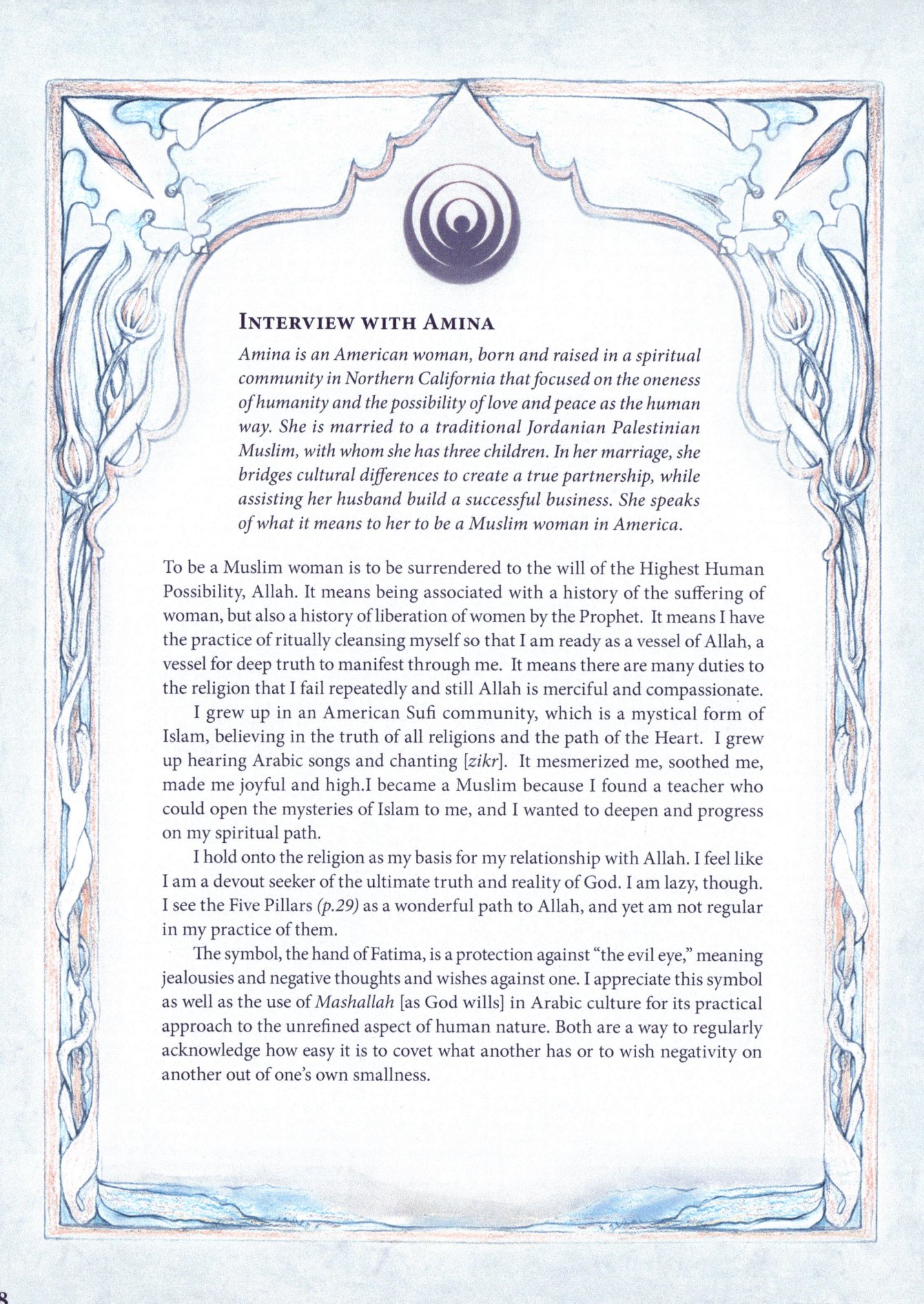

Amina is an American woman, born and raised in a spiritual community in Northern California that focused on the oneness of humanity and the possibility of love and peace as the human way. She is married to a traditional Jordanian Palestinian Muslim, with whom she has three children. In her marriage, she bridges cultural differences to create a true partnership, while assisting her husband build a successful business. She speaks of what it means to her to be a Muslim woman in America.

To be a Muslim woman is to be surrendered to the will of the Highest Human Possibility, Allah. It means being associated with a history of the suffering of woman, but also a history of liberation of women by the Prophet. It means I have the practice of ritually cleansing myself so that I am ready as a vessel of Allah, a vessel for deep truth to manifest through me. It means there are many duties to the religion that I fail repeatedly and still Allah is merciful and compassionate.

I grew up in an American Sufi community, which is a mystical form of Islam, believing in the truth of all religions and the path of the Heart. I grew up hearing Arabic songs and chanting [*zikr*]. It mesmerized me, soothed me, made me joyful and high. I became a Muslim because I found a teacher who could open the mysteries of Islam to me, and I wanted to deepen and progress on my spiritual path.

I hold onto the religion as my basis for my relationship with Allah. I feel like I am a devout seeker of the ultimate truth and reality of God. I am lazy, though. I see the Five Pillars *(p.29)* as a wonderful path to Allah, and yet am not regular in my practice of them.

The symbol, the hand of Fatima, is a protection against "the evil eye," meaning jealousies and negative thoughts and wishes against one. I appreciate this symbol as well as the use of *Mashallah* [as God wills] in Arabic culture for its practical approach to the unrefined aspect of human nature. Both are a way to regularly acknowledge how easy it is to covet what another has or to wish negativity on another out of one's own smallness.

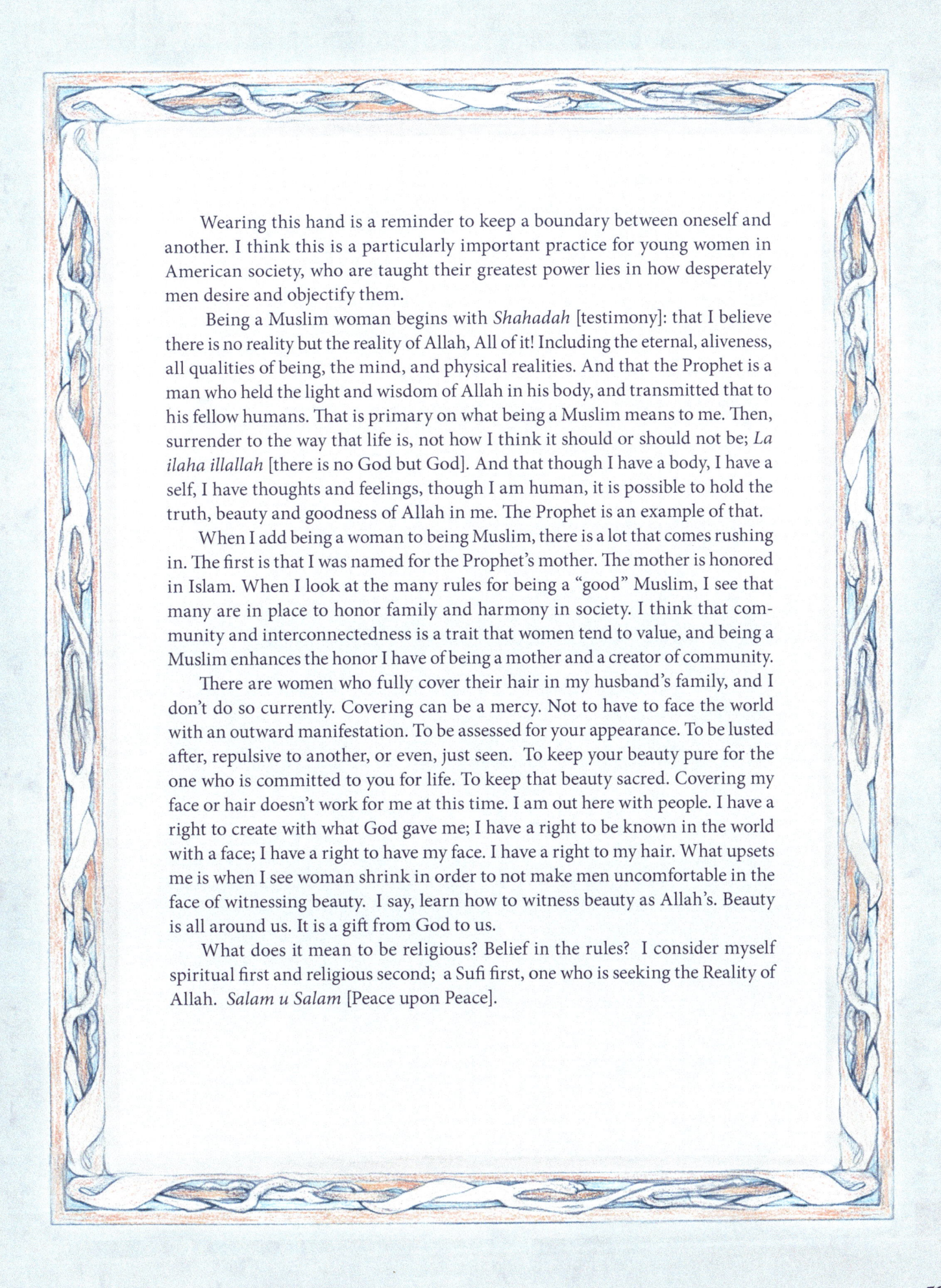

Wearing this hand is a reminder to keep a boundary between oneself and another. I think this is a particularly important practice for young women in American society, who are taught their greatest power lies in how desperately men desire and objectify them.

Being a Muslim woman begins with *Shahadah* [testimony]: that I believe there is no reality but the reality of Allah, All of it! Including the eternal, aliveness, all qualities of being, the mind, and physical realities. And that the Prophet is a man who held the light and wisdom of Allah in his body, and transmitted that to his fellow humans. That is primary on what being a Muslim means to me. Then, surrender to the way that life is, not how I think it should or should not be; *La ilaha illallah* [there is no God but God]. And that though I have a body, I have a self, I have thoughts and feelings, though I am human, it is possible to hold the truth, beauty and goodness of Allah in me. The Prophet is an example of that.

When I add being a woman to being Muslim, there is a lot that comes rushing in. The first is that I was named for the Prophet's mother. The mother is honored in Islam. When I look at the many rules for being a "good" Muslim, I see that many are in place to honor family and harmony in society. I think that community and interconnectedness is a trait that women tend to value, and being a Muslim enhances the honor I have of being a mother and a creator of community.

There are women who fully cover their hair in my husband's family, and I don't do so currently. Covering can be a mercy. Not to have to face the world with an outward manifestation. To be assessed for your appearance. To be lusted after, repulsive to another, or even, just seen. To keep your beauty pure for the one who is committed to you for life. To keep that beauty sacred. Covering my face or hair doesn't work for me at this time. I am out here with people. I have a right to create with what God gave me; I have a right to be known in the world with a face; I have a right to have my face. I have a right to my hair. What upsets me is when I see woman shrink in order to not make men uncomfortable in the face of witnessing beauty. I say, learn how to witness beauty as Allah's. Beauty is all around us. It is a gift from God to us.

What does it mean to be religious? Belief in the rules? I consider myself spiritual first and religious second; a Sufi first, one who is seeking the Reality of Allah. *Salam u Salam* [Peace upon Peace].

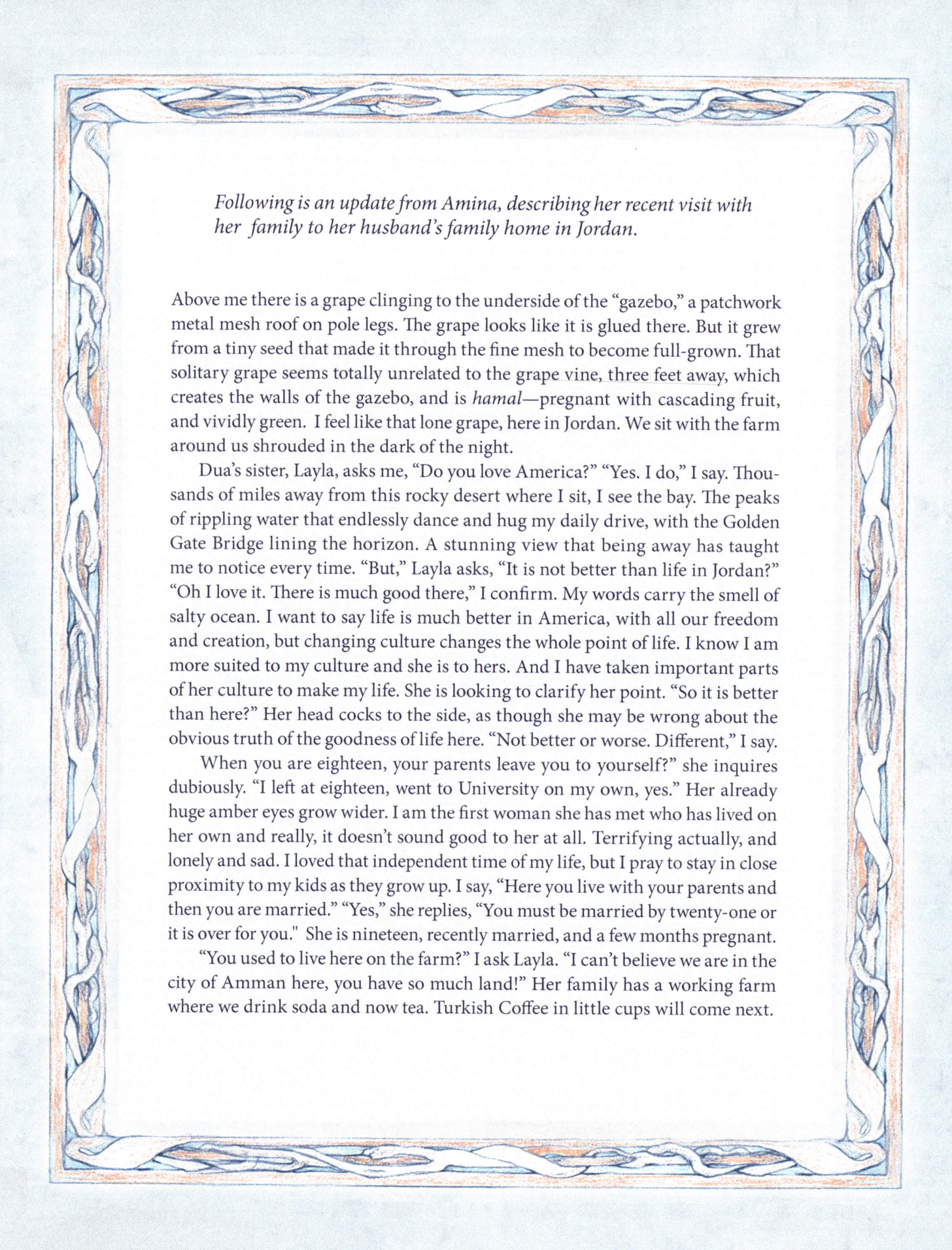

Following is an update from Amina, describing her recent visit with her family to her husband's family home in Jordan.

Above me there is a grape clinging to the underside of the "gazebo," a patchwork metal mesh roof on pole legs. The grape looks like it is glued there. But it grew from a tiny seed that made it through the fine mesh to become full-grown. That solitary grape seems totally unrelated to the grape vine, three feet away, which creates the walls of the gazebo, and is *hamal*—pregnant with cascading fruit, and vividly green. I feel like that lone grape, here in Jordan. We sit with the farm around us shrouded in the dark of the night.

Dua's sister, Layla, asks me, "Do you love America?" "Yes. I do," I say. Thousands of miles away from this rocky desert where I sit, I see the bay. The peaks of rippling water that endlessly dance and hug my daily drive, with the Golden Gate Bridge lining the horizon. A stunning view that being away has taught me to notice every time. "But," Layla asks, "It is not better than life in Jordan?" "Oh I love it. There is much good there," I confirm. My words carry the smell of salty ocean. I want to say life is much better in America, with all our freedom and creation, but changing culture changes the whole point of life. I know I am more suited to my culture and she is to hers. And I have taken important parts of her culture to make my life. She is looking to clarify her point. "So it is better than here?" Her head cocks to the side, as though she may be wrong about the obvious truth of the goodness of life here. "Not better or worse. Different," I say.

When you are eighteen, your parents leave you to yourself?" she inquires dubiously. "I left at eighteen, went to University on my own, yes." Her already huge amber eyes grow wider. I am the first woman she has met who has lived on her own and really, it doesn't sound good to her at all. Terrifying actually, and lonely and sad. I loved that independent time of my life, but I pray to stay in close proximity to my kids as they grow up. I say, "Here you live with your parents and then you are married." "Yes," she replies, "You must be married by twenty-one or it is over for you." She is nineteen, recently married, and a few months pregnant.

"You used to live here on the farm?" I ask Layla. "I can't believe we are in the city of Amman here, you have so much land!" Her family has a working farm where we drink soda and now tea. Turkish Coffee in little cups will come next.

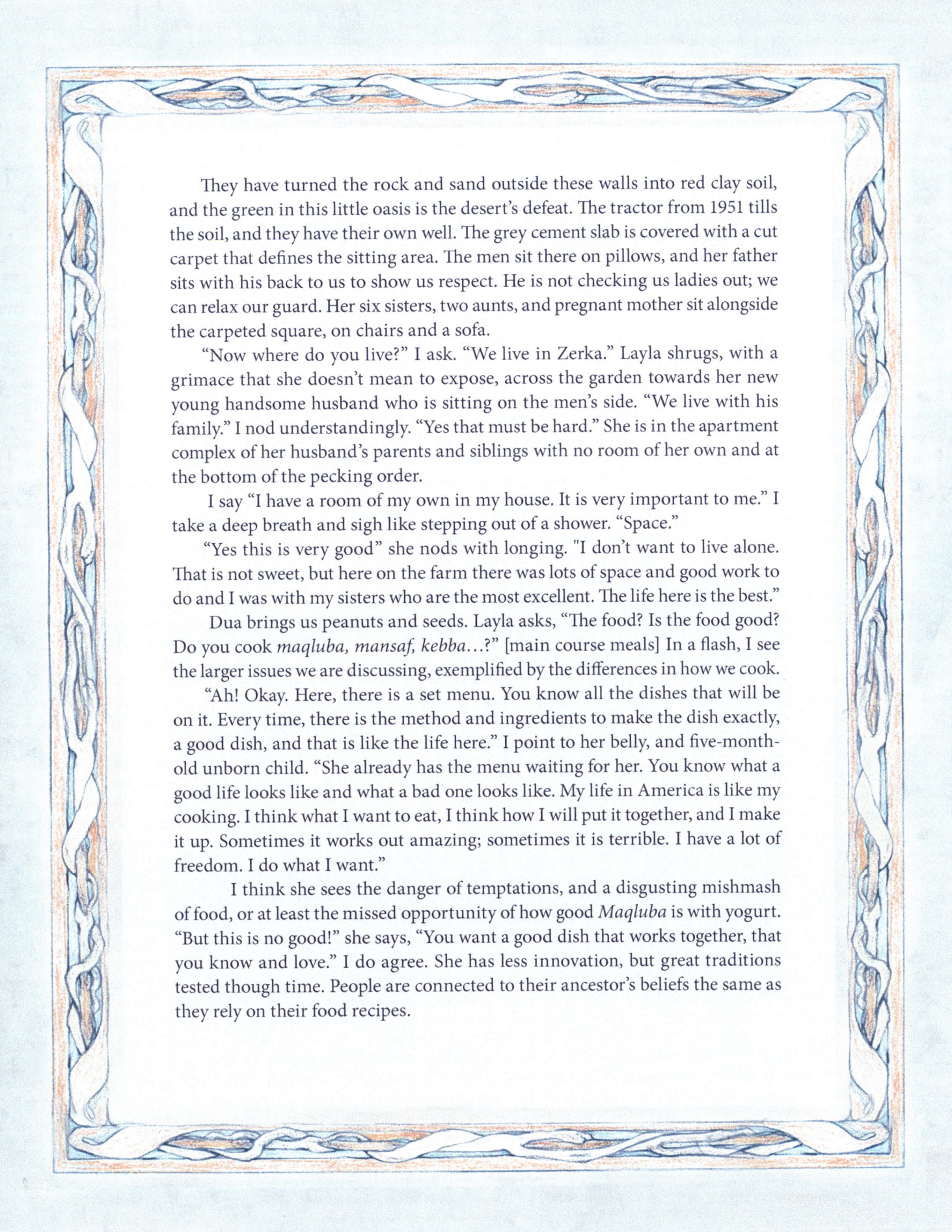

They have turned the rock and sand outside these walls into red clay soil, and the green in this little oasis is the desert's defeat. The tractor from 1951 tills the soil, and they have their own well. The grey cement slab is covered with a cut carpet that defines the sitting area. The men sit there on pillows, and her father sits with his back to us to show us respect. He is not checking us ladies out; we can relax our guard. Her six sisters, two aunts, and pregnant mother sit alongside the carpeted square, on chairs and a sofa.

"Now where do you live?" I ask. "We live in Zerka." Layla shrugs, with a grimace that she doesn't mean to expose, across the garden towards her new young handsome husband who is sitting on the men's side. "We live with his family." I nod understandingly. "Yes that must be hard." She is in the apartment complex of her husband's parents and siblings with no room of her own and at the bottom of the pecking order.

I say "I have a room of my own in my house. It is very important to me." I take a deep breath and sigh like stepping out of a shower. "Space."

"Yes this is very good" she nods with longing. "I don't want to live alone. That is not sweet, but here on the farm there was lots of space and good work to do and I was with my sisters who are the most excellent. The life here is the best."

Dua brings us peanuts and seeds. Layla asks, "The food? Is the food good? Do you cook *maqluba, mansaf, kebba*…?" [main course meals] In a flash, I see the larger issues we are discussing, exemplified by the differences in how we cook.

"Ah! Okay. Here, there is a set menu. You know all the dishes that will be on it. Every time, there is the method and ingredients to make the dish exactly, a good dish, and that is like the life here." I point to her belly, and five-month-old unborn child. "She already has the menu waiting for her. You know what a good life looks like and what a bad one looks like. My life in America is like my cooking. I think what I want to eat, I think how I will put it together, and I make it up. Sometimes it works out amazing; sometimes it is terrible. I have a lot of freedom. I do what I want."

I think she sees the danger of temptations, and a disgusting mishmash of food, or at least the missed opportunity of how good *Maqluba* is with yogurt. "But this is no good!" she says, "You want a good dish that works together, that you know and love." I do agree. She has less innovation, but great traditions tested though time. People are connected to their ancestor's beliefs the same as they rely on their food recipes.

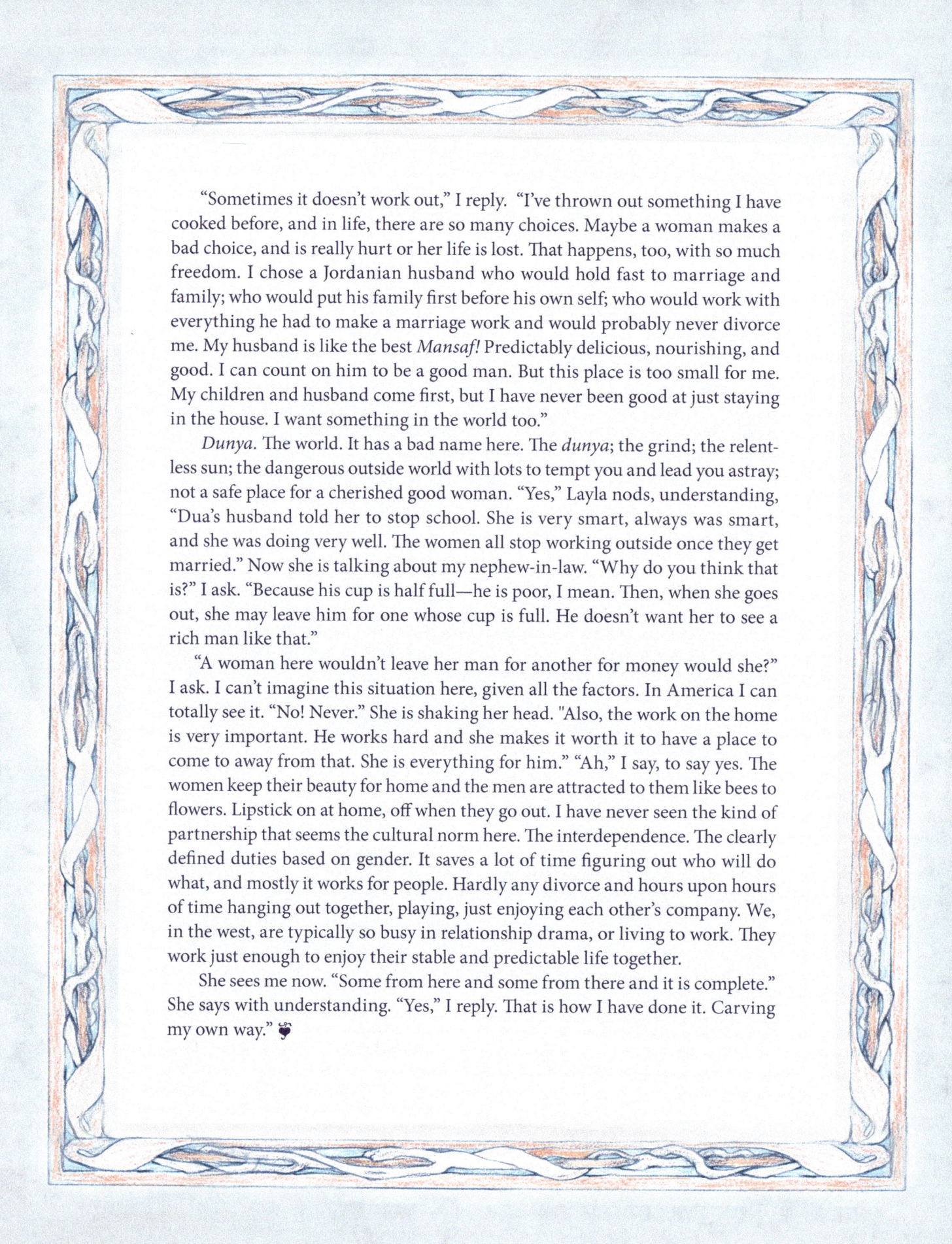

"Sometimes it doesn't work out," I reply. "I've thrown out something I have cooked before, and in life, there are so many choices. Maybe a woman makes a bad choice, and is really hurt or her life is lost. That happens, too, with so much freedom. I chose a Jordanian husband who would hold fast to marriage and family; who would put his family first before his own self; who would work with everything he had to make a marriage work and would probably never divorce me. My husband is like the best *Mansaf!* Predictably delicious, nourishing, and good. I can count on him to be a good man. But this place is too small for me. My children and husband come first, but I have never been good at just staying in the house. I want something in the world too."

Dunya. The world. It has a bad name here. The *dunya*; the grind; the relentless sun; the dangerous outside world with lots to tempt you and lead you astray; not a safe place for a cherished good woman. "Yes," Layla nods, understanding, "Dua's husband told her to stop school. She is very smart, always was smart, and she was doing very well. The women all stop working outside once they get married." Now she is talking about my nephew-in-law. "Why do you think that is?" I ask. "Because his cup is half full—he is poor, I mean. Then, when she goes out, she may leave him for one whose cup is full. He doesn't want her to see a rich man like that."

"A woman here wouldn't leave her man for another for money would she?" I ask. I can't imagine this situation here, given all the factors. In America I can totally see it. "No! Never." She is shaking her head. "Also, the work on the home is very important. He works hard and she makes it worth it to have a place to come to away from that. She is everything for him." "Ah," I say, to say yes. The women keep their beauty for home and the men are attracted to them like bees to flowers. Lipstick on at home, off when they go out. I have never seen the kind of partnership that seems the cultural norm here. The interdependence. The clearly defined duties based on gender. It saves a lot of time figuring out who will do what, and mostly it works for people. Hardly any divorce and hours upon hours of time hanging out together, playing, just enjoying each other's company. We, in the west, are typically so busy in relationship drama, or living to work. They work just enough to enjoy their stable and predictable life together.

She sees me now. "Some from here and some from there and it is complete." She says with understanding. "Yes," I reply. That is how I have done it. Carving my own way." ♥

السَّلَامُ

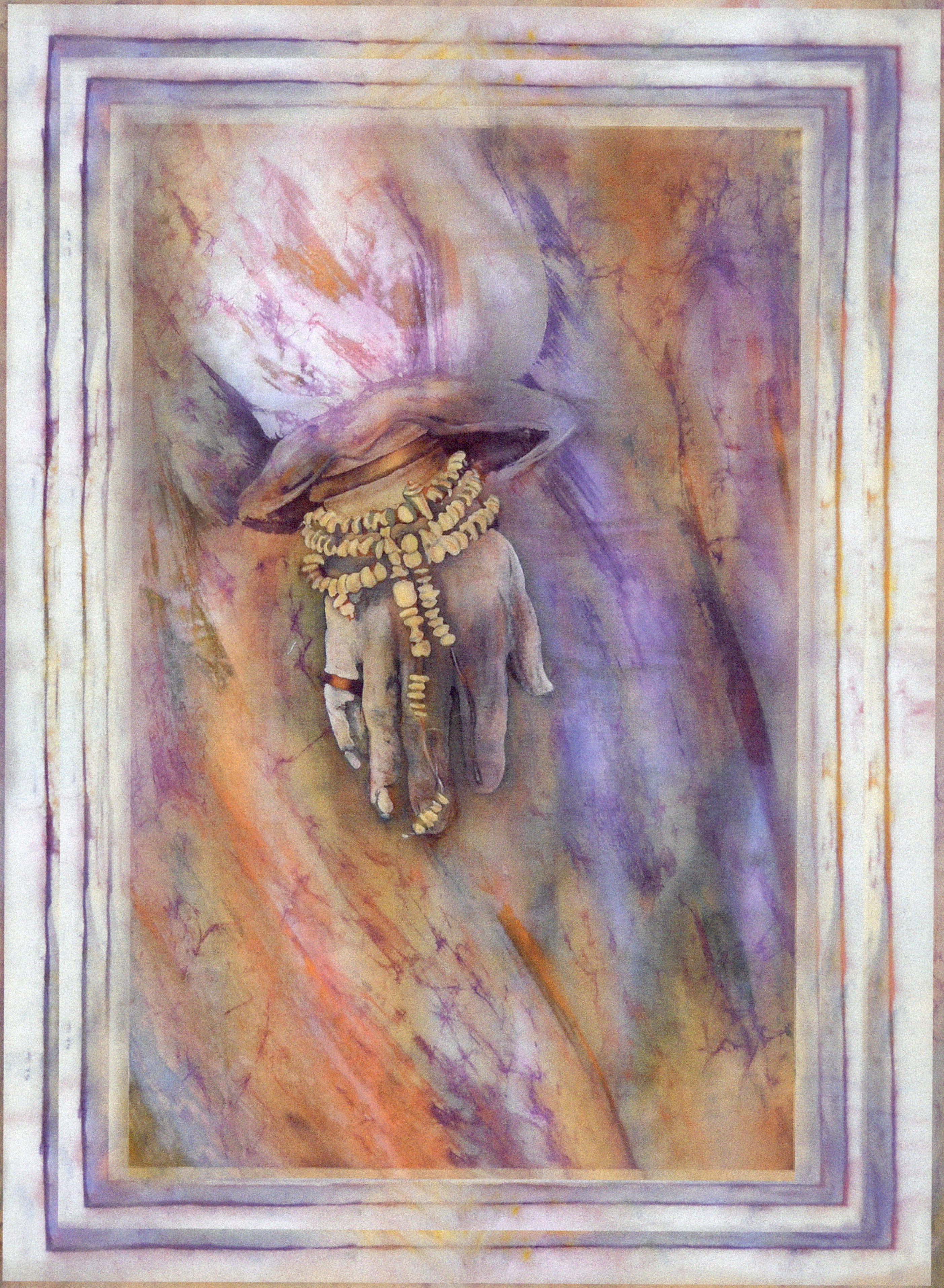

Surrender

All of the prophets and saints have understood the practice of surrender to the will of God. A simple practice of surrender is to find a place on the earth that is comfortable and clean, and lie face down. Spread out the arms and legs into a five-pointed star. Take a moment to breathe in this position, and consider what your destiny is as a human being on this planet. Tradition says that only humans do not know that we are here to praise. The entire world is vibrating with the hum of *Alhamdulillah*—All Praise to Allah. As human beings it is our responsibility to evoke this praise and gratitude and so spread luminosity in the world.

Throughout all time and space we exist in the Generosity of Allah, most merciful and compassionate. From the moment of one's birth and first breath in the element of air, beyond our mother's womb, this lifelong cartography of the seen and unseen worlds is established. The reality that maps one's orientation throughout life as a Muslim affirms the Generosity of God.

The generosity of divine Mercy and Compassion embraces all of existence. The birth of the Prophet Muhammad, known as the Seal of the Prophets within Islam, is one confirmation of this generosity for the Muslim.

Qutayelah, a wise woman of Mecca, foretold the birth of Prophet Muhammad to his father, Abdullah. As described in *Birth Stories of the Prophets*, by Dede Khan, she had a dream in which an angel told her to recognize and greet the father of the coming Prophet by the unique light emanating from his forehead. When she saw Abdullah coming out of the *Kaaba* with his father, Qutayelah identified Abdullah by the sign upon his forehead, and rushed to tell him of his destiny.

The practice of reading the forehead is still a skill among certain schools of Sufi mystics. The life force and vitality, the balance and fullness of breath in the body, the radiance of the countenance, and the vibrational field of Love are important signs of identification. At a time of crisis in my own life, the Sufi teacher, Murshida Vera Corda, read the foreheads of all those close to me and gave me instruction for rebalancing and renewing these relationships.

Abdullah, father of Muhammad, died shortly after the consummation of his marriage. Amina was pregnant with Muhammad. This sudden death of her husband left Amina alone to raise her son. She was a noblewoman and managed to raise her unusual, kind and thoughtful son with the help of the community.

Dreams that she experienced during her pregnancy were recorded. Early in the pregnancy she dreamed that the Angel Gabriel came to greet her. After this dream, unusual lightning appeared in the skies as far as Syria. This electrical storm was followed by an earthquake. Famine, due to drought, was relieved during Amina's pregnancy, as rains fell throughout the deserts of Africa and Arabia. The angel Gabriel appeared to Amina several times. He instructed her to call the child Muhammad, meaning, "He who praises God." Gabriel told her that this son was to be blessed on earth and in the heavens. Amina was humble before the Angel Gabriel and praised and thanked God for this great blessing in her life.

Stars of blue etched with gold swirled above her head and body during her time of labor and childbirth. The whirling colors are said to have hypnotized her and brought her into a state of ecstasy. In this state she heard the soothing voice of Asiya, sister and wife of Pharaoh and savior of baby Musa—Moses, and Mariam, mother of Jesus. A white dove with an emerald beak appeared. The wings of the dove caressed the sides of her swollen belly, which is similar to the soothing practice of effleurage, sometimes used by midwives during birthing. The birth proceeded painlessly and her son, Muhammad, was born.

Three angels, one carrying a silver ewer, one an emerald bowl, and the third, a beautiful white silk towel, surrounded the infant. Seven times, the angels washed the child and carried him away on strong-winged backs.

The Persian leader, Anushirvan dreamed of a new sun rising and, on this night, the fire that had burned on the Zoroastrian Persian altar for a thousand years was extinguished, cold and dead. Muslim history records that the Jews also foretold that a special star would appear on this night, the start of *Ahmad*, the Star of the new prophet.

The custom of the upper classes of Mecca, to which Amina belonged, was to send babies to the villages away from the dust and atmosphere of the city. Halima, whose name means the gentle one, was the milk mother for two years to the Prophet Muhammad in the desert. Within the desert aristocracy, it was an honored custom for a child to be fed by the milk mother. Halima returned Muhammad to his mother in Mecca, but due to epidemics he lived with Halima for up to six years, according to some accounts.

According to legend, while he is a young boy living in the desert with his milk mother, he was herding cattle when two angels appeared, threw him upon the ground, and cut open his breast. When Halima questioned Muhammad about this experience he told her that the two men in brilliant white clothing threw him down and removed a black spot from his heart, which the angels disposed of immediately. They then closed his chest again and disappeared. The angels purified Muhammad's heart—bestowing upon him the first seal of prophethood.

> There came unto me two men clothed in white,
> With a gold basin full of snow.
> Then they laid hold upon me,
> And split open my breast.
>
> They brought forth my heart.
> This likewise, they split open
> And took from it a black clot,
> Which they cast away.
>
> Then they washed my heart
> And my breast with the snow.
>
> —Quran, Sura 94: 1

Galaxies

The desert stretches skyward.
Evening rolls down the sequence
of color to black.
Out past the tents, the faqiri moon,
a rim-slip of silver, sets.

Now the Milky Way is everything—
Glisten is flung from there, out of the pools
of paradise where the Mothers of Islam bathe:

Amina, and Halima—the wet nurse
are first with splash and laughter;
then wives: Khadija and Aisha;
Umm Habiba, Umm Salama, Sawda, Hafsa, Rayhana,
Safiyya, Marya, Zaynab, Juwayriyya, and Maymuna—
daughters: Zaynab, Ruqayya, Umm Kulthum, and Fatima,
A shower of blessings to all!

Honored by the Prophet, each woman
a galaxy, a night breeze, a mysterious pearl;
each one a solar system, complete in the white
blaze of her name. They lighten the sky,
beauty mark of the heavens, and heighten my astonishment
until I'm milk-marked and speechless. They say:
    Those earthly years
    we ringed 'round him,
    held everything firm, as tent pegs do,
    we kept him love-heavy;
    husband, father, light—of—a—life-time
    we star in a thousand family stories.
                  Write them.

                    —Tamam Kahn

Zakat—Giving to Others

The sacred is woven into every aspect of the religion of Islam and its expression in daily life. The unique life story of Khadija, the first wife of Muhammad and the first Muslim, can provide insight into this ideal.

Khadija is a role model for many reasons. Her life is one of *abd'Allah,* servant to Allah and Prophet Muhammad. This represents the balance between the exoteric and esoteric, the mundane and the sacred, the active and the passive. She is the successful business executive and family organizer. She is the loving mother and supportive wife. Her life is one of generosity, as she praises Allah for both the gifts and hardships of her existence. She balances the breath of *baraka* (blessing) with giving back to her family and community, to those less fortunate, and to the destitute ones.

This generosity is *Zakat,* the fourth pillar of Islam. The Muslim household is directed to give one fortieth of its resources to the poor and all those in need, annually, at the end of the month of *Ramadan.* This is formal *Zakat.* There is also the principal of generosity that is continual *Zakat.* As a tool for training the ego, try doing hidden acts of generosity with no human to witness or applaud.

This generosity directs one to share with those less fortunate the material necessities of food, clothing and shelter. It also includes the generosity of sharing one's knowledge. It is the kind word, the loving glance, the helpful prayer or direction. The directions for this, as for all Muslim life, are found in the Quran and in the Hadith.

> *Behold, the God-conscious will find themselves amid gardens and springs, enjoying all that their Sustainer will have granted them because, verily they were doers of good in the past.*
>
> *They would lie asleep during but a small part of the night and would pray for forgiveness from their innermost hearts, and would assign in all that they possessed a due share unto such as might ask for help and such as might suffer privation.*
>
> —Quran, Sura 1: 5-19

KHADIJA BINT KHUWAYLID

Khadija Bint Khuwaylid (may Allah be pleased with her) came from a Quraysh tribe of Mecca. Her father, the leader Khuwaylid, and family were wealthy nobles. He was killed in a battle while she was still a young woman. Khadija was educated and raised to be independent. Her camel caravans worked the trade routes to and from Mecca. Her house, one of the richest in Mecca, overlooked the Kaaba. She dressed elegantly, with some accounts comparing her to a queen. Her private residence and garden were known for their refinement, luxury, and beauty. She married within the noble class and, when her second husband died, she became a wealthy widow.

As a beautiful, rich, intelligent, yet aging, woman, the most important nobles of the Quraysh proposed to her. Pursued by the men of Mecca to remarry, she remained steadfast in her refusal throughout the hounding of these suitors. One evening Khadija dreamed of a brilliant sun descending closer and closer to the earth, until it came to rest within her home. After the dream she queried her wise cousin, Waraqa ibn Nawfal, to interpret the dream. He informed her that she would marry a brilliant man, whose name would be known throughout the world. She committed to the dream of this ideal man and continued to refuse the many marriage proposals.

She held the reputation of being a woman of generous heart who assisted all those in need. Known as the Lady of the Quraysh in Mecca, Khadija is given the name The Mother of Orphans for her endless generosity. It was a time when female infanticide was not unusual. She helped destitute mothers and fathers in saving daughters from this fate.

An astute and successful business executive, running the import and export caravans she inherited, Khadija first interacted with Muhammad when she interviewed him to manage a caravan to Syria. At the time of their meeting, Muhammad was a young and handsome man in his early twenties. He had a reputation in the community of being an honest man, so Khadija employed him, entrusting him with her rich cargo. The young Muhammad proved himself successful and trustworthy in Syria, returning home with a large profit for Khadija. Shortly after his return, Khadija proposed marriage to Muhammad.

After receiving the blessing of Abu Talib, the Prophet's uncle, the couple married. Muhammad was twenty-five years old and Khadija was forty at the time of their wedding. Considering aging in the sixth century, Khadija was definitely an older woman.

There was great love and respect between Muhammad and Khadija. The couple lived happily for the next fifteen years in Mecca, raising children and running the family business.

After the age of forty, Khadija gave birth to seven children. The sons of their union do not survive. Their first child was a son, named Qasim, who died when he was only two years old. Two more sons, Tayyib and Tahir, were also born, but they died in infancy. Their four daughters, Zeinab, Ruqayya, Umm Kulthum and Fatima all survive childhood.

Throughout the city of Mecca, Muhammad becomes known as *al-Amin*, the "trustworthy one."

Muhammad was always reflective and introspective. Every year he made a retreat in the month of *Ramadan* in a cave on Mount Hira, which is close to Mecca. Sometimes Khadija joined him in fast and prayer. Other times she brought food and water to sustain him during his retreat. She often was the only one who knew where he went. When Muhammad was the age of forty and Khadija fifty-five, Muhammad returned at the end of the month of Ramadan in the middle of the night, shaking and calling to Khadija, "Cover me, cover me up!" This is the Night of Power in which Muhammad receives the first revelation of Quran through the angel Gabriel. The angel embraces him and commands:

Read, in the Name of your Lord who created, created man from a clot,
   Read, and your Lord is the Most Gracious,
     Who taught with the pen, taught man what he did not know.

—Quran, Sura 96: 1-5

Khadija quickly wrapped a blanket around the quaking Muhammad. After she waited for him to stop shaking, she asked him what had happened. He told her of the marvelous being, the angel who appeared to him while he is in the cave.

Astounded by the beauty and majesty of Gabriel, Muhammad was shivering in fear and shock. At this time, he is not clear if this is all his imagination or if he is losing his mind.

Khadija takes Muhammad to see her cousin, Waraqa ibn Nawfal, who is a scholar in the Holy books of the Jews and Christians. He confirmed that Muhammad is the Prophet foretold by Moses and Jesus. He foretold of the difficulties that Muhammad and Khadija would experience. He emphasized the history of the previous prophets to them, outcast and expelled from their own tribe and community.

As a final affirmation of this Prophet, Waraqa felt between Muhammad's shoulder blades and found a small, round, slightly raised irregularity in the skin, about the size of a pigeon's egg. This sign confirmed for Waraqa that Muhammad was the next Prophet after Jesus. This mark is known as "the seal of the Prophet."

Khadija and Muhammad worked together in the unfoldment of Islam. Khadija was the first Muslim to publicly perform the First Pillar of Islam: "I bear witness that there is no god but God, and I bear witness that Muhammad is the servant and the Messenger of God."

Throughout the challenges, Khadija remained a loyal and patient helpmate to Muhammad. She spent all her wealth spreading the message of Prophet Muhammad. During these tumultuous early times, she was at the forefront of support, housing and feeding the growing community of Muslim converts.

The community is ostracized and persecuted. The fledgling community flees Mecca, some to Abyssinia, where Negus, the Christian ruler, welcomed them. The *Quraysh* of Mecca were intent on the failure and destruction of Muhammad and his message. As Waraqa foretold, the time came when Muhammad, Khadija, and the first Muslims and the members of his tribe, the Banu Hashim, were forced out of the city of Mecca.

The families camped in the mountains, exposed to bitter cold in the winter and fierce heat in the summer, with few amenities, little food and minimum shelter. A prohibition was enforced that allowed no buying and selling with the Muslims. Intermarriage was prohibited with the new sect. Secret sympathizers sent food and clothing to the community. There are stories of horses and riders being sent off riderless with the prayer that they would reach the community, which was taboo to visit. Throughout the hardships of exposure to extreme hunger and thirst, heat and cold, the faith of the first Muslims intensifies, and they put their trust in the wisdom and goodness of Allah.

After three years of hardship, the Muslims were permitted to return to Mecca. This is a time of mourning for the Prophet as his uncle and supporter, Abu Talib, who was in his eighties, did not survive the hardships. Khadija also died this year, only months later during Ramadan, at the age of sixty-five. Prophet Muhammad mourned the loss of his confidant and strongest ally who supported him and their community with her loving and generous nature.

The Prophet and Khadija shared twenty-five years of monogamous marriage and companionship. They survived the challenges of persecution, loss of children, and times of great hardship. Khadija remained a strong and helpful partner to Muhammad. She was the mother of his only children who survived to adulthood. She is known as *Khair-un-nisa*, the best of women. She is also called *Tahira*, meaning pure.

Many difficult years followed for the family, as the Prophet worked at spreading the message of Compassion and Mercy of Allah. As the first *Umm al-Mu'min*, Mother of the Faithful, Khadija lays the foundation of Islamic spirituality and family life.

She is called the midwife of Islam for her support and faith in Muhammad. The wealthy, respected businesswoman and financier died in 619, during the persecution of the first Muslims by the Quraysh in Mecca, during extreme food deprivations. The love between Khadija and the Prophet Muhammad extended beyond her death, as he continued to honor her throughout his life.

These are messages of the divine writ, full of wisdom,
Providing guidance and grace unto the doers of good,
Who are constant in prayer and dispense charity;

For it is they, they who in their innermost heart are certain of the life to come.
It is they who follow guidance that comes to them from their Sustainer;
And it is they, they who shall attain to a happy state!

—Quran, Sura 31: 2-5

INTERVIEW WITH MAHEERA

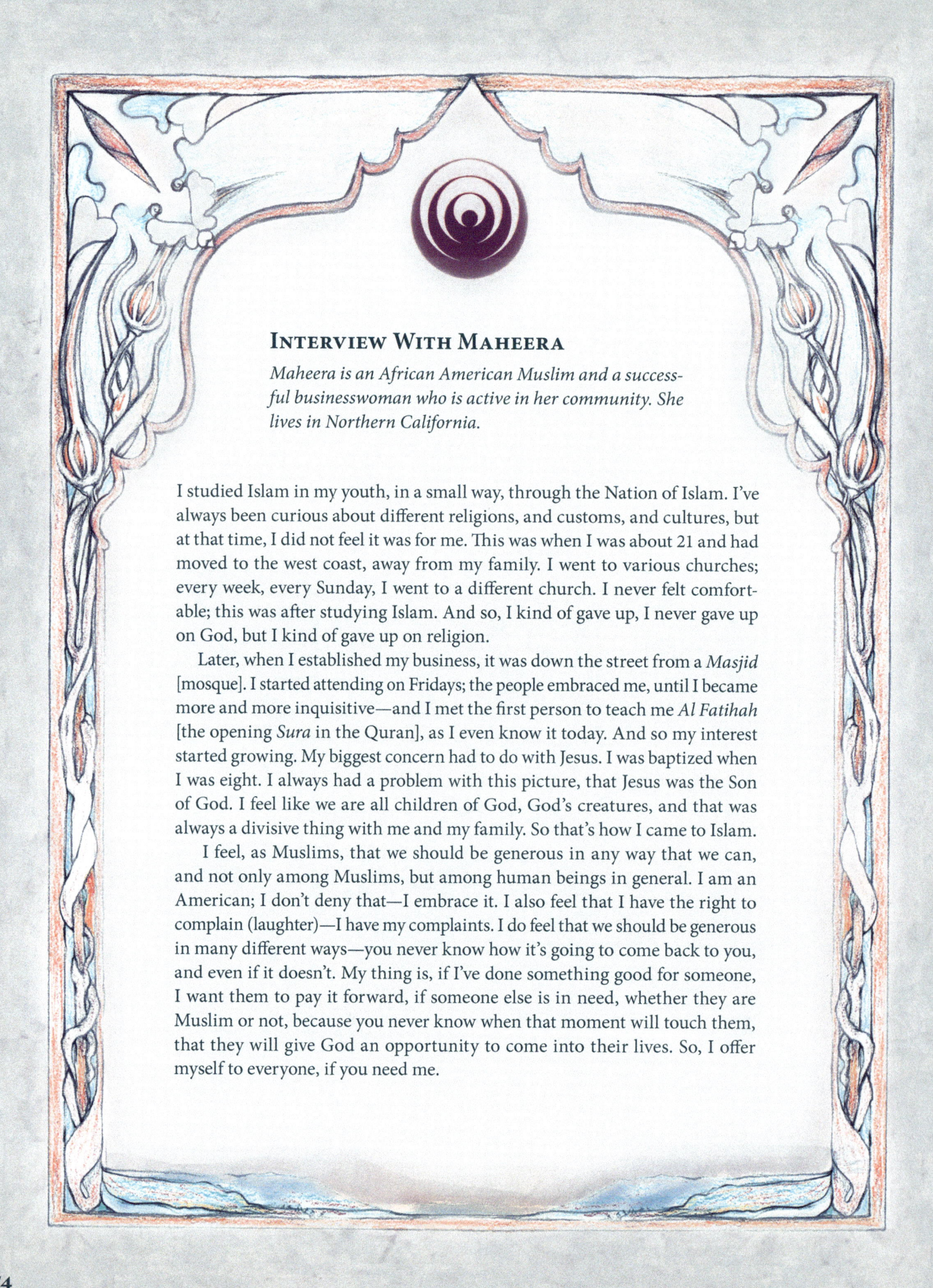

Maheera is an African American Muslim and a successful businesswoman who is active in her community. She lives in Northern California.

I studied Islam in my youth, in a small way, through the Nation of Islam. I've always been curious about different religions, and customs, and cultures, but at that time, I did not feel it was for me. This was when I was about 21 and had moved to the west coast, away from my family. I went to various churches; every week, every Sunday, I went to a different church. I never felt comfortable; this was after studying Islam. And so, I kind of gave up, I never gave up on God, but I kind of gave up on religion.

Later, when I established my business, it was down the street from a *Masjid* [mosque]. I started attending on Fridays; the people embraced me, until I became more and more inquisitive—and I met the first person to teach me *Al Fatihah* [the opening *Sura* in the Quran], as I even know it today. And so my interest started growing. My biggest concern had to do with Jesus. I was baptized when I was eight. I always had a problem with this picture, that Jesus was the Son of God. I feel like we are all children of God, God's creatures, and that was always a divisive thing with me and my family. So that's how I came to Islam.

I feel, as Muslims, that we should be generous in any way that we can, and not only among Muslims, but among human beings in general. I am an American; I don't deny that—I embrace it. I also feel that I have the right to complain (laughter)—I have my complaints. I do feel that we should be generous in many different ways—you never know how it's going to come back to you, and even if it doesn't. My thing is, if I've done something good for someone, I want them to pay it forward, if someone else is in need, whether they are Muslim or not, because you never know when that moment will touch them, that they will give God an opportunity to come into their lives. So, I offer myself to everyone, if you need me.

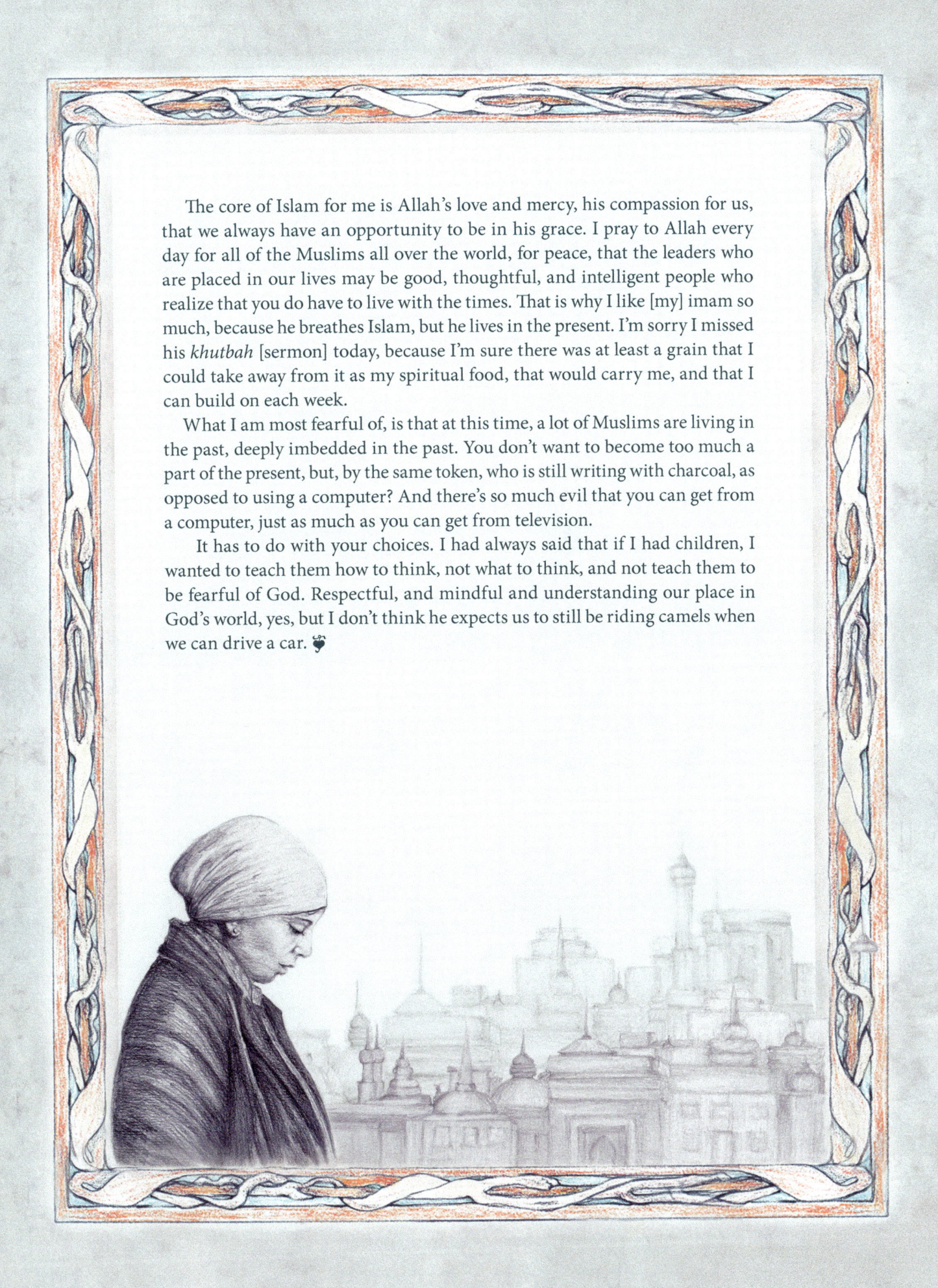

The core of Islam for me is Allah's love and mercy, his compassion for us, that we always have an opportunity to be in his grace. I pray to Allah every day for all of the Muslims all over the world, for peace, that the leaders who are placed in our lives may be good, thoughtful, and intelligent people who realize that you do have to live with the times. That is why I like [my] imam so much, because he breathes Islam, but he lives in the present. I'm sorry I missed his *khutbah* [sermon] today, because I'm sure there was at least a grain that I could take away from it as my spiritual food, that would carry me, and that I can build on each week.

What I am most fearful of, is that at this time, a lot of Muslims are living in the past, deeply imbedded in the past. You don't want to become too much a part of the present, but, by the same token, who is still writing with charcoal, as opposed to using a computer? And there's so much evil that you can get from a computer, just as much as you can get from television.

It has to do with your choices. I had always said that if I had children, I wanted to teach them how to think, not what to think, and not teach them to be fearful of God. Respectful, and mindful and understanding our place in God's world, yes, but I don't think he expects us to still be riding camels when we can drive a car.

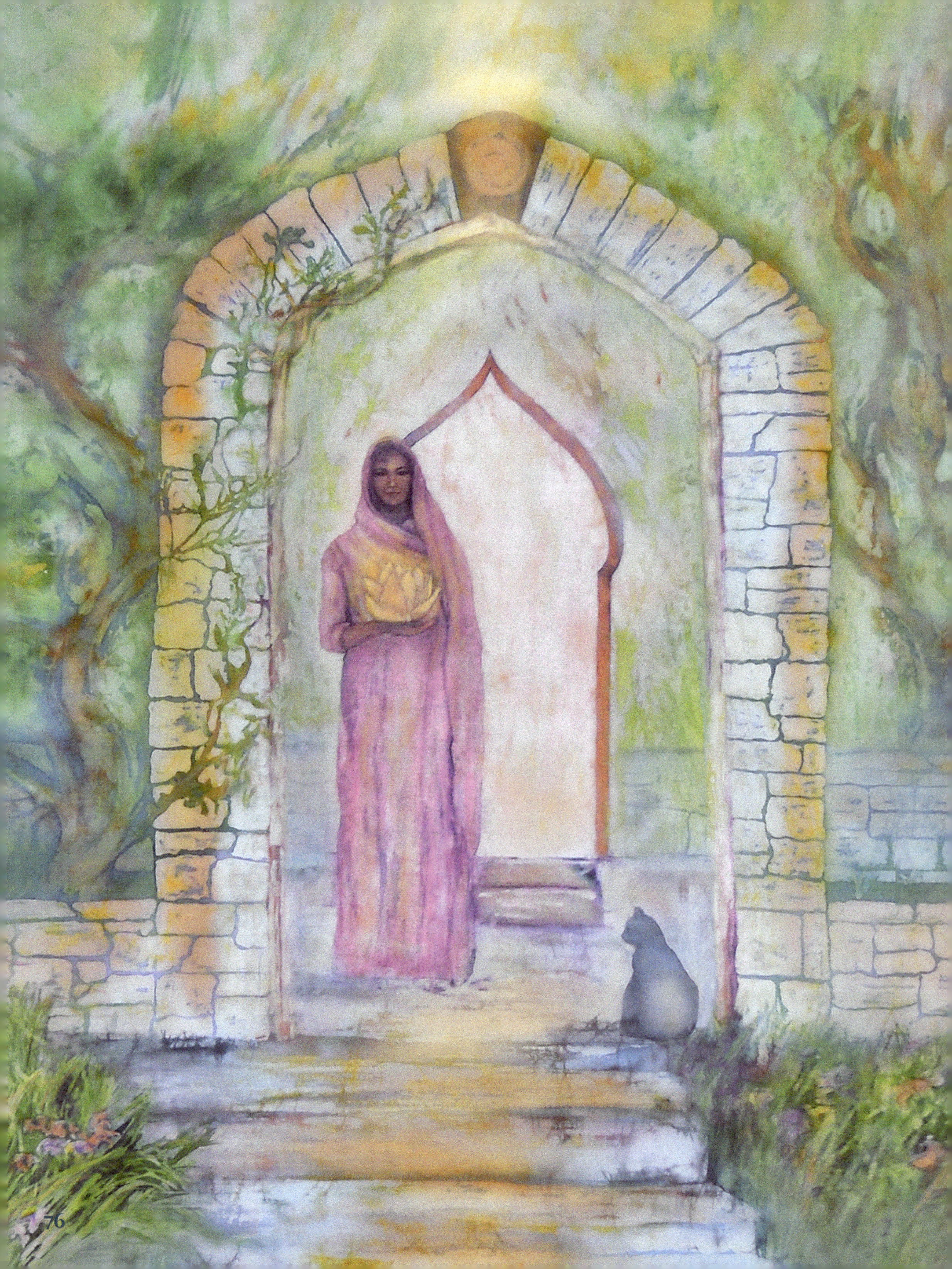

CREATING HEART SPACE:
RECIPES FOR THE SACRED

DIVINE ARCHETYPES—GENEROSITY

The ninety-nine attributes of God represent different archetypes that exist in the human and universal consciousness. Some of those representing generosity are:
Ya Wahab, Ya Karim, Ya Rezaq, Ya Ghani.

These sacred sounds may be spoken aloud or silently intoned on the breath to experience the subtle and different sacred qualities of generosity. Experiment to find one that most resonates with you in this moment.

Ya Wahab—The Bestower; The Giver. The wise say that repetition of this holy name brings *Baraka*, blessing, the gift of security and inspiration in and from God.

Ya Karim—The Generous; the Bountiful. The wise say that repetition of this holy name strengthens faith in God and nourishes generosity.

Ya Rezaq—The Provider; The Sustainer; The Maintainer. The wise say that repetition of this holy name gives succor, or support, in times of hardship.

Ya Ghani—The Rich; the Independent; the Self-Sufficient. The wise say that repetition of this holy name gives contentment and freedom from jealousy.

Walking Meditation
Find a place outdoors, in a forest, on the beach, or in a garden. Concentrate on the reality of abundant blessing and generosity. Breath in "Ahl"; breathe out "Lah." Let the breath come into balance as you inhale for a count of four and exhale for a count of four, with the rhythm of "Ahl–Lah," as the breath gently flows in and out. Walk four steps on the inhalation, four steps on the exhalation. Allah Allah Allah Allah—walk with this concentration for around ten minutes.

Secret Service
Do one act of hidden generosity daily for seven days. Try to do this at the same time every day.

The Rose and Islam—
Fragrance of Generosity

The rose is known as the queen of flowers and mirror of beauty. It is an archetype of completeness and perfection. The rose is a symbol of the generosity of Allah, giving both fragrance and fruit, sustaining body, heart, and soul.

The fragrance of the rose is said to be pleasing to angels and saints and to assist in our listening to the spirit of guidance.

Honored within Islam, the rose is associated with the Prophet Muhammad, Mevlana Jelaluddin Rumi, Mariam (Mary) mother of Isa (Jesus), other saints and friends of the Friend, peace and blessings be upon them. There is a saying that the rose is born of the sweat of the Prophet's brow. The artifacts of the Prophet, garments and hair from his beard, are said to smell of roses, even centuries later. This can be experienced in Konya at the Turbe (Tomb) of Mevlana Jelaluddin Rumi. Pilgrims stand next to the glass case protecting beard hairs of Prophet Muhammad, as this pilgrim, the author of this book, did. The delicious fragrance of roses is perceptible as a living gift from the Prophet.

The first roses may have been cultivated in ancient Persia. Wild roses grow throughout Turkey, the Middle East and India. It is an essential ingredient in cuisine, infusing food and drink with unique culinary qualities. The essence of rose has uses both medicinally and cosmetically.

There is a story that Shah Jahan, the seventeenth-century Mughal emperor who built the Taj Mahal, filled the moat surrounding the castle in Agra with rose petals and rose water for his marriage celebration. Guests were ferried by boat through this rose liquid. The heat of the Indian sun began the natural distillation process of isolating the oil, which floated to the surface. The fragrance delighted his young wife, Mumtaz Mahal, and their guests.

All of what we call the Middle East is rich with wild roses. Muslim poets, Sufis, botanists and gardeners all study the rose. The Sufi orders treasure roses. There is a saying in Sufism that the presence of the Beloved (God) is beyond any human description, but that the scent of the rose is as close as one can get to conveying the feeling of that presence. The rose is an essential element in the Persian garden.

Roses are traditional at the *Urs* celebrations of the saints. The term, *Urs*, refers to the anniversary of a saint's passing, his time of reunion with God. One can see the tombs of saints and prophets covered with roses and rose petals. Each participant often leaves these celebrations with the gift of a rose.

The rose is a symbol of the marriage of the spiritual and natural worlds, a royal archetype of manifest beauty in all of its wild, cultured, and cultivated forms. The symbol of the rose is the unfolding self in submission to Allah, spiraling into manifestation from the bud stage, to live a life of beauty. Petals fall and the rose hip forms. The spiraling cycle of creation continues in the truth that from Allah we come, to Allah we shall return.

The fragrance of the rose calms the mind and revivifies the spirit. It touches the heart, and is associated with the heart chakra. Rose fragrance nourishes the nerves and soothes the stressed psyche. The essential oil of the rose is a tool to balance and unify the exoteric with the esoteric, the masculine and the feminine, within the chamber of the heart. With this unity of self comes the opening to inner peace.

Perfume of generosity—Rose

Place essence of rose on the heart chakra, in the center of the breastbone, for peace, tranquility and inspiration. Listen to the poetry of the fragrance as it arises in the breath. Flower of generosity—Rose.

Place a rose in a hidden location for Allah—the library, the bus station, the bakery, the bookstore. Allow the generosity to manifest in this gift of nature. It has been said that women, perfume and prayer are loveable to the Prophet.

> *To remain forever in the world you love is an*
> *Ambition beyond reach.*
> *Remember the date palm that still stands*
> *After the gardener's demise.*
> *That sweetness is eternal.*
>
> —Sha'wana

HONOR THE EARTH—PLANT A ROSE

Plant a rose bush in the ground or in a pot, a miniature or a tree. Allow your heart's longing to choose the color. Consider your relationship to this plant as you create a healthy home for it to grow. Through this interaction and contemplation with the world of nature we can glean tools to understand the self. Experience the generosity of the rose. Listen for a poem or music in the fragrance of the rose. Inshallah (God Willing) this rose will bloom long after your passage from the earth, continuing to give the essence of its nature—beauty. In giving, the essence of our nature is generosity.

In love nothing exists between breast and breast.
Speech is born out of longing,
True description from the real taste.
The one who tastes, knows.
The one who explains, lies.
How can you describe the true form of something
In whose Presence you are blotted out?
And in whose Being you still exist
And Who lives as a sign for your journey.

—Rabi'a of Basra

يا حي يا قيوم

The Gift of the Silk Route

4

Women in Early Islam

It is said that the Holy Quran is written in the desert sands, on the shoulder blade of a camel, and in the hearts of pure men and women. The women of Prophet Muhammad's family were some of the first believers and pure-hearted Muslims.

The teachings of Muhammad and the arrival of the Quran transformed the culture and society of the Arabian Peninsula and the Silk Route. The value placed upon education and the directive that all, men and women, pursue knowledge is inherent in the teachings of the Prophet. Muhammad introduced legal rights for women relative to property, marriage and divorce. It is most unfortunate that these religious laws are not respected by the radical fundamentalists who are violently destroying opportunity and lives, and who choose not to follow the Messenger or the Message.

Islam and the Sufi tradition are rich with women mystics, although their stories are often anonymous and hidden. Today we have increasing access to more translation and compilation of these histories than ever before.

DREAM SEQUENCE

The moon is full. We've ridden for hours into the desert. The camels are grumpy. It is silent except for the soft chatter and laughter of the caravan. The desert has turned from tans and browns and grays under the broiling sun to indigo and sparkling flashes of gold under the moonlight. A quiet surrounds me, a silence stretched in all directions. We put out the prayer rugs in the direction of Mecca for the night prayer, Isha. After the last bow, and the greeting of the angel, with peace on the right, and the greeting of the angel with peace on the left, I continue to sit, listening to the silence of the drifting desert mountains, listening for our human story and for the story of the women. There is only silence and moonlight.

Muhammad's Wives and the Women of Islam

Khadija Bint Khuwaylid

The year that Khadija died is called the Year of Sorrows. It is more than difficult to imagine the persecutions of the Muslims in these early years: the poverty, the times of extreme hunger and thirst. Sometimes there was neither food nor water. Harsh wind and desert sand storms were part of their rigorous life. The strength that came from mutual belief and devotion to the Prophet Muhammad and the new religion of Islam, as well as the extremely raw experience of the desert, gave the growing community unity.

These are the conditions and circumstances of Fatima's childhood and the conditions and circumstances at the end of Khadija's life. The first wife of Prophet Muhammad, Khadija was visited many times by the angels. Because Muhammad was too poor to offer the traditional bridal gift at the time of marriage, legends suggest that the angel Gabriel gave her gems. At the time of her death, her burial shroud is said to have been woven by angels and delivered by Gabriel. It is said the Prophet told her they would be joined after the earthly life, and where to find him in paradise. Khadija and Muhammad shared a fruitful and monogamous companionship until her death in 619. Several of the wives of the Prophet experienced dreams of Muhammad prior to marriage with him that foretold their alliance.

Sawda bint Zam'ah

The first woman Muhammad married after the death of Khadija is Sawda bint Zam'ah. She was a widow of forty with a son. By joining Sawda in legal marriage, the Prophet rescued her from the existent tribal society of the time that provided no future but destitution or enslavement for single women. The ages of most of the other wives, also previously widowed or divorced, was between forty and fifty. Several had children that joined the household of the Prophet. Aisha was the only "virginal" wife.

Certainly those who criticize Islam's Prophet as promiscuous and a philanderer do not have an understanding of the history of the time or the harsh conditions of tribal desert society that left women and children most vulnerable.

Aisha bint Abu Bakr

Aisha, daughter of Khalif Abu Bakr, is considered the favorite wife and companion of Prophet Muhammad. She is known as *Umm Al Mumineen*, Mother of the Faithful. Deeply devoted to Muhammad and Islam since her girlhood, she was one of the main contributors of Hadith. She was a *Hafiz*, one who has completely memorized the Quran. Adroit in legal understanding of the new Muslim society, she was a respected source of Islamic wisdom throughout her lifetime, and generously shared this knowledge.

Muhammad died in her small home, a modest hut, with his head in Aisha's lap, and he was buried under the floor of this dwelling. Aisha was eighteen years old when she became a widow. Aisha and Fatima, the daughter of Muhammad, were the nearest to the Prophet in life and at the time of his departure from the earth.

Muhammad's further marriages, for political, compassionate and personal reasons, were to Hafsa bint Umar, Zaynab bint Khuzayma, Umm Salama Hind bint Abi Umayya, Zaynab bint Jahsh, Juwayriyya bint al-Harith, Rayhana bint Zayd, Umm Habiba Ramla bint Abi Sufyan, Safiyya bint Huyeiy Ibn Akhtab, Maria al-Qibtiyya, Maymuna bint al-Harith, each of whom contributed uniquely to the early days of Islam.

Fatima Al-Zahra bint Muhammad

Fatima is conceived with the blessings of paradise. Divine food is delivered to Muhammad prior to her conception. The angel Gabriel brings the Prophet a plate of dates and grapes from heaven and commands him to eat this food. He is then commanded to go to Khadija, and Fatima is conceived. And the Prophet confirms that Fatima is conceived from the fruits of paradise.

While Khadija is pregnant with Fatima, she experiences an easy pregnancy. The growing infant speaks to Khadija from the womb. Muhammad rejoices when he hears of this occurrence, affirming that Fatima will begin the maternal line of his successors.

It was also a difficult time for Khadija. Once revered by the tribe of Quraysh, particularly the women, she is now abandoned with her young husband Muhammad, two daughters from a prior marriage, and the blessings of more children to come and the newly forming religion.

As legend has it: No midwives would assist her. When the birthing time comes, four beautiful women come to assist her: Eve; Miriam, sister of Moses; Assiya, wife of the Pharaoh; and Mariam, mother of Jesus.

These untraditional midwives deliver Fatima, who is given the name *Al-Zahra* (the shining one), because of the bioluminescence she carries. She is known as a model of Islam.

Fatima is left motherless at a young age when Khadija dies at age sixty-three. She marries Ali, and four children are born from the union: Hasan the eldest; Husain; Zaynab; and Umm Kulthum the youngest daughter. Fatima dies from an injury received when Umar pushes open a door that hits her in the stomach while she was pregnant. The infant dies and Fatima passes away a few months later. There are stories of miracles from her generosity.

In her lifetime she was given many names: *Al-Tahera*, the virtuous or pure; *Al-Zahra*, woman of light; *Al-Siddiqa*, she who is honest and sincere; *Al-Mubaraka*, the blessed one; *Al Batool*, the chaste; *Al-Zakiya*, the pure; *Al-Radhiya*, the satisfied; *Al-Mardhiya*, the one pleasing to Allah. Some say she is the Islamic Mary, the one to whom one can pray for supplication; the one who transmits the mercy of Allah through the brilliance of her nature.

Muhammad asked his favorite daughter, Fatima, if she accepted Ali in marriage. She replied that she would accept upon one condition that did not concern Ali. "If that condition is fulfilled, I will accept. If not, I will never accept to marry Ali." When asked by the Prophet what this condition was, she replied:

"I hear you continuously, day and night, praying for your community. You say 'O My Lord! Give me permission to lead my community to you! Forgive them; purify them! Take away their sins and difficulties and burdens!' I hear you and know how much you suffer for your community. I know from what you have said that when you pass away, you will still be saying 'My community!' to your Lord, in your grave and on Judgment Day. My father, I see you suffering so much for your community. Since that love of your community is also in my heart, I want your community as my dowry. If you accept, I will marry Ali."

Muhammad waited for guidance as to whether it was proper for him to give Fatima this dowry. In a vision Gabriel appeared with the message, "God sends you His greetings and accepts Fatima's request." Muhammad then gave her what she asked for as her dowry. Fatima, educated and respected, following in her father's footsteps, took every member of the Muslim community into the space of her heart and under her wing, reflecting both the love of her father and her surrender to her destiny as a Muslim woman.

Muhammad instructed his wife, Aisha, to prepare the wedding feast for Fatima and Ali. They served the guests with dates, grapes and sweet water. The marriage feast also included the traditional sheep.

Resolving Conflict

Another beautiful story is told of a time of discord in the marriage of Ali and Fatima. Muhammad, who was visiting at the time, had them lie down on the floor next to each other and place the palm of the right hand on the diaphragm of the other, stop talking and just breathe together. This simple solution quickly and deeply resolved the dispute.

What is most poignant and inspiring in both of these stories of Fatima and Muhammad is Fatima's ability to articulate her needs and desires. In the first story there is the desire to share the responsibility for the growing Muslim community with her father, to be in the function of *Abdullah* (servant of God) with him. In the second story she clearly speaks her need. She is overwhelmed and crying, "Help!"

For a moment, we may consider our own needs and desires. Are we able to articulate and voice these needs and desires to ourselves, to someone we love and respect, to our larger community?

BIBI HAYATI KERMANI

The Sufi mystic Bibi Hayati is best known for her ecstatic poetry. Sincere in prayer and devotion to Allah from an early age, she married her teacher within the Nimatullahi Sufi Order, Nur 'Ali Shah.

Before there was a trace of this world of men,
I carried the memory of a lock of your hair,
A stray end gathered within me, though unknown.

Inside that invisible realm,
Your face like the sun longed to be seen,
Until each separate object was finally flung into light.

From the moment of Time's first-drawn breath,
Love resides in us,
A treasure locked into the heart's hidden vault:

Before the first seed broke open the rose bed of Being.
An inner lark soared through your meadows,
Heading toward Home.

What can I do but thank you, one hundred times?
Your face illumines the shrine of Hayati's eyes,
Constantly present and lovely.

—Bibi Hayati, c. 1853, CE

RABIA AL-ADAWIYYA

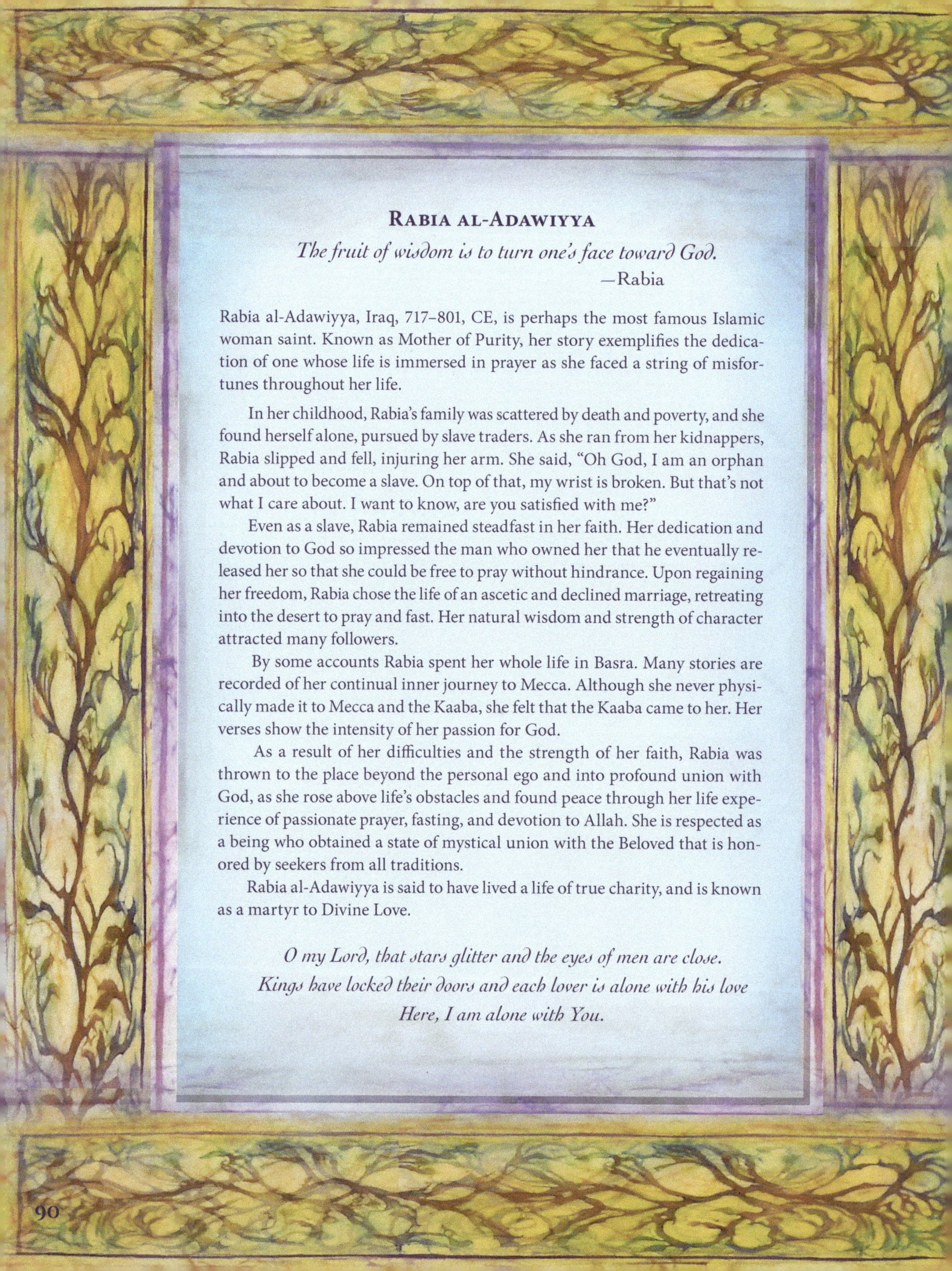

The fruit of wisdom is to turn one's face toward God.
—Rabia

Rabia al-Adawiyya, Iraq, 717–801, CE, is perhaps the most famous Islamic woman saint. Known as Mother of Purity, her story exemplifies the dedication of one whose life is immersed in prayer as she faced a string of misfortunes throughout her life.

In her childhood, Rabia's family was scattered by death and poverty, and she found herself alone, pursued by slave traders. As she ran from her kidnappers, Rabia slipped and fell, injuring her arm. She said, "Oh God, I am an orphan and about to become a slave. On top of that, my wrist is broken. But that's not what I care about. I want to know, are you satisfied with me?"

Even as a slave, Rabia remained steadfast in her faith. Her dedication and devotion to God so impressed the man who owned her that he eventually released her so that she could be free to pray without hindrance. Upon regaining her freedom, Rabia chose the life of an ascetic and declined marriage, retreating into the desert to pray and fast. Her natural wisdom and strength of character attracted many followers.

By some accounts Rabia spent her whole life in Basra. Many stories are recorded of her continual inner journey to Mecca. Although she never physically made it to Mecca and the Kaaba, she felt that the Kaaba came to her. Her verses show the intensity of her passion for God.

As a result of her difficulties and the strength of her faith, Rabia was thrown to the place beyond the personal ego and into profound union with God, as she rose above life's obstacles and found peace through her life experience of passionate prayer, fasting, and devotion to Allah. She is respected as a being who obtained a state of mystical union with the Beloved that is honored by seekers from all traditions.

Rabia al-Adawiyya is said to have lived a life of true charity, and is known as a martyr to Divine Love.

O my Lord, that stars glitter and the eyes of men are close.
Kings have locked their doors and each lover is alone with his love
Here, I am alone with You.

I am fully qualified to work as a doorkeeper,
And for this reason:
What is inside me, I don't let out;
What is outside me, I don't let in.
If someone comes in, he goes right out again.
He has nothing to do with me at all.
I am a Doorkeeper of the Heart,
Not a lump of wet clay.

In two ways have I loved Thee: selfishly,
And with a love that is worthy of Thee.
In selfish love, my joy in Thee I find,
While to all else and others, I am blind.
But in that love which seeks Thee worthily,
The veil is raised that I may look on Thee.
Yet is the praise in that or this, not mine;
In this and that, the praise is wholly Thine.

—Rabia

Cultural Inheritance of the Silk Route

The Silk Road, extending 4,000 miles from eastern China to the Mediterranean Sea, was an ancient trade route, its name derived from the lucrative trade in Chinese silk that took place along its length, beginning during the Han dynasty (206 B.C.–220 A.D.). The Road became the highway of philosophy, architecture, art, algebra, science, of war and weapons, healing, morality and justice, cultural interchange and religion.

Along with the rich interchange of science, philosophy, art and culture, the religion and the stories of the Prophet Muhammad traveled quickly by camel, by the wind, by the perfume, by the stories, by the new sacred text, Holy Quran. Like the Internet highway of today, the silk route changed the known world.

One of the outcomes of this time is what the poets have called the Hidden Treasure, the flowering of Sufism and Islamic Mysticism. Although we know primarily the stories and poetry of the male mystics of this time, the one known as Ibn 'Arabi is profound in his teaching on the feminine nature of the Soul.

We see in his work one of the forerunners and foundations of SoulWork, a sacred psychology rooted in Sufism. We see this inherent wisdom decoded by 'Arabi mirrored by Jung in his twentieth-century development of archetypal psychology.

Ibn 'Arabi remained a lifelong student of mysticism. He honored his women teachers, notably, Nuna Fatima bint Ibn al-Muthanna (Fatima of Cordoba) and Shams Umm al-Fuqara', with whom he studied while living in Seville.

A rich tapestry of culture evolves on the Silk Route from Morocco, through Arabia and Syria, China and Europe, along with unique religious interpretation of the message of the Prophet, of the new religion of Islam cross-pollinating through the Mediterranean, traveling from Arabia west through the northern rim of Africa, west into Spain, Portugal, Italy and France. The religion traveled east into China, India and Persia, seeding the way of the Prophet in people ready for the message of Islam. Among the more distinct cultural attributes were the harem and the veil.

I believe in the religion of Love,
Whatever direction its caravans may take,
For Love is my religion and my faith.

—Ibn 'Arabi

The Myth of the Harem

Colonialist orientalism is rich with many exotic tales of the harem. In reality, the term harem (or *"purdah"* in South Asian societies) simply means the section of the house protected and dedicated to the use of the women. The word originates from the Arabic root *"harama,"* which means forbidden because sacred or important. During the Sultanate of the Ottoman empires, the Harem was a forbidden sanctuary and the permanent house of the Sultan's women, their female serving staff, young children of both sexes, and eunuchs, castrated male slaves.

The seclusion of women within the palace harems was not the romantic fantasy portrayed in fictionalized accounts. In the harems of the Ottoman Empire, the politically powerful sultans were the only males over the age of seven allowed within this restricted area. As in any microcosm of society, levels of status varied based on birth origin and race. For some women the harem was a lifelong prison while others rose to exert great power beyond the confines of their seclusion. Yet, even within this enforced isolation, members of the harem pursued arts and learning, as the harem became a school of literature, art, music and religion.

The harem was the sole possession of the sultan, although the women held there included Turkish, Greek, Chinese, European, Moroccan, and other tribal women. In addition to the wives and concubines of the male royalty, the harem included the Sultan's mother and daughters, and other female relatives, slaves to serve them, and the eunuchs, who were usually slaves who had been castrated before puberty. The eunuchs served as guards for the harem, and held an important place in palace culture.

The sultans, no less than their regal equivalents in the west, were capable of dire behaviors. A devastating tragedy took place under Padishah Ibrahim I (1615-1648). When he heard rumors from his lover, Sechir Para (Sugar Cube), that one of his concubines was sporting with a man outside of the palace, he raged for days and had his chief eunuch torture a few of the harem girls to discover the identity of the mystery girl. None of them would speak, so Ibrahim tied up every single one of his 280 harem women to weighted sacks and had them thrown into the Bosporus River in Istanbul. Only one girl survived (other than the Valide Sultan [the Queen Mother], her *kadins* [companions], and Sechir Para, who were spared) because her sack was not sufficiently tied and she was rescued by a French ship. The Valide Sultan became jealous of Sechir Para's power after the drownings, and had Sechir Para strangled. Ibrahim was told that she had died of a mysterious illness.

The Mother Sultan, or first wife of the sultan, was an important figure in the Sultan's Court and held great influence, playing a meaningful role in Ottoman history. Other wives, sisters and mothers of sultans also played a significant, if somewhat hidden, role. It is said that at times the empire was ruled from the harem. Hürrem Sultan, wife of Süleyman The Magnificent, mother of Selim II, and Kösem Sultan, mother of Murad IV, were the two most powerful women in Ottoman history.

Eventually, extreme greed and the excessive wealth of the Ottomans led to extravagances and amoral behavior that caused the decay and downfall of the empire. After World War I, and Ataturk's movement towards an independent and secular Turkey, the status of women in Turkey changed, but the legend of the Harem remains.

The pursuit of arts, learning and religion were cultivated in the harem. At that location and time there was, in all probability, no place outside of the harem where such a rich learning environment existed for women to engage in, and pursue knowledge of, the wisdom and mysteries of the feminine aspect. What value is there for women in this modern age to seek a society apart, at times, a solely female refuge? What secluded inner harems do we benefit from, places for the personal discovery of our deepest intentions?

We may only speculate what women's wisdom was cultivated within the harem. What can we discover in our own hidden societies, our hidden rooms, as well as the hidden rooms within ourselves where exotic secrets of the feminine are waiting to be uncovered? And, where are we held apart and away from ourselves or from our deepest intentions?

The Veil—the Hijab, the Burqa, the Chador

Contrasting the harem and the veil has led to extreme views of Middle Eastern women in Western society. Stories from history and images in current media emphasize the custom of veiling in the Middle East. This vision of extreme modesty and strict separation of the sexes is in direct contrast to the legends of harems, belly dancers and exotic sensuality.

The Quran called for both women and men to dress modestly and to behave with dignity and respect towards others. It was customary for both sexes to wear long, loose-fitting robes that did not emphasize the contour of the body. Wearing that type of clothing also made it easier to kneel and prostrate oneself in daily prayer.

Many Muslim women veil their heads only during times of prayer and when entering a mosque, holy site or sacred gathering. The exact dictate of the Prophet Muhammad is a controversial issue among theologians.

> *The Believers, men and women, are protectors, one of another: they enjoin what is just and forbid what is evil: they observe regular prayers, practice regular charity, and obey God and His prophet. On them will God pour His mercy.*
>
> *For God is exalted in power, wise. God hath promised to believers, men and women, gardens under which rivers flow, to swell therein, and beautiful mansions, in garden of everlasting bliss is the good pleasure of God, that is the supreme felicity.*
>
> —Quran, Sura 16: 97

The word *hijab* has its root in *hajaba*, meaning to hide from sight or hide with a curtain. In the ancient Arab world, caliphs, kings, and princes often sat behind a curtain to avoid the gaze of members of their court. This practice was later introduced into Islam in the practice of separating the sexes. The custom *of hijab*, or veiling, varies from culture to culture, as does wearing a headscarf. While *"hijab"* generally refers to covering the hair and arms, the term *"niqab"* means covering of the face as well. The headscarf is mandatory for women in some parts of the Middle East, while it is prohibited in others.

Biologically, the odor and scent of human excretions dictates much of the unconscious behavior between the sexes. Covering the hair with a hijab or *chador* prevents almost all female pheromones from escaping in public. The *burqa,* which covers the entire body from head to toe with minimal slit for the eyes, prohibits any release or escape of female pheromones. Beneath the *burqa,* many women wear brightly colored clothes and other feminine adornments—saved for those who are closest to her.

Orthodox Jews and Christians both follow directives relative to covering the hair. In some Islamic cultures, the removal of all bodily hair by women is considered ideal. This does not include the hair of the head as it does in Orthodox Judaism. As with any cultural convention, judgements based on ideas of what is appropriate from a point of view outside of the context of the culture is naturally limiting.

Girls usually begin taking on the custom of hijab between age seven and puberty. The transition from girlhood into womanhood is accentuated by the custom of veiling, as the growing girl begins to identify with the world of women as opposed to that of children. In certain cultures it is the sign of a good Muslim family to begin the veiling of girls before they enter their teens, around age nine or ten.

In many Islamic cultures, there is a belief that men are unable to control their passions, so it is up to the woman to avoid exposing men to the temptation of any glimpse of a woman's face or body. This lack of responsibility on the part of men is obviously limiting to both men and women, but it has also served as the excuse for extreme oppression and violence toward women who did not follow strict traditions of covering. This belief is not in accord with the respect Muhammad afforded women, but rather reflects a deviation from the original message of Islam.

Significant research has been conducted on the wearing of the veil and the response of Westerners to the image that it has conveyed. Scholars such as Katherine Bullock argue that the image of the veil as a symbol of the oppression of women serves western political ends—fostering a sense of "otherness" between Western Women and Islamic societies. She contends that the ideas of liberation and equality that support this view are based on a Western perspective that does not take into account the history on which the hijab is based.

While covering of the head has been standard practice for centuries, women held an important place in early Islamic society and, in fact, their rights deteriorated with the onset of Colonialism in the late nineteenth century. After Napoleon's invasion of Egypt in 1798, veiling became more widespread and increased during the European occupation of the Middle East (1830–1956).

In the late 1970's a re-veiling movement began in Turkey, Iran, and other Middle Eastern societies in which young women chose to cover, unlike their mothers and grandmothers who fought against the veil. This return to tradition was a typical response to what some see as a deterioration of practices that threaten the order created by such practices. Ideally, indigenous women should be given the opportunity to determine for themselves what is oppressive for them, and the notion that veiling is oppressive for all women needs to be examined as a projection of a stereotype based on Western standards and a misunderstanding of the long tradition of the hijab.

Reducing the issue of subjugation of Islamic women to a headscarf is an oversimplification that ignores history and cultural context. Many women find it quite liberating to be free of the sexual projections of men, a view that has been expressed by young women who have chosen the hijab, even as mothers and grandmothers fought against it. This focus on a particular article of clothing ignores the myriad varieties of experience and expression unique to any human, and, as in any stereotype, confines Islamic women within a narrow definition.

It is difficult for non-Muslim women to understand the respect and fondness that many Muslim women have for this practice. The response of many Westerners to covering the hair and body is to see it as direct oppression. For some women in areas of the world where the veil is legally dictated, that is, no doubt, the case. However, the context of the veil within Muslim societies must also be considered. Many young women find freedom in wearing a veil or headscarf that conceals the precious and delicate gift of their sexuality.

In American society where sexuality is explicitly expressed, a modest approach to public appearance shifts the attention away from the sexual projections of men upon women. The refinement of what is most intimate within a woman is saved for the people closest to her. This approach may be difficult for women from Western societies to understand, but perhaps a deep consideration of the history of sexual harassment that most Western women have endured will lead to empathy and understanding.

As we challenge these stereotypes and explore a deeper understanding of traditional Muslim women in society, we are faced with the very real oppression against women from groups such as the Taliban and other extremist religious fundamentalists. Reclaiming the beautiful symbolism of the veil, and the comfort and protection it provides for many women who chose the hijab, is one simple step that we can take toward peace.

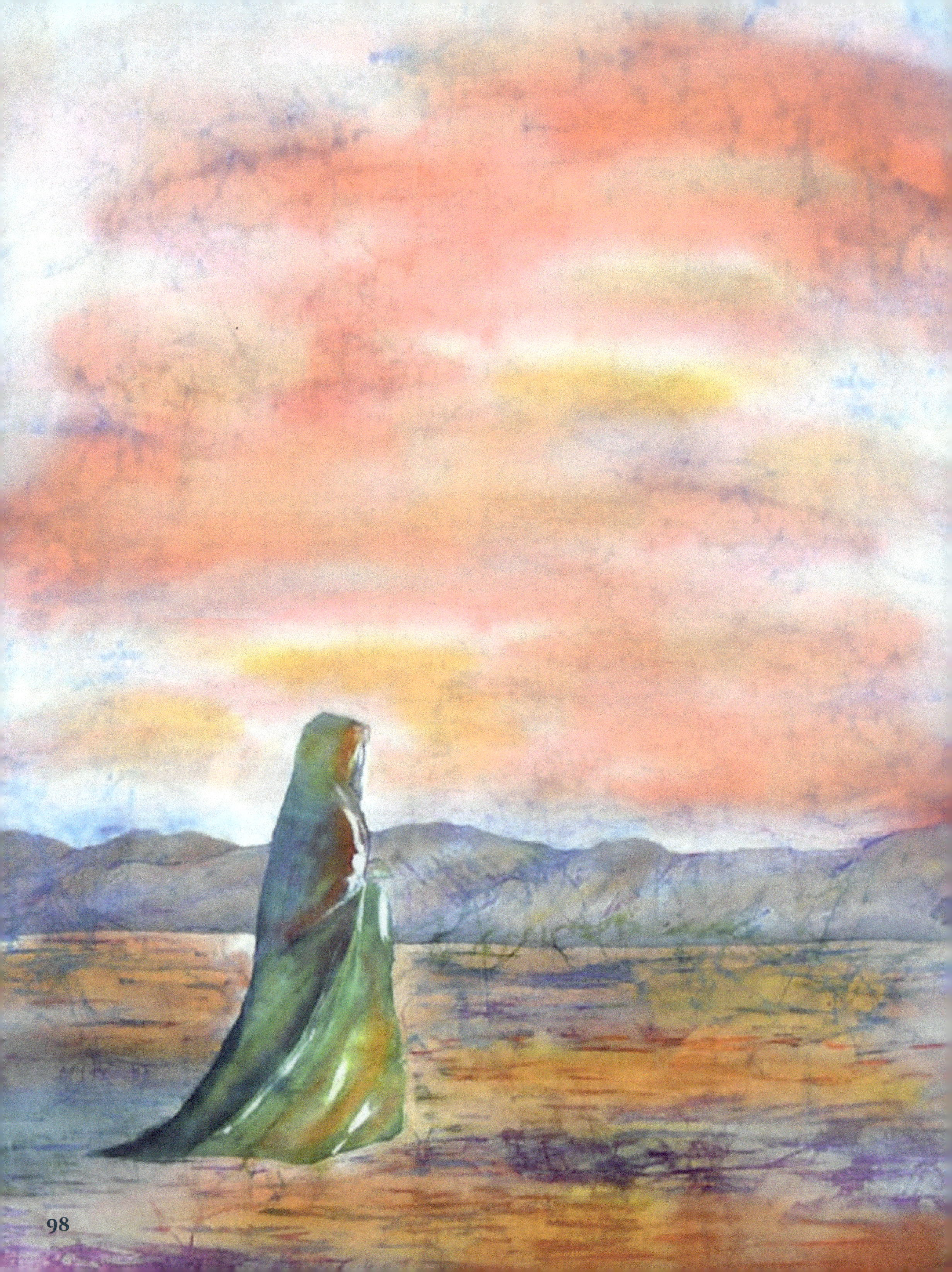

The Veil of Love's Mysteries

In Sufism, the veil is viewed in a different context, symbolizing obstacles that separate one from his or her divine nature, or levels of uncovering at various stages on the path. At the same time, veils of spiritual protection are essential as we operate in the world. This mystical interpretation of the veil can be used as a daily practice, with the breath, as we see the veils that both cover our true selves and protect our delicate inner natures. While the veils of personality are essential to our being in the world, knowledge of these layers brings awareness and awakening into our daily lives. As the onion has layers removed, one by one, to reveal the great emptiness at the center, so do veils cover the golden nature of the heart and of the being, until they are removed and the brilliance of the heart is revealed.

Haram, Shirk, and Khamr
Guidelines for Living

Haram

The Arabic term *haram* literally means, "forbidden," and defines what is prohibited under Islamic law. It identifies that which is immoral for the individual and society according to the dictates of the Quran. The opposite of *haram* is *halal*, or that which is allowed. There are many similarities within the Jewish, Christian and Muslim approach to moral code, each being rooted in the patriarchal lineage of Abraham and Moses.

When viewed from a historical and societal vantage point, these guidelines were essential in the formation of a stable society. In general, what is forbidden in the Christian and Jewish religion is considered haram in Islam, although there are some variations.

Shirk

La ilaha Il Allah Hu—Nothing Exists but God—or Allah; Unity, permeates the totality of creation, both the seen and unseen realms. The ultimate error is to compare Allah to any of creation, as Allah encompasses all of creation.

Shirk is the most extreme action of that which is *haram*—it means essentially polytheism, or idolatry, placing a person or object in a position equal to Allah. The story of the Children of Israel worshipping a golden calf for which Moses ordered their execution is told in the Quran as well as in the Old Testament.

This edict is viewed and expressed in many ways within Islam and Sufism. Within traditional Sunni Islam, there is no intermediary in any sense. Any rendering of Muhammad or other saints and prophets is strictly forbidden as that limits them to the rendered image, as in reality God is far beyond any possible depiction.

In Shia and in Sufism, the roles of *Pir* (guide), *Imam* (prayer leader), or *Murshid* (teacher) play an important function. Ideally, the spiritual guide is viewed as someone who guides the seeker towards a direct relationship with God, rather than as someone to be worshipped. Those individuals who are elevated to positions of spiritual leadership have undergone intensive training for the position, and checks and balances are in place to ensure right use of the power inherent in such a position of leadership. Some traditions believe that those individuals new to the path benefit from guidance from a teacher as well as from transmissions of *baraka*, or energy that can be transmitted from the teacher to the student, or *mureed*.

The *Pir* also carries out an important function as leader of a spiritual body—a single voice to direct the many. In the Sufi tradition, leaders guide the sacred ceremony of the *zikr* (remembrance of God), but they lead as part of the organism of the group. Ultimately, this position is viewed as an extension of Allah's grace, originating from the ultimate Source and guided by only that Source. As human beings, spiritual guides are subject to the whims of the ego, but ideally, once a person has been elevated to such a rank, they are able to observe this aspect of the *nafs* (ego) and not become lost within it. This ideal is realized in varying degrees, and ultimately the spiritual seeker is encouraged to look within to open the inner eye, the teacher of the heart, thus cultivating divine discernment.

> *Ultimately, all belongs to Allah, returns to Allah,*
> *And is an expression of the profound grace*
> *Beyond our human comprehension,*
> *Which is the unified grace of the Beloved; Allah.*

Khamr

The *khamr* refers to intoxicants, which are considered *haram*, or forbidden in traditional Islam. Anything that fogs the mind or causes a person not to think clearly is *khamr*. This restriction has proved useful for creating a stable society. The simple statement that one needs to be of clear mind in order to pray and to remember the Beloved seems self explanatory and is similar to restrictions in traditional Buddhism and other religious traditions.

The Wine of Sufism

References to wine and drunkenness are common in the ecstatic poetry of the Sufis. However, these references have an esoteric meaning rather than a literal one. The love of the Beloved is equated with the finest wine, cured and fermented through time. The state of ecstasy that some mystics experience is equated with drunkenness in an allegorical sense—intoxication with the divine wine of love. The term *saqi* refers to the wine pourer, or wine bearer, and is considered a high spiritual station in some Sufi communities, but is an allegory for the wine of love.

It is important to remember that the state of sobriety within the ecstatic state is an even more refined level of being. "Practice sobriety within the ecstasy" is an instruction often given. Even when whirling into the starry nature of being, the dervish can remain absolutely present. While some Sufi communities do partake of mild intoxicants, this is rare, and intoxication is not encouraged.

Earthly Union and Mystical Marriage

Marriage, the family, and the extended family are foundational to Muslim life. Although Islam does not emphasize celibacy, emphasis is placed on marriage, as a foundation to a stable community within a strong society. The extended family ideally protects and sustains the individual. Maintaining a successful marriage is considered a high spiritual practice.

Shifting Traditions

Polygyny, which is the form of polygamy when a man takes more than one wife, was commonly practiced at the time of the Prophet Muhammad. Within Islam there is the allowance for a man to take up to four wives. However, in the twenty-first century, this is no longer a common practice. Polygamy, and in particular, polygyny, was practiced centuries before the Quran was transmitted. This practice served the society of the time for social and economic reasons.

Today, polygamy is dying out as a common practice. In the early twentieth century more than one wife was the norm in much of the Middle East, through all classes of society. A man who had more than one wife had increased wealth. In an agricultural society, more wives meant more workers.

Islam advises all mature Muslims to marry. Marriage customs vary around the world, adapting to the culture and at the same time, honoring the Islamic code. There are elaborate kinship rules directing whom one may morally marry. According to the code, the rule is for a Muslim woman to marry a Muslim man. A Muslim man may marry any woman who is a monotheist.

The legal ceremony of marriage is performed by an *Imam* or *Mullah* (learned teacher), who reads the terms of the marital contract aloud. In some cases the marital contract is read three times, in some cases thirteen times, to assure that there is no misunderstanding between husband, wife, and families. The signed Islamic legal contract completes the union.

INTERVIEW WITH RAAUFA—HAFIZ QURAN

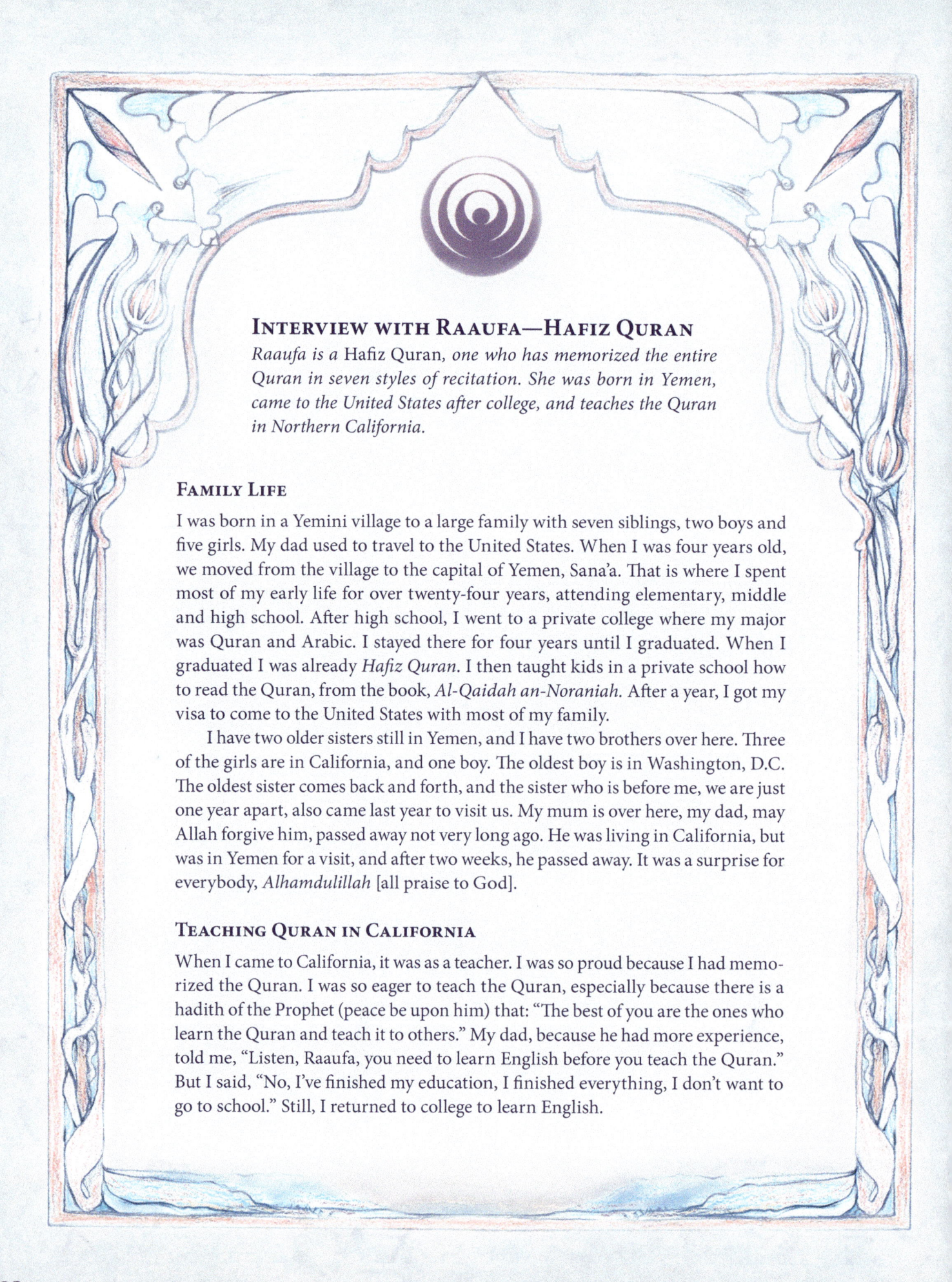

Raaufa is a Hafiz Quran, *one who has memorized the entire Quran in seven styles of recitation. She was born in Yemen, came to the United States after college, and teaches the Quran in Northern California.*

FAMILY LIFE

I was born in a Yemini village to a large family with seven siblings, two boys and five girls. My dad used to travel to the United States. When I was four years old, we moved from the village to the capital of Yemen, Sana'a. That is where I spent most of my early life for over twenty-four years, attending elementary, middle and high school. After high school, I went to a private college where my major was Quran and Arabic. I stayed there for four years until I graduated. When I graduated I was already *Hafiz Quran.* I then taught kids in a private school how to read the Quran, from the book, *Al-Qaidah an-Noraniah.* After a year, I got my visa to come to the United States with most of my family.

I have two older sisters still in Yemen, and I have two brothers over here. Three of the girls are in California, and one boy. The oldest boy is in Washington, D.C. The oldest sister comes back and forth, and the sister who is before me, we are just one year apart, also came last year to visit us. My mum is over here, my dad, may Allah forgive him, passed away not very long ago. He was living in California, but was in Yemen for a visit, and after two weeks, he passed away. It was a surprise for everybody, *Alhamdulillah* [all praise to God].

TEACHING QURAN IN CALIFORNIA

When I came to California, it was as a teacher. I was so proud because I had memorized the Quran. I was so eager to teach the Quran, especially because there is a hadith of the Prophet (peace be upon him) that: "The best of you are the ones who learn the Quran and teach it to others." My dad, because he had more experience, told me, "Listen, Raaufa, you need to learn English before you teach the Quran." But I said, "No, I've finished my education, I finished everything, I don't want to go to school." Still, I returned to college to learn English.

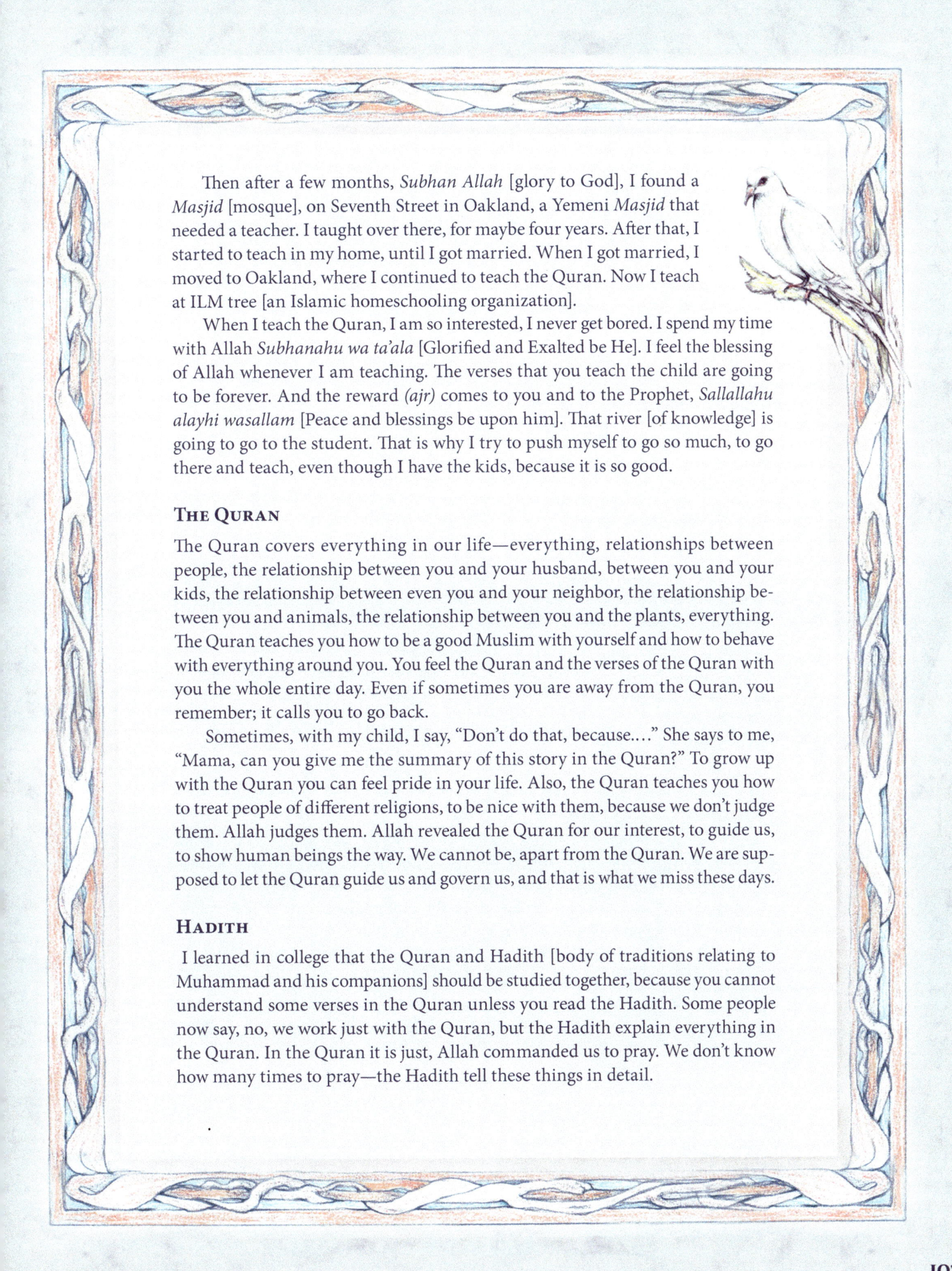

Then after a few months, *Subhan Allah* [glory to God], I found a *Masjid* [mosque], on Seventh Street in Oakland, a Yemeni *Masjid* that needed a teacher. I taught over there, for maybe four years. After that, I started to teach in my home, until I got married. When I got married, I moved to Oakland, where I continued to teach the Quran. Now I teach at ILM tree [an Islamic homeschooling organization].

When I teach the Quran, I am so interested, I never get bored. I spend my time with Allah *Subhanahu wa ta'ala* [Glorified and Exalted be He]. I feel the blessing of Allah whenever I am teaching. The verses that you teach the child are going to be forever. And the reward *(ajr)* comes to you and to the Prophet, *Sallallahu alayhi wasallam* [Peace and blessings be upon him]. That river [of knowledge] is going to go to the student. That is why I try to push myself to go so much, to go there and teach, even though I have the kids, because it is so good.

The Quran

The Quran covers everything in our life—everything, relationships between people, the relationship between you and your husband, between you and your kids, the relationship between even you and your neighbor, the relationship between you and animals, the relationship between you and the plants, everything. The Quran teaches you how to be a good Muslim with yourself and how to behave with everything around you. You feel the Quran and the verses of the Quran with you the whole entire day. Even if sometimes you are away from the Quran, you remember; it calls you to go back.

Sometimes, with my child, I say, "Don't do that, because…." She says to me, "Mama, can you give me the summary of this story in the Quran?" To grow up with the Quran you can feel pride in your life. Also, the Quran teaches you how to treat people of different religions, to be nice with them, because we don't judge them. Allah judges them. Allah revealed the Quran for our interest, to guide us, to show human beings the way. We cannot be, apart from the Quran. We are supposed to let the Quran guide us and govern us, and that is what we miss these days.

Hadith

I learned in college that the Quran and Hadith [body of traditions relating to Muhammad and his companions] should be studied together, because you cannot understand some verses in the Quran unless you read the Hadith. Some people now say, no, we work just with the Quran, but the Hadith explain everything in the Quran. In the Quran it is just, Allah commanded us to pray. We don't know how many times to pray—the Hadith tell these things in detail.

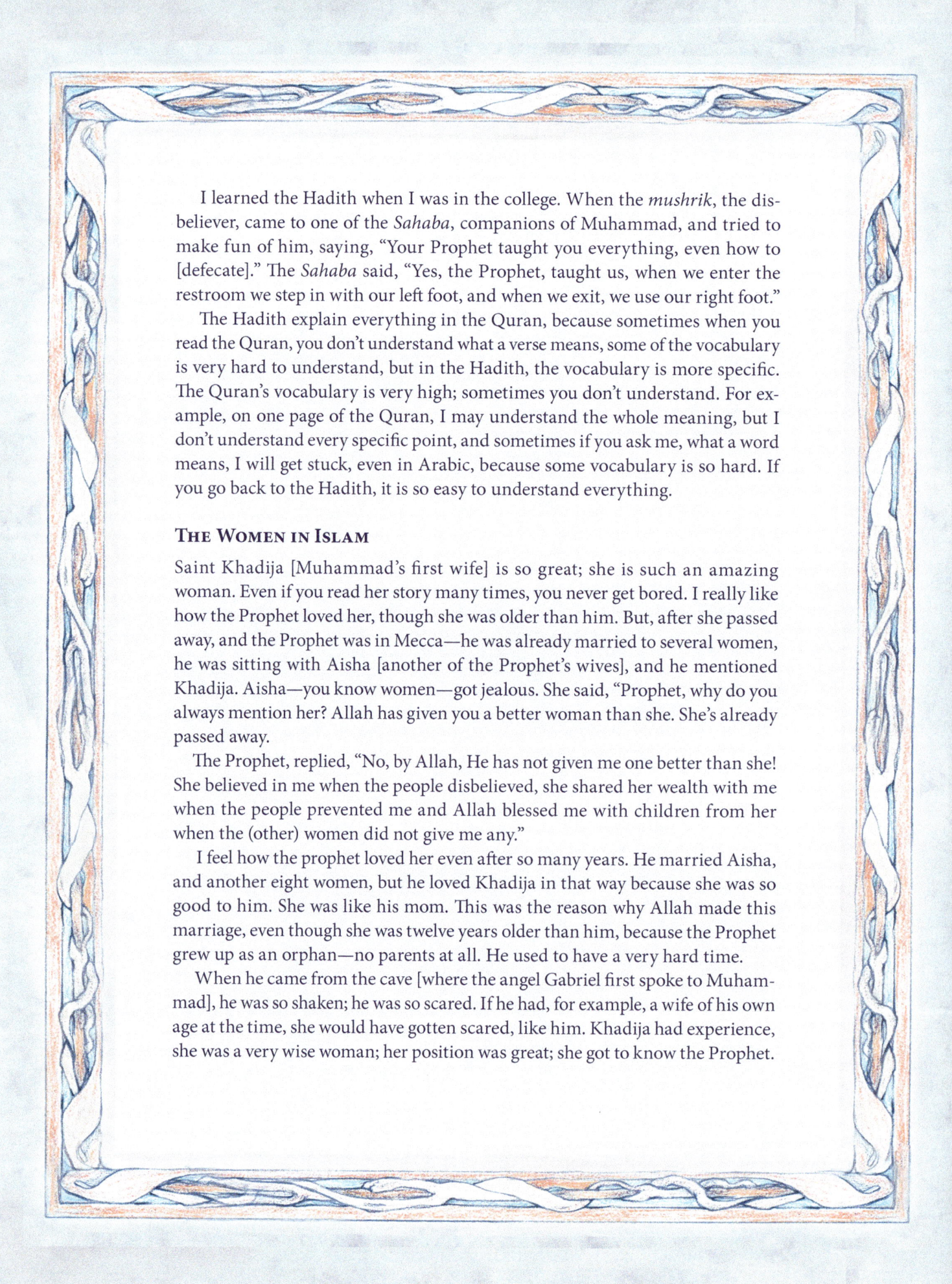

I learned the Hadith when I was in the college. When the *mushrik*, the disbeliever, came to one of the *Sahaba*, companions of Muhammad, and tried to make fun of him, saying, "Your Prophet taught you everything, even how to [defecate]." The *Sahaba* said, "Yes, the Prophet, taught us, when we enter the restroom we step in with our left foot, and when we exit, we use our right foot."

The Hadith explain everything in the Quran, because sometimes when you read the Quran, you don't understand what a verse means, some of the vocabulary is very hard to understand, but in the Hadith, the vocabulary is more specific. The Quran's vocabulary is very high; sometimes you don't understand. For example, on one page of the Quran, I may understand the whole meaning, but I don't understand every specific point, and sometimes if you ask me, what a word means, I will get stuck, even in Arabic, because some vocabulary is so hard. If you go back to the Hadith, it is so easy to understand everything.

The Women in Islam

Saint Khadija [Muhammad's first wife] is so great; she is such an amazing woman. Even if you read her story many times, you never get bored. I really like how the Prophet loved her, though she was older than him. But, after she passed away, and the Prophet was in Mecca—he was already married to several women, he was sitting with Aisha [another of the Prophet's wives], and he mentioned Khadija. Aisha—you know women—got jealous. She said, "Prophet, why do you always mention her? Allah has given you a better woman than she. She's already passed away.

The Prophet, replied, "No, by Allah, He has not given me one better than she! She believed in me when the people disbelieved, she shared her wealth with me when the people prevented me and Allah blessed me with children from her when the (other) women did not give me any."

I feel how the prophet loved her even after so many years. He married Aisha, and another eight women, but he loved Khadija in that way because she was so good to him. She was like his mom. This was the reason why Allah made this marriage, even though she was twelve years older than him, because the Prophet grew up as an orphan—no parents at all. He used to have a very hard time.

When he came from the cave [where the angel Gabriel first spoke to Muhammad], he was so shaken; he was so scared. If he had, for example, a wife of his own age at the time, she would have gotten scared, like him. Khadija had experience, she was a very wise woman; her position was great; she got to know the Prophet.

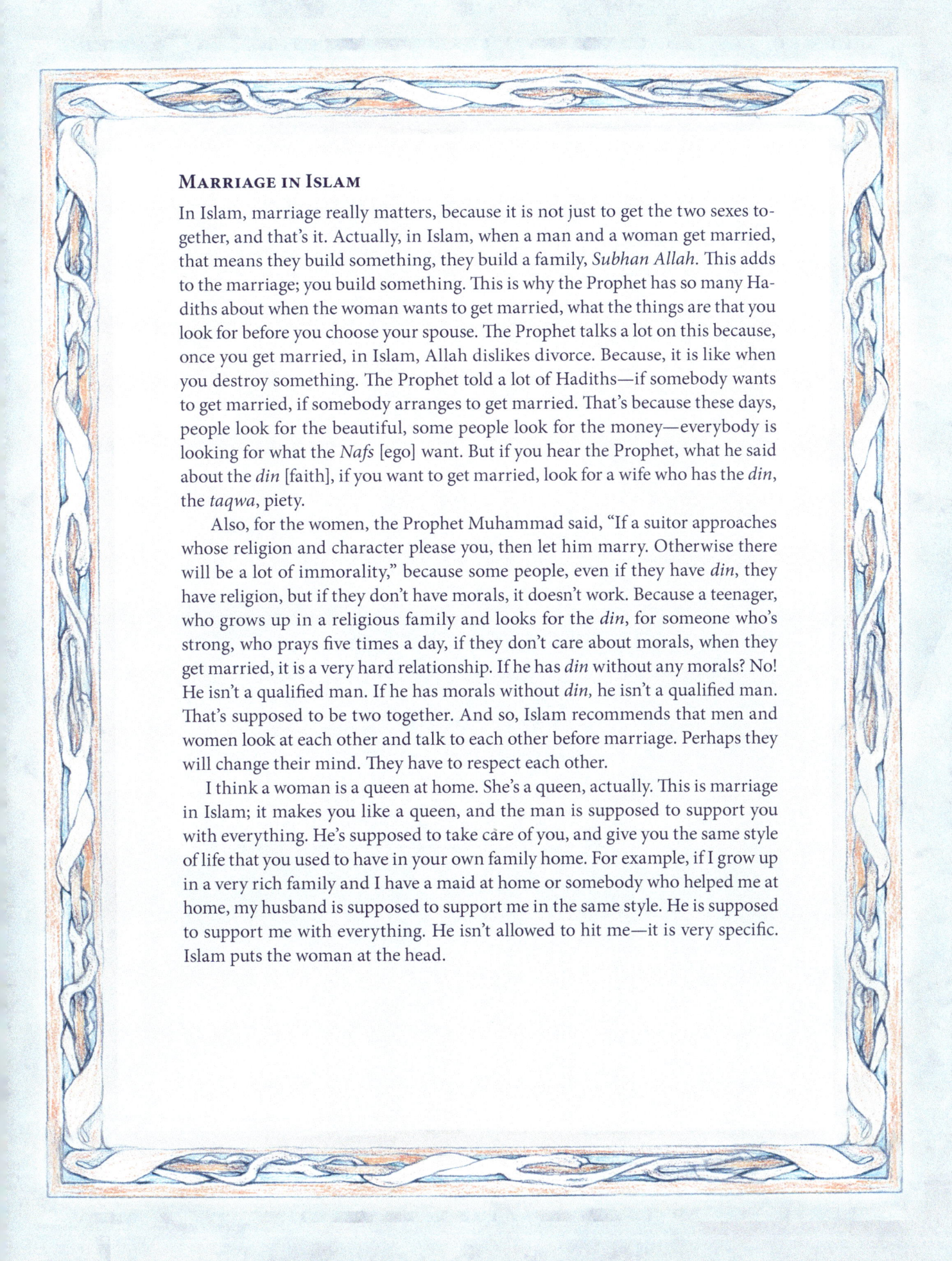

Marriage in Islam

In Islam, marriage really matters, because it is not just to get the two sexes together, and that's it. Actually, in Islam, when a man and a woman get married, that means they build something, they build a family, *Subhan Allah*. This adds to the marriage; you build something. This is why the Prophet has so many Hadiths about when the woman wants to get married, what the things are that you look for before you choose your spouse. The Prophet talks a lot on this because, once you get married, in Islam, Allah dislikes divorce. Because, it is like when you destroy something. The Prophet told a lot of Hadiths—if somebody wants to get married, if somebody arranges to get married. That's because these days, people look for the beautiful, some people look for the money—everybody is looking for what the *Nafs* [ego] want. But if you hear the Prophet, what he said about the *din* [faith], if you want to get married, look for a wife who has the *din*, the *taqwa*, piety.

Also, for the women, the Prophet Muhammad said, "If a suitor approaches whose religion and character please you, then let him marry. Otherwise there will be a lot of immorality," because some people, even if they have *din*, they have religion, but if they don't have morals, it doesn't work. Because a teenager, who grows up in a religious family and looks for the *din*, for someone who's strong, who prays five times a day, if they don't care about morals, when they get married, it is a very hard relationship. If he has *din* without any morals? No! He isn't a qualified man. If he has morals without *din*, he isn't a qualified man. That's supposed to be two together. And so, Islam recommends that men and women look at each other and talk to each other before marriage. Perhaps they will change their mind. They have to respect each other.

I think a woman is a queen at home. She's a queen, actually. This is marriage in Islam; it makes you like a queen, and the man is supposed to support you with everything. He's supposed to take care of you, and give you the same style of life that you used to have in your own family home. For example, if I grow up in a very rich family and I have a maid at home or somebody who helped me at home, my husband is supposed to support me in the same style. He is supposed to support me with everything. He isn't allowed to hit me—it is very specific. Islam puts the woman at the head.

MULTIPLE WIVES IN ISLAM

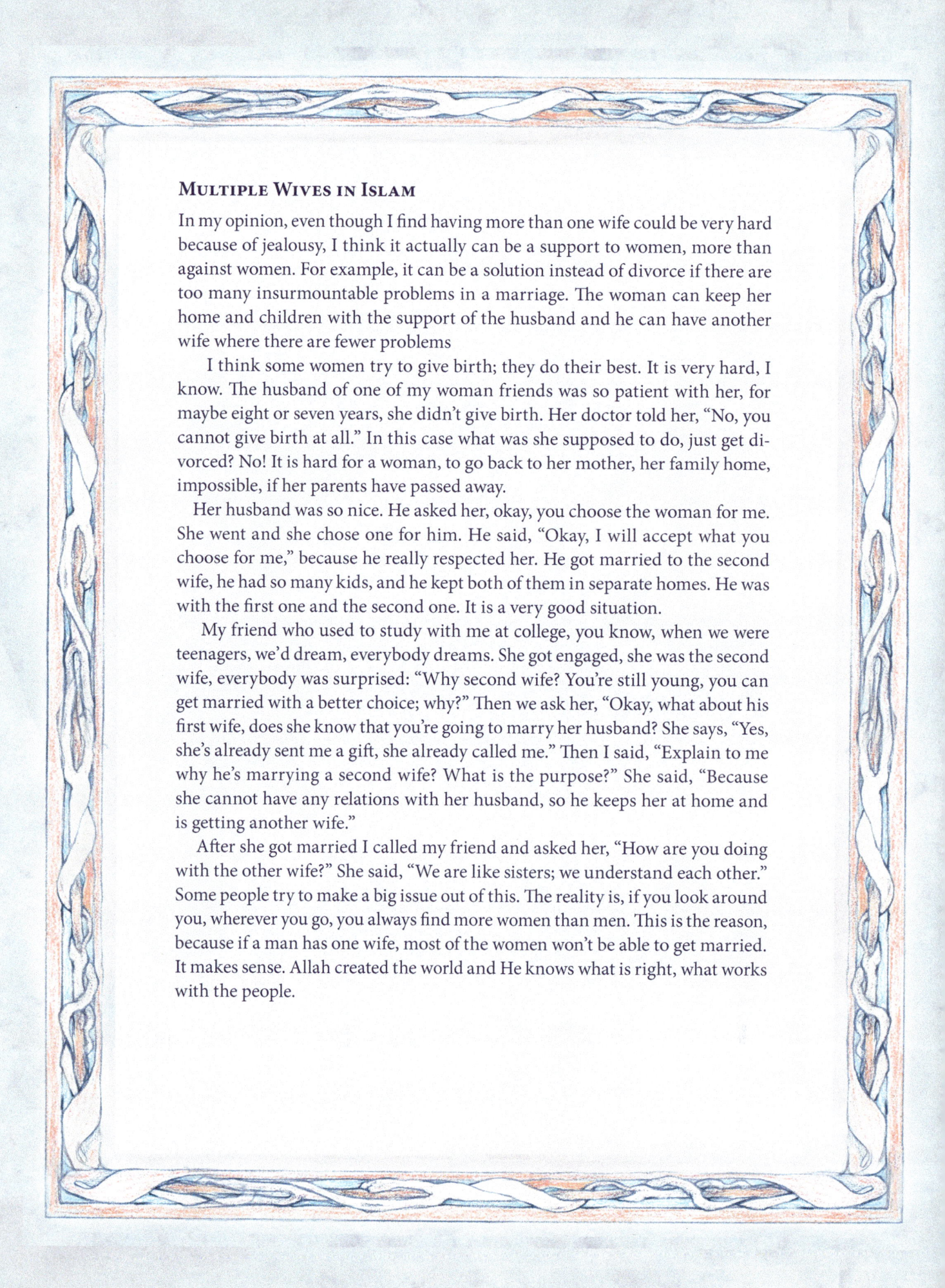

In my opinion, even though I find having more than one wife could be very hard because of jealousy, I think it actually can be a support to women, more than against women. For example, it can be a solution instead of divorce if there are too many insurmountable problems in a marriage. The woman can keep her home and children with the support of the husband and he can have another wife where there are fewer problems

I think some women try to give birth; they do their best. It is very hard, I know. The husband of one of my woman friends was so patient with her, for maybe eight or seven years, she didn't give birth. Her doctor told her, "No, you cannot give birth at all." In this case what was she supposed to do, just get divorced? No! It is hard for a woman, to go back to her mother, her family home, impossible, if her parents have passed away.

Her husband was so nice. He asked her, okay, you choose the woman for me. She went and she chose one for him. He said, "Okay, I will accept what you choose for me," because he really respected her. He got married to the second wife, he had so many kids, and he kept both of them in separate homes. He was with the first one and the second one. It is a very good situation.

My friend who used to study with me at college, you know, when we were teenagers, we'd dream, everybody dreams. She got engaged, she was the second wife, everybody was surprised: "Why second wife? You're still young, you can get married with a better choice; why?" Then we ask her, "Okay, what about his first wife, does she know that you're going to marry her husband? She says, "Yes, she's already sent me a gift, she already called me." Then I said, "Explain to me why he's marrying a second wife? What is the purpose?" She said, "Because she cannot have any relations with her husband, so he keeps her at home and is getting another wife."

After she got married I called my friend and asked her, "How are you doing with the other wife?" She said, "We are like sisters; we understand each other." Some people try to make a big issue out of this. The reality is, if you look around you, wherever you go, you always find more women than men. This is the reason, because if a man has one wife, most of the women won't be able to get married. It makes sense. Allah created the world and He knows what is right, what works with the people.

Zakat and Generosity

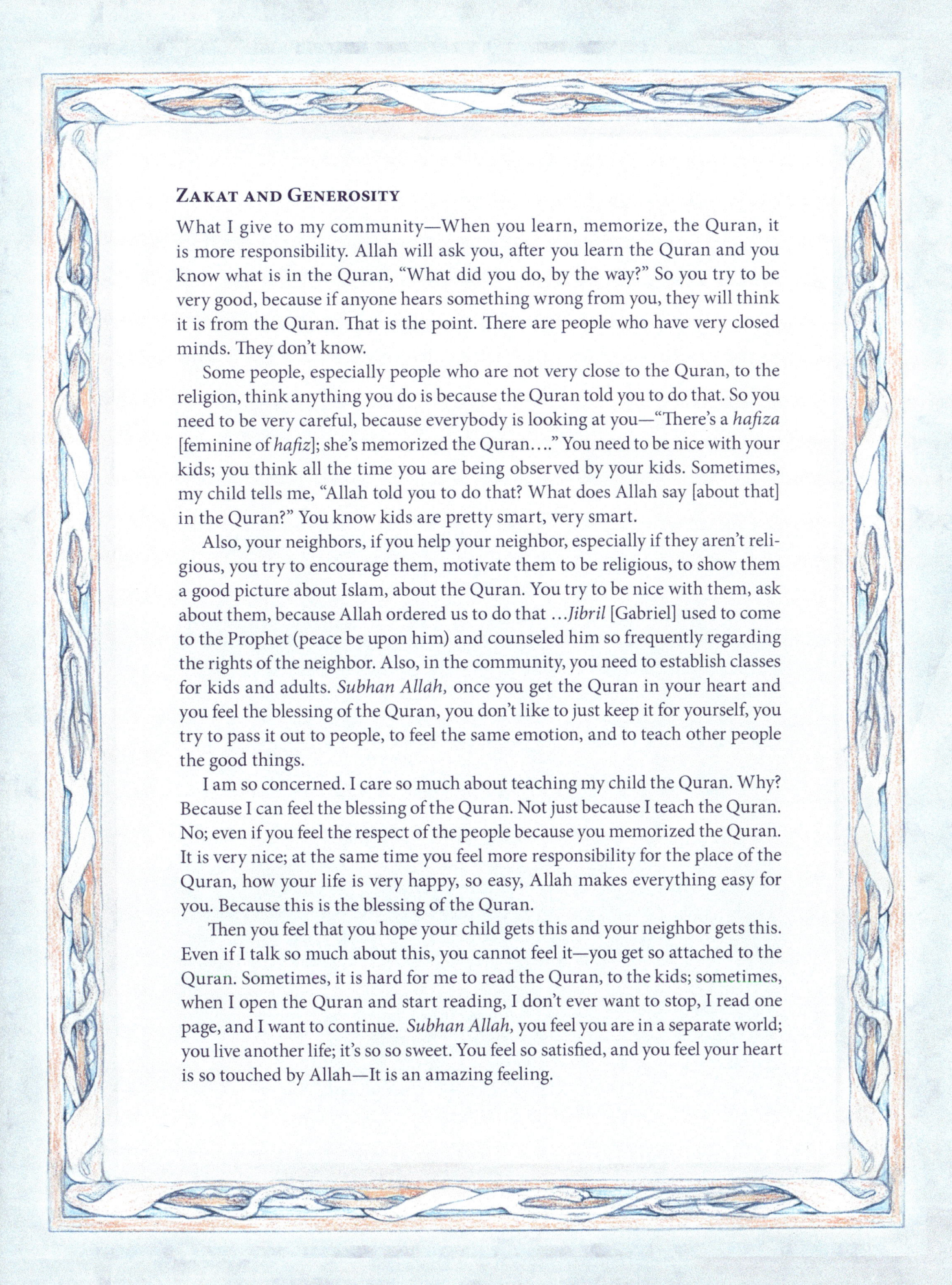

What I give to my community—When you learn, memorize, the Quran, it is more responsibility. Allah will ask you, after you learn the Quran and you know what is in the Quran, "What did you do, by the way?" So you try to be very good, because if anyone hears something wrong from you, they will think it is from the Quran. That is the point. There are people who have very closed minds. They don't know.

Some people, especially people who are not very close to the Quran, to the religion, think anything you do is because the Quran told you to do that. So you need to be very careful, because everybody is looking at you—"There's a *hafiza* [feminine of *hafiz*]; she's memorized the Quran…." You need to be nice with your kids; you think all the time you are being observed by your kids. Sometimes, my child tells me, "Allah told you to do that? What does Allah say [about that] in the Quran?" You know kids are pretty smart, very smart.

Also, your neighbors, if you help your neighbor, especially if they aren't religious, you try to encourage them, motivate them to be religious, to show them a good picture about Islam, about the Quran. You try to be nice with them, ask about them, because Allah ordered us to do that …*Jibril* [Gabriel] used to come to the Prophet (peace be upon him) and counseled him so frequently regarding the rights of the neighbor. Also, in the community, you need to establish classes for kids and adults. *Subhan Allah,* once you get the Quran in your heart and you feel the blessing of the Quran, you don't like to just keep it for yourself, you try to pass it out to people, to feel the same emotion, and to teach other people the good things.

I am so concerned. I care so much about teaching my child the Quran. Why? Because I can feel the blessing of the Quran. Not just because I teach the Quran. No; even if you feel the respect of the people because you memorized the Quran. It is very nice; at the same time you feel more responsibility for the place of the Quran, how your life is very happy, so easy, Allah makes everything easy for you. Because this is the blessing of the Quran.

Then you feel that you hope your child gets this and your neighbor gets this. Even if I talk so much about this, you cannot feel it—you get so attached to the Quran. Sometimes, it is hard for me to read the Quran, to the kids; sometimes, when I open the Quran and start reading, I don't ever want to stop, I read one page, and I want to continue. *Subhan Allah,* you feel you are in a separate world; you live another life; it's so so sweet. You feel so satisfied, and you feel your heart is so touched by Allah—It is an amazing feeling.

Receiving Support

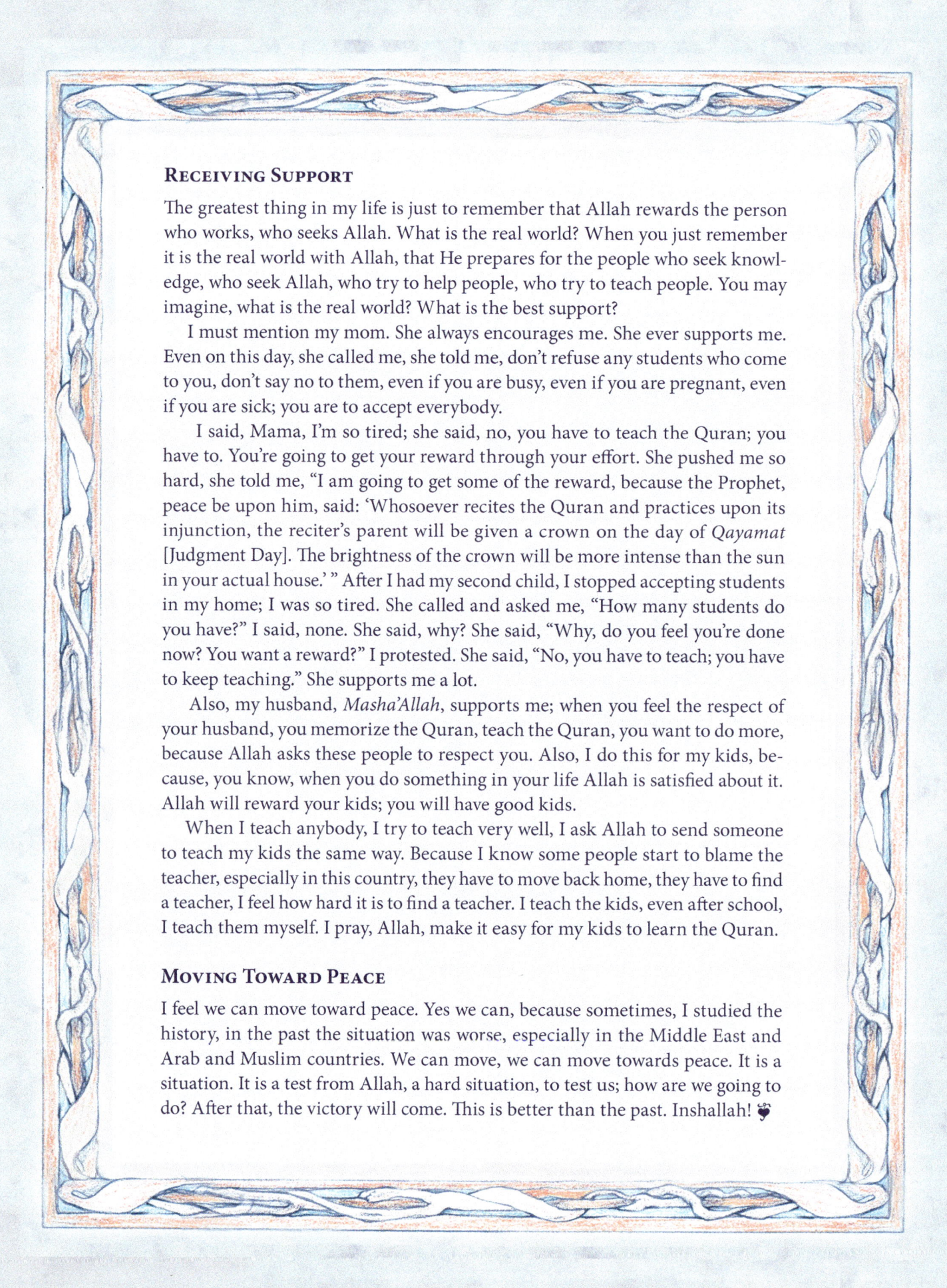

The greatest thing in my life is just to remember that Allah rewards the person who works, who seeks Allah. What is the real world? When you just remember it is the real world with Allah, that He prepares for the people who seek knowledge, who seek Allah, who try to help people, who try to teach people. You may imagine, what is the real world? What is the best support?

I must mention my mom. She always encourages me. She ever supports me. Even on this day, she called me, she told me, don't refuse any students who come to you, don't say no to them, even if you are busy, even if you are pregnant, even if you are sick; you are to accept everybody.

I said, Mama, I'm so tired; she said, no, you have to teach the Quran; you have to. You're going to get your reward through your effort. She pushed me so hard, she told me, "I am going to get some of the reward, because the Prophet, peace be upon him, said: 'Whosoever recites the Quran and practices upon its injunction, the reciter's parent will be given a crown on the day of *Qayamat* [Judgment Day]. The brightness of the crown will be more intense than the sun in your actual house.'" After I had my second child, I stopped accepting students in my home; I was so tired. She called and asked me, "How many students do you have?" I said, none. She said, why? She said, "Why, do you feel you're done now? You want a reward?" I protested. She said, "No, you have to teach; you have to keep teaching." She supports me a lot.

Also, my husband, *Masha'Allah*, supports me; when you feel the respect of your husband, you memorize the Quran, teach the Quran, you want to do more, because Allah asks these people to respect you. Also, I do this for my kids, because, you know, when you do something in your life Allah is satisfied about it. Allah will reward your kids; you will have good kids.

When I teach anybody, I try to teach very well, I ask Allah to send someone to teach my kids the same way. Because I know some people start to blame the teacher, especially in this country, they have to move back home, they have to find a teacher, I feel how hard it is to find a teacher. I teach the kids, even after school, I teach them myself. I pray, Allah, make it easy for my kids to learn the Quran.

Moving Toward Peace

I feel we can move toward peace. Yes we can, because sometimes, I studied the history, in the past the situation was worse, especially in the Middle East and Arab and Muslim countries. We can move, we can move towards peace. It is a situation. It is a test from Allah, a hard situation, to test us; how are we going to do? After that, the victory will come. This is better than the past. Inshallah! ❦

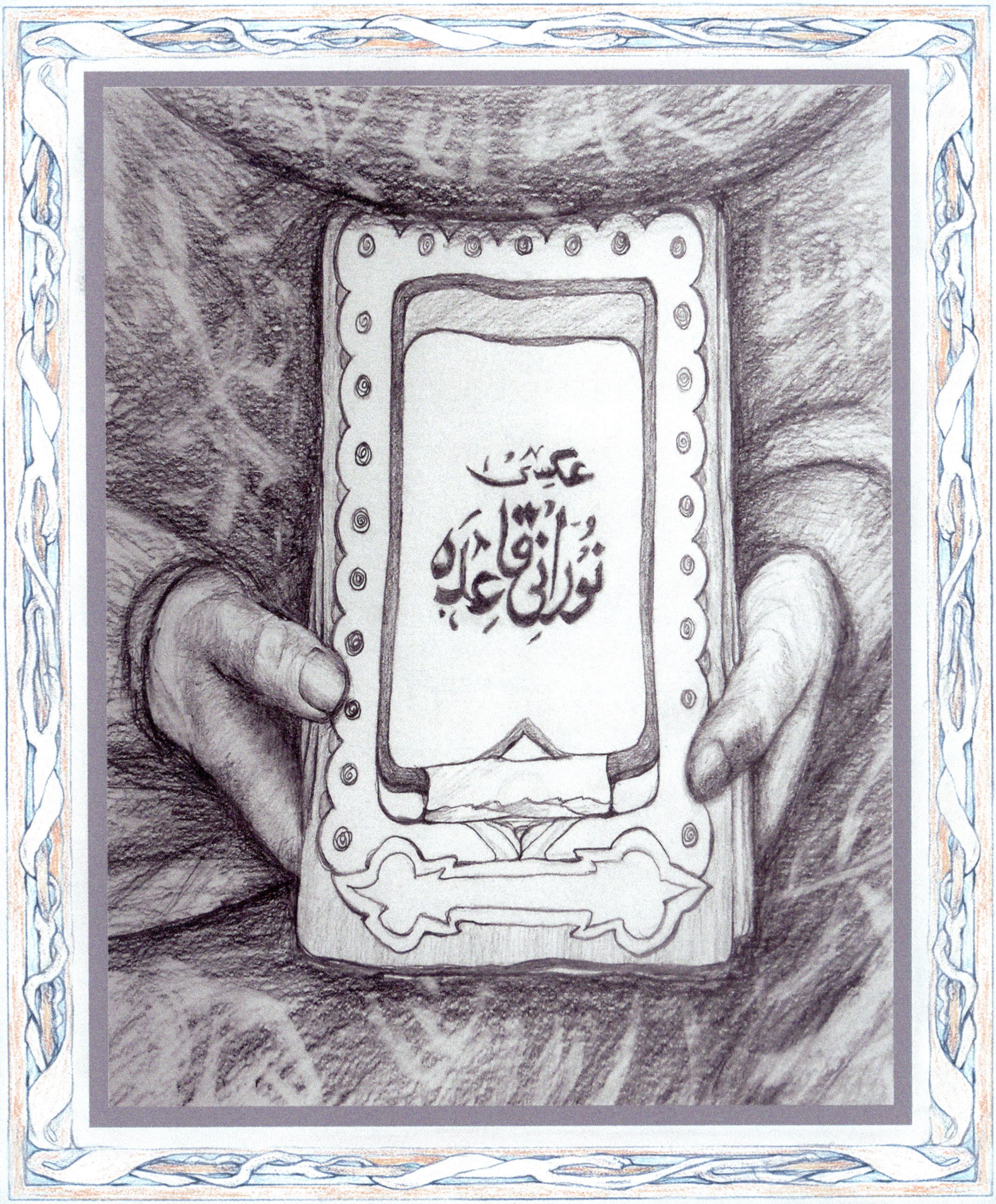
عکس
نورانی قاعده

Some Cultural Marriage Customs

In many societies, the *Lailat el Henna,* or Henna Night, occurs the night before the wedding ceremony and celebration. This is a special time for the women to join in honoring the bride. Henna paste is arranged in mounds on trays for the intricate process of beautifying the bride. In some cultures, hands, palms, fingernails, the soles of the feet, and toenails are all covered in traditional designs. Henna parties of women can go on all night. Some traditions only use the henna on the hands and fingernails.

A close woman friend or relative holds an open Quran before the face of the bride as she crosses the threshold into the home. Traditionally, a sheep is slaughtered on the threshold; the bride steps over warm blood, and the wedding party feasts on the offering. It is not only sorrow, but also ancient tribal custom that calls for the bride to weep upon leaving her childhood home as she enters the home of her husband to begin her new life with his family.

Within certain Muslim societies, the mother-in-law can be just as important as one's husband, and in some cultures, she controls the life of the household and the bride, directing the rhythm of her new life. This relationship can be one of a kind matriarchal guidance or more challenging to the young bride. The archetype of the difficult mother-in-law is ubiquitous throughout the world and Islamic societies are no exception.

In Egypt and other parts of the Middle East, there is the custom of building on top of the existing house or adding on when one becomes married. This custom supports the extended multi-generational family.

Marriage as Mystical Union

In the Sufi tradition, marriage also connotes a state of Divine Union with the Beloved. In modern society women can live independently without the physical need to depend on a male for security reasons, although the institution is still a foundation of any stable society. Women who do not marry out of choice, or from circumstance, can explore the notion of mystical union—of deep constant connection with Divine Source.

The *Urs,* or Wedding Day, is celebrated on the day of the death of an important spiritual figure. On the day of death, it is said that the person achieves the ultimate union with source, the mystical wedding. The mystic prepares for this ultimate divine union by cultivating states of unity while living upon earth. Whether or not this is supported by the earthly institution of marriage, any woman can know deep union with her source.

In the oral tradition, there is a story that Fatima once went to her father, Muhammad, in a state of deep fatigue and frustration. She complained of the endless amount of work and her inability to complete her responsibilities. To Fatima's delight, her father told her that he had the solution, the perfect gift to help her find the fortitude to continue. Prophet Muhammad then gave instruction to Fatima in repetition of the following three *wazifas* or names of God: *Subhan Allah*—God is all purity; *Alhamdulillah*—All praise to God; *Allah ho Akbar*—All power is in God. Also translated as Peace is Power by the twentieth century Sufi mystic, Murshid Sam Lewis. The phrase *Allah ho Akbar* is a powerful phrase that has gotten an undeserved reputation because of its misuse by extremists in the execution of violence.

And if you have reason to fear that you might not act equitably towards orphans, then marry from among (other) women such as are lawful to you—even two or three or four: but if you have reason to fear that you might not be able to treat them with equality, fear that you might not be able to treat them with equal fairness, then (only) one—or (from among) those whom you rightfully possess. This will make it more likely that you will not deviate from the right course.

And give unto women their marriage portions in the spirit of a gift, but if they, of their own accord, give up unto you aught thereof, then enjoy it with pleasure and good cheer.

—Quran, Sura 4: 3-4

112

CREATING HEART SPACE
RECIPES FOR THE SACRED

The Body Prayer of Hazrat Fatima

Abu Huraira, companion to the Prophet, said that when Fatima went to the Prophet and asked him for a servant, he said, "Let me guide you to something which is better than a servant. Say, *'Subhan Allah'* (Glory be to God), thirty three times, *'Alhamdulillah'* (Praise be to God), thirty three times and *'Allah ho Akbar'* (God is most great) thirty-three times."

Take back this beautiful expression from the misuse of extremists by saying it thirty three times, either aloud or silently, at each time of prayer and when you go to bed.

To prepare for the practice, begin to allow the thoughts of the day to drift away. Cultivate the state of the observer, watching thoughts come and go. Practice the experience of accessing and balancing the body, mind, and spirit.

By focused movement, such as rhythmic walking, accompanied by prayer, chanting, and spoken meditation, a grounded transcendental experience is possible.

Subhan Allah, Alhamdulillah, Allah ho Akbar

SEATED MEDITATION

Once comfortably seated, take a moment to stretch and shake out stress and stale energy. As you repeat the sacred phrases, gently drop the chin toward the chest in order to speak the phrase into the heart.

Subhan Allah (Glory be to God), Say this into the heart thirty three times,
Alhamdulillah (Praise be to God), thirty three times into the heart,
Allah ho Akbar (God is most great), thirty three times into the heart.

Continue to sit, breathing in and out through the nose, feeling these attributes permeate your being. Reflect on this experience, taking a moment to record any significant experience in your journal.

WALKING MEDITATION

Stand up. Stretch and shake out any tension. Let the body tell you where it needs extra attention. Notice the condition of the knees and hips.

Place the three *wazifas* in the hara center (abdomen), the solar plexus, and the heart chakra.

Subhan Allah
Place the palms in front of the hara center, about three fingers below the belly button for women, and about one finger below for men. This is the center of gravity of the body. Focus here provides grounding and balance. Connection with the hara center might be felt as a luminous ball, or as a portal. Each person will find their own place of deep connection with their center of gravity.

Place the left palm on top of the right and let the thumbs and shoulders relax. Begin to walk in a clockwise direction intoning *Subhan Allah* for four steps on the out-breath and repeat for the in-breath. Do this for about five minutes. This is a *wazifa* of all pervading unity.

Alhamdulillah
Place the hands on the heart. The spiritual heart, or heart chakra is located at the center of the sternum. Connecting with the heart chakra going through to the back of the body, between the shoulder blades, can strengthen the experience of this important spiritual organ.

Let the head drop to the heart chakra for the sound of "Al", and raise upward while looking upward, allowing the head to fall slightly back, for "Hamdulillah". Walk five minutes with *Alhamdulillah*, in a counterclockwise direction, let the arms rise upwards in praise as the head falls back and the eyes look upward. This is a *wazifa* of praise.

Allah Ho Akbar
Place the arms at the solar plexus, approximately where the diaphragm sits in the lower chest. Gently hold the left arm with the right hand and the right arm with the left hand. Allow the head to travel, beginning by looking over the left shoulder and then slowly through the center point and ending the motion by looking over the right shoulder. The prayer of looking from horizon to horizon imbues the atmosphere with the power and peace of Allah.

Walk in a clockwise direction for five minutes intoning this *wazifa* with this mudra (crossed arms). An alternate mudra is to bend the arms at the elbow, lower arms raised, and hands into gentle fists. The gaze is directly forward and unwavering. Allow the posture to be relaxed yet fully engaged and strong. Walk with purpose and faith for five minutes intoning *Allah ho Akbar*.

Art Meditation on the Hand of Fatima

Collect art supplies to trace your own hand on a sheet of paper.

Trace the right hand on the blank sheet of paper, choosing your own colors. In each of the fingers write a one-word intention, i.e., forgiveness, surrender, prayer, gratitude, freedom.

In the center of the palm, draw a symbol with space in the middle for one word that unifies your personal and planetary intention and prayers in this moment, i.e., LOVE in the center of a circle. Use color as inspired to complete the hand. Fatima's hand is the hand of loving service.

Conclude this exercise inhaling *Rahman*, exhaling *Rahim*, breathing in compassion and exhaling mercy.

سُبْحَانَ ٱللَّٰه

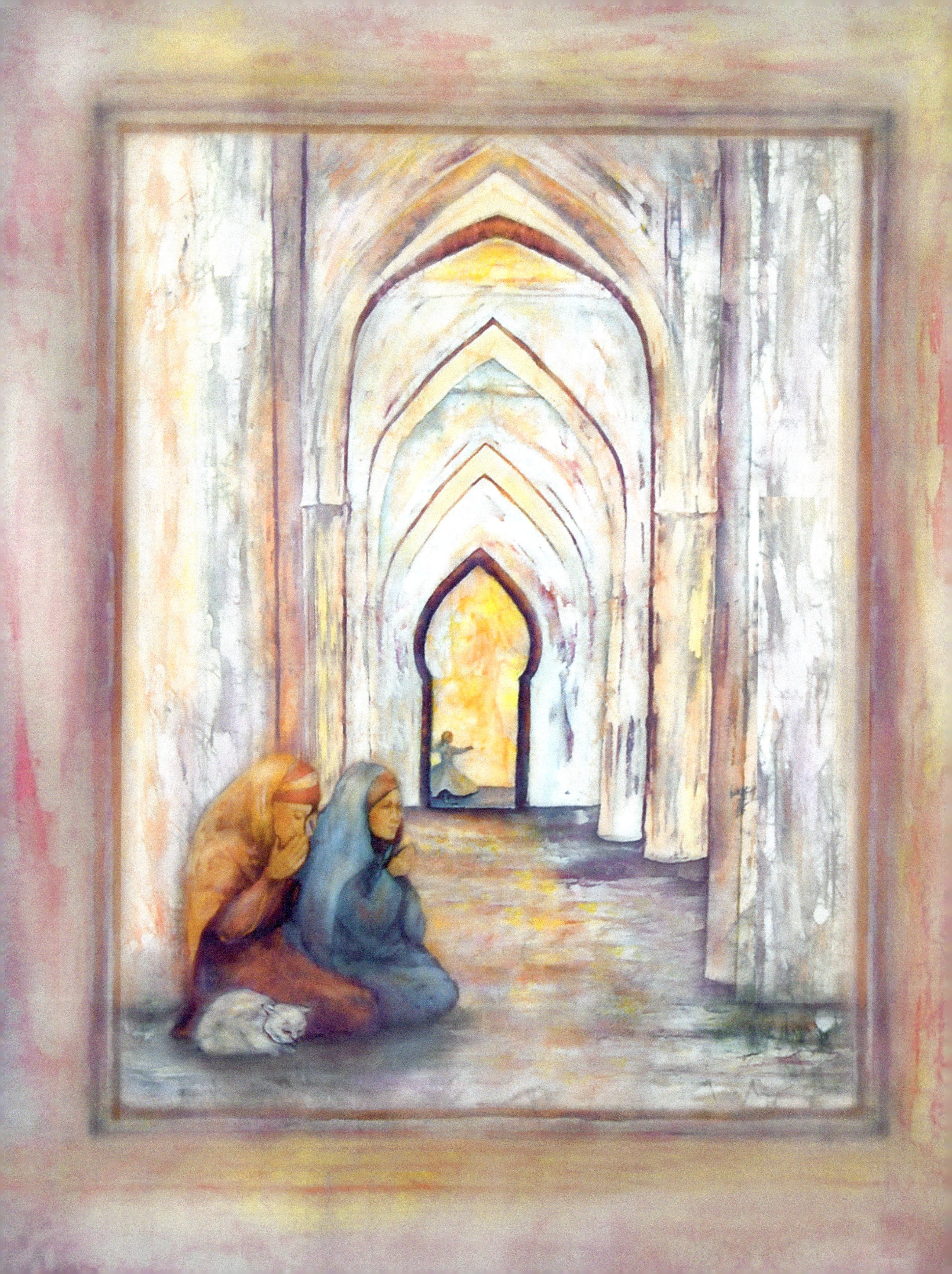

PRAYER
5

Concentrated Conversation with Self and Divinity

Prayer of some kind exists in all spiritual traditions, and ranges from petitioning a divine source for assistance, to cultivating a direct state of union, to embodying a ritual with full attention. In the Sufi tradition, the dervish endeavors to maintain a constant state of prayerful union. The Muslim action of breaking the day into a rhythm of shared prayer provides a focal point for remembrance throughout the action of the day. Variations of the action of prayer share a common thread of developing and practicing concentrated connection with the Infinite Source.

PETITION

The act of asking the Benevolent Presence for assistance has been with humanity throughout time. Great comfort is given to the petitioner through the action of prayer. Experiments have shown that praying over a plant increases its vitality. Anecdotes abound of miraculous responses to desperate prayers of petition. It is said that the prayer, "God Help Me," is always answered with grace, even when that answer is not immediately apparent.

Another view of asking for something through prayer is that it suggests a separation from God. In the Sufi tradition, many believe that the Beloved is with us always, so there is nothing to ask, as this presence already knows all of our needs and desires.

PRAYER AS UNION

Some practitioners view prayer as the direct action of using breath and repetition of sacred phrases. This experiential practice contains the intention of all action as an expression of prayer—that prayer is a home that one returns to as regularly as possible, a home that provides nourishment for development of peace in the world. Sufism and other mystical traditions tend towards this active practice of prayer.

Contemplative Prayer

Meditative traditions practice remembrance of unity through breath and stillness. This place of quiet and reflection develops deep concentration, which supports other prayerful states. In some cases, thoughts are observed as clouds, passing across the clear blue sky of the mind. Mantric practices, such as the wazifa (sacred phrase) practice of the Sufi, allow the mind to have a point of concentration that supports the prayer. The breath remains the root at the center of the practice.

Regular Shared Prayer

In the Islamic tradition, the shared practice of prayer forms the warp and weft of the fabric of daily life. As each cycle of a day progresses, like the Book of Hours of the early Christians, the practicing Muslim faces Mecca, and bows in remembrance and affirmation of the faith. Prior to the prayer, the body is washed in a specific fashion with the concentration on light, and on letting go of the detritus of life.

When Muslims gather in prayer, the practice is to stand shoulder to shoulder, so that the line of the faithful is connected—to bow and rise as one, and to feel the great equalizing force of shared faith.

The Sunni tradition calls for five intervals of prayer throughout the day, and the Shia tradition specifies three daily prayers. There are exceptions for travel and for other situations in life. The prayer practiced in the mosque or on the solitary prayer rug is the root from which the life of compassion and surrender sprouts.

The Muslim is advised to pray for protection from temptation daily. Praying with the intention of surrender to God, the most Merciful and Compassionate Creator, allows the practitioner to be in perfect harmony with the created universe, turning in rhythm with the geometry and music of the seen and unseen realms of existence.

Zikr—Embodiment of Shared Prayer

In the Sufi tradition, shared prayer includes a ceremony of song and motion called *zikr*, or remembrance, with innumerable variations throughout the world. In the basic *zikr* form, practitioners stand in a circle, shoulder to shoulder, with hands clasped. A *wazifa*, or sacred phrase, is sung in repetition, usually accompanied by rhythm and music, as the circle gently steps and moves as one. The rhythm of the breath is an essential aspect of the *zikr* practice.

As the *zikr* progresses, the energy increases, sometimes resulting in ecstatic dance and music, and other times leading to quiet, unified motion. Some traditions practice the *zikr* seated, containing the energy while it builds. In some Sufi communities, women and men share the *zikr* circle, in others, women and men share the *zikr* in separate circles, and in others, the women hold their own ceremony, separate from the men. Many women express gratitude for the freedom of sharing *zikr* in a safe and relaxed circle along with their Sufi sisters.

All *zikr* is practiced with the intention of dissolving into a state of deep union with the Beloved, moving past individual distinctions, into a unified body of prayer. Traditionally, the zikr begins or ends with the prayer, "May any benefit received this night go to the service and healing of all of humanity."

Angels

Angels are neither male nor female. To our human understanding we might consider them androgynous. Stories are told of a romantic love between angels and humans. Angels are in continual praise of the Creator and Nourisher of all the worlds—of all the universes. The angel, *Jibreel* (Gabriel), appears many times within the Quran. The greatest of all Islamic angels, *Jibreel* delivers and reveals the messages of the Holy Quran to Muhammad. *Jibreel* visits and guides Amina, mother of Prophet Muhammad, and Mary, mother of Prophet Jesus. He guides Noah in the building of the Ark, and saves Abraham from his condemnation to death by fire ordered by Nimrod. Gabriel is mentioned by name three times in the Quran.

Satan—or *Iblis* in Arabic—is made of fire and was cast out of the Heavens by God for refusing to bow down to the created human form, Adam. While *Iblis* does not obey the command to prostrate before Adam, his story differs from the Christian version in that he is not a figure that is against God. He proceeds to successfully tempt Adam and Eve to eat of the forbidden Tree, as in the Christian tradition.

Prophet Muhammad calls *Mikael*, archangel Michael in the Christian hierarchy of angels, *wazir,* vizier, or minister. *Mikael* assists *Jibreel* in instructing Muhammad, and is said to protect mosques and sacred places dedicated to worship of the One God.

Azrael—Azrael—is mentioned in the Quran as the Angel of Death. From Hadith we learn that *Azrael* carries the scroll with all the names and stories of every human recorded.

The Mihrab or Prayer Niche

The *Mihrab* is the prayer niche within the mosque, which orients towards the Kaaba, the stone building in the court of the Great Mosque at Mecca that contains the sacred black stone. The Kaaba, located in Mecca, is the goal of *Hajj*, the Islamic pilgrimage and the direction toward which all Muslims turn in daily prayer. Some radical feminists liken the *Mihrab* to the vagina, opening to the Womb of Allah.

Since there are no artistic renderings of the Prophet Muhammad, the wives of the Prophet, daughter Fatima, and other Islamic figures, the Mosque is void of portraiture, personal or individual expression. The beauty of Allah is expressed through the natural world and found in the calligraphy, architecture, and unique styles of art that have emerged from this path of submission to God.

Sura An Nur

Allah is the Light of the heavens and the earth. The example of His light is like a niche within which is a lamp, the lamp is within glass, the glass as if it were a pearly [white] star lit from [the oil of] a blessed olive tree, neither of the east nor of the west, whose oil would almost glow even if untouched by fire. Light upon light. Allah guides to His light whom He wills. And Allah presents examples for the people, and Allah is Knowing of all things.

—Quran, Sura 24: 35

DREAM SEQUENCE

I am in the rain forest, thick, warm, humming vibrant greenness all around. There are huge ferns and trees, tangled vines, birds singing and flying overhead, and in the branches of lower vegetation. I am running on a dirt trail that is just large enough for one person. It feels good to run and I keep moving, amazed to be in this beautiful place. After some time, I see a woman in Hijab (the traditional covering for the hair and neck that is worn by Muslim women) in the distance. Running closer, I see that she is older, her face a map of a full life, and her shoulders tired from life's burdens. She stands at a crossroads where four trails come together emanating the aura of an eccentric authority figure.

There is a large, rectangular, flip board, a bulletin board on one side with notes tacked to it, and a chalkboard with erasers and writing on the other side. She is cleaning and organizing the notes on the bulletin board side. I want to read what they say, and so move closer. She grabs my shoulders and turns me towards her, shaking me, and shouting in my face, nose to nose, "Ask for what you really want!" I wake up, knowing that this is Mama Feriste, Mother of Dervishes, even though we have never met before.

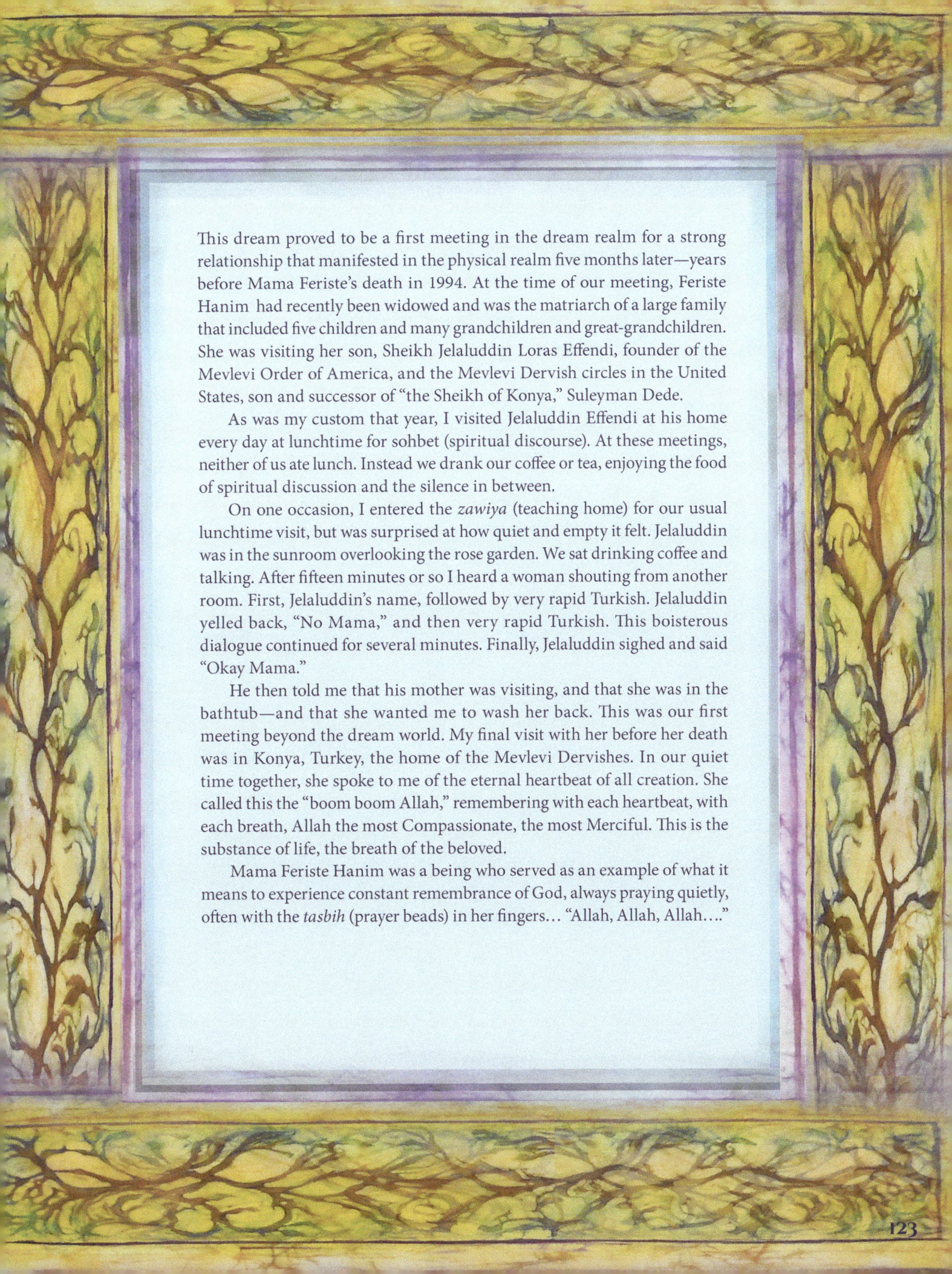

This dream proved to be a first meeting in the dream realm for a strong relationship that manifested in the physical realm five months later—years before Mama Feriste's death in 1994. At the time of our meeting, Feriste Hanim had recently been widowed and was the matriarch of a large family that included five children and many grandchildren and great-grandchildren. She was visiting her son, Sheikh Jelaluddin Loras Effendi, founder of the Mevlevi Order of America, and the Mevlevi Dervish circles in the United States, son and successor of "the Sheikh of Konya," Suleyman Dede.

As was my custom that year, I visited Jelaluddin Effendi at his home every day at lunchtime for sohbet (spiritual discourse). At these meetings, neither of us ate lunch. Instead we drank our coffee or tea, enjoying the food of spiritual discussion and the silence in between.

On one occasion, I entered the *zawiya* (teaching home) for our usual lunchtime visit, but was surprised at how quiet and empty it felt. Jelaluddin was in the sunroom overlooking the rose garden. We sat drinking coffee and talking. After fifteen minutes or so I heard a woman shouting from another room. First, Jelaluddin's name, followed by very rapid Turkish. Jelaluddin yelled back, "No Mama," and then very rapid Turkish. This boisterous dialogue continued for several minutes. Finally, Jelaluddin sighed and said "Okay Mama."

He then told me that his mother was visiting, and that she was in the bathtub—and that she wanted me to wash her back. This was our first meeting beyond the dream world. My final visit with her before her death was in Konya, Turkey, the home of the Mevlevi Dervishes. In our quiet time together, she spoke to me of the eternal heartbeat of all creation. She called this the "boom boom Allah," remembering with each heartbeat, with each breath, Allah the most Compassionate, the most Merciful. This is the substance of life, the breath of the beloved.

Mama Feriste Hanim was a being who served as an example of what it means to experience constant remembrance of God, always praying quietly, often with the *tasbih* (prayer beads) in her fingers… "Allah, Allah, Allah…."

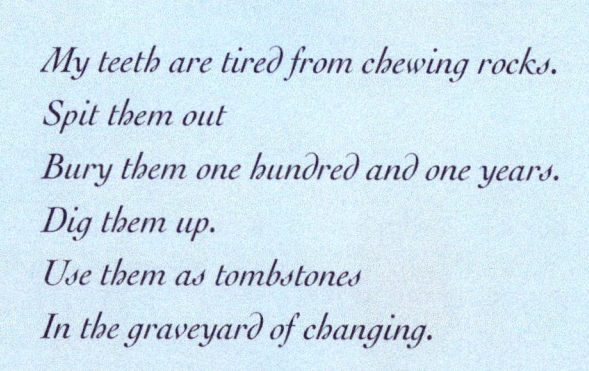

My teeth are tired from chewing rocks.
Spit them out
Bury them one hundred and one years.
Dig them up.
Use them as tombstones
In the graveyard of changing.

—Mariam Baker

BEAUTY AND HARMONY

What is true beauty and harmony? In the Islamic and Sufi traditions, these attributes are represented by a certain refinement, love of a pleasing atmosphere, scents, fine foods, and most important, considering the comfort of others. While the Beloved is manifest in all things, the nature of the Beloved is harmony.

The Way, also known as Tariqat of the Whirling (Mevlevi) Dervishes, is based around the life and poetry of the mystic poet, Jelaluddin Rumi. Tariqat is the path of return to our Source, through returning to our own heart—meaning, "way, path or method."

At the anniversary of his death, the community of dervishes celebrates the mystical union in honor of Rumi's return home to the Beloved, turning in *Sema*, the almost 800-year-old ritual.

URS OF RUMI: THE MYSTICAL MARRIAGE—
THE NIGHT OF TURNING TOWARD UNITY

For the mystic, marriage and union are ultimately with God, Allah, the only Beloved. Students of the Whirling Dervish, Mevlevi school of Sufism celebrate this mystical marriage each year on the anniversary of the death of the poet Rumi, the patron saint of the Whirling Dervishes.

While in many Mevlevi communities, women and men participate in the turning ritual together, this is a relatively recent accommodation initiated in the 1960s and 1970s by the Sufi saint and visionary, Suleyman Dede. In some Mevlevi schools, women are still not allowed to participate in the turning ritual, but must observe from a separate chamber. Considering that this commingling is occurring in cultures where men and women do not regularly interact, such group participation is a radical departure from the norm.

In 1994 and 1997, I was privileged to participate in the sacred ritual of the great whirling dance of the dervishes at the tomb of Jelaluddin Rumi in Konya, Turkey, as part of a delegation of women and men turning together. This was one of the first times that women and men were able to share this great moving prayer in public in Turkey. Tears streamed down the faces of women in the audience as our group helped to support the fulfillment of Suleyman Dede's, dream, that men and women would turn together in prayer at the tomb of Pir Mevlana Jelaluddin Rumi.

Once a year, on December seventeenth, the day of Rumi's death, the dervishes celebrate what is called Shebi Arus—the Wedding Night. This winter celebration marks the high holy days of the whirling dervishes. The poetry of Rumi and the ritual of the Mevlevi are rooted in the wisdom of the Quran. The sea of swirling white, supported by the zikr, represent beauty and harmony made manifest. The Sema, or sacred ceremony of turning, has been performed by semazens in growing numbers since Rumi's passing in 1273.

The *semazen* (one who is initiated in the practice of the Turn) begins preparation and purification for the Wedding Night by a process of stripping away the material, emotional, psychic, and worldly attachments and possessions. Thus begins the purification on every level that is as much a part of the ceremony as the turning itself.

All clothing and jewelry are removed for ritual ablutions. Some *semazens* choose to anoint themselves with rose oil or rosewater, in honor of the Rose of Konya (Rumi) and the sweetness of Love. There is a saying that the closest one can get to the Beloved on the earthly plane is through the scent of a rose. With each ablution, the *semazen* prays for purification. Some choose a fast of silence, abstaining from words and food till after the ceremony, to strengthen their intention and prayer.

Preparation is a time of contemplation. The long hours of practice of the turn are completed. *Inshallah*—God willing—each *semazen* is ready with endurance and commitment to perform the great whirling dance—for the wedding night has arrived. All will join as one in preparing the sacred space for this ceremony.

The participants share the concentration of ironing the yards and yards of white and black material that form the sacred costumes worn only for the sacred ceremony of *Sema* and *Shebi Arus*. Each costume entails hours of holding, pressing, hanging, laying out, holding, pressing, spraying. The semazens work together in twos, threes, and fours, often in silence or sharing the prayer of the *zikr* Allah.

The *semazens* begin assisting in dressing one another two hours in advance of the ceremony. Each garment is kissed in respect and in greeting of the symbolism it carries. The tall camel's hair hat that each *semazen* wears, called a *sikke*, represents the tombstone for the ego. The long white dress worn by each *semazen*, called a *tenure* (ten'-yur-ay), represents the ego's shroud. Lead weights around the hem of the *tenure* support the turning. *Tenure*, literally translated, means skin of light.

A rich sweetness is shared as *semazens* help one another dress. Once dressed, a silent line of *semazens* is formed. In reverence, they await the moment of entry into the *Semahane,* or sacred space where the whirling is to be performed. As they stand in the line, deep in prayer, the arms are crossed over the heart, resting on the shoulders, testifying to the unity of the Beloved.

I am so hot in this waiting,
The wedding gown is heavy and I sweat.
Waiting and waiting,
Heavy in my waiting,
The call to prayer cries:
Why wait? The groom is here.

—Mariam Baker

At the beginning of the ritual, the *semazen* covers the *tenure* with a long black cloak, called a *hurke*. After entry into the *Semahane*, with the permission of the leader, the *semazens* begin circumnambulating the space three times in a slow measured step, formally bowing to each other in recognition of the eternal soul. Before the turning begins, the *semazen* removes the black cloak, carefully placing it in the assigned spot with three folds: one in the name of Love, one in the name of Beauty, and one in the name of Unity. This dropping of the heavy black cloak, revealing the white radiance of the tenure beneath, is visually and spiritually moving, as the *semazens* whirl out from under the cloak of worldly attachments into the infinite. The spiritual rebirth in the truth of the One is acknowledged.

During the ceremony, the Whirling Dervish becomes the witness of Allah's compassion and mercy, dissolving into love and the sacrifice of the ego to love. The act of turning in unity with the other *semazens* is one of total submission and the annihilation of self to unity into the Beloved. The ceremony concludes with the dervish's renewed return and commitment to service of life and truth, and submission to the One. The shield of the heart is pierced and the deep longing of the soul is fulfilled in remembrance of Love, Harmony and Beauty.

Those witnessing the sacred ritual of the whirling dervishes are also recipients of a deep measure of peace and fulfillment as the dervishes complete the great ecstatic dance with a prayer, either spoken aloud or into the heart.

Spontaneity comes licking
The toes of my grief.
Praise leads me by the nose
To the sweetness of melting.
Exaltation dissolves the separateness
And I am His bride.

—Mariam Baker

Fasting

Mystics throughout the ages have advocated fasting. There are many kinds of fasts. There is the fast from food and drink, the fast from habitual behavior and thought, the fast from speech.

> *Consider fasting for one day or one afternoon;*
> *Consider fasting from hypnotic thought;*
> *Fast from gossip;*
> *Fast from judgment of self and others;*
> *Fast from sunrise to sunset in support of world peace or inner peace.*

Consider choosing something to give up for a specific period of time and dedicate this time to awakening, to a deepening of your inner state.

> *Die before death (a saying of the Prophet Muhammad).*
> *Be grateful now.*
> *Forgive yourself and others Now.*
> *Do not wait until your last breath to realize this gift of human incarnation.*
> *Surprise yourself! Be happy—Be grateful.*

The Fast of Ramadan

The fast of all liquids and food from sunrise to sunset during the month of Ramadan is an important part of Muslim spiritual practice and is considered *Sunnah,* or associated with the Prophet Muhammad. The time of Ramadan is a period of deepening one's attunement with Allah, of prayer and of gratitude for the food that sustains us.

The first food to break the Ramadan fast is the date, in the tradition of the Prophet. Ramadan is the ninth month of the Islamic calendar, which is based on the lunar cycle, so its timing varies each year. Pope John Paul II advocated fasting in unity with Muslims.

> *O ye who believe! Fasting is prescribed to you as it was prescribed to those before you,, that ye may learn self-restraint.*
> —Quran, Sura 2: 184-185

For twenty-four hours, practice saying thank you for everything that is given to you. For the following twenty-four hours, practice saying thank you for everything that is withheld from you.

Observe the results of this exercise. Record the effects of this practice of simple gratitude in your journal.

Thirsty, yet no water quenches this thirst.
You say: go jump in the well.
Disappear in the dark, cool, sweet
Mystery of love.
— Mariam Baker

INTERVIEW WITH AMALA

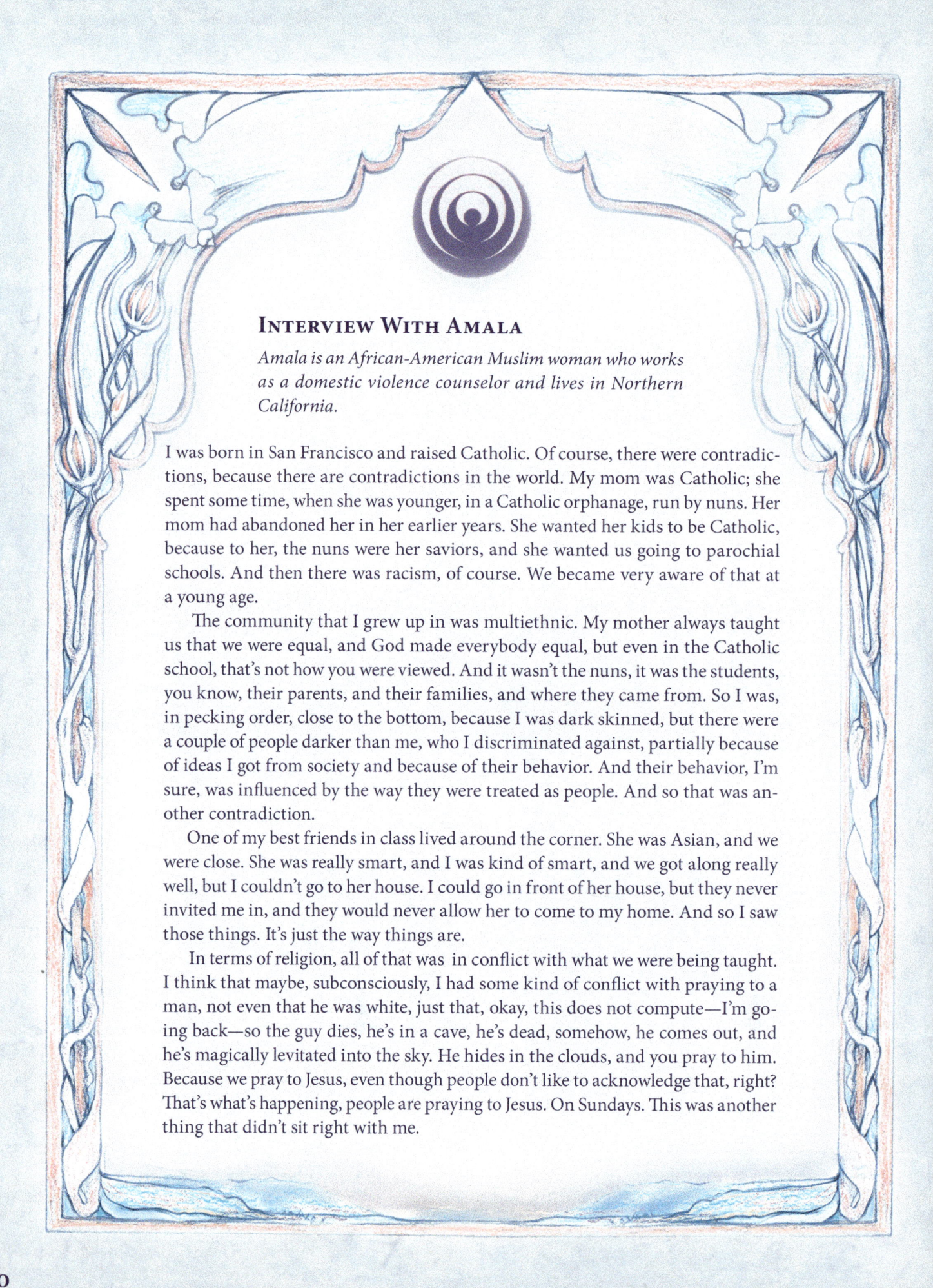

Amala is an African-American Muslim woman who works as a domestic violence counselor and lives in Northern California.

I was born in San Francisco and raised Catholic. Of course, there were contradictions, because there are contradictions in the world. My mom was Catholic; she spent some time, when she was younger, in a Catholic orphanage, run by nuns. Her mom had abandoned her in her earlier years. She wanted her kids to be Catholic, because to her, the nuns were her saviors, and she wanted us going to parochial schools. And then there was racism, of course. We became very aware of that at a young age.

The community that I grew up in was multiethnic. My mother always taught us that we were equal, and God made everybody equal, but even in the Catholic school, that's not how you were viewed. And it wasn't the nuns, it was the students, you know, their parents, and their families, and where they came from. So I was, in pecking order, close to the bottom, because I was dark skinned, but there were a couple of people darker than me, who I discriminated against, partially because of ideas I got from society and because of their behavior. And their behavior, I'm sure, was influenced by the way they were treated as people. And so that was another contradiction.

One of my best friends in class lived around the corner. She was Asian, and we were close. She was really smart, and I was kind of smart, and we got along really well, but I couldn't go to her house. I could go in front of her house, but they never invited me in, and they would never allow her to come to my home. And so I saw those things. It's just the way things are.

In terms of religion, all of that was in conflict with what we were being taught. I think that maybe, subconsciously, I had some kind of conflict with praying to a man, not even that he was white, just that, okay, this does not compute—I'm going back—so the guy dies, he's in a cave, he's dead, somehow, he comes out, and he's magically levitated into the sky. He hides in the clouds, and you pray to him. Because we pray to Jesus, even though people don't like to acknowledge that, right? That's what's happening, people are praying to Jesus. On Sundays. This was another thing that didn't sit right with me.

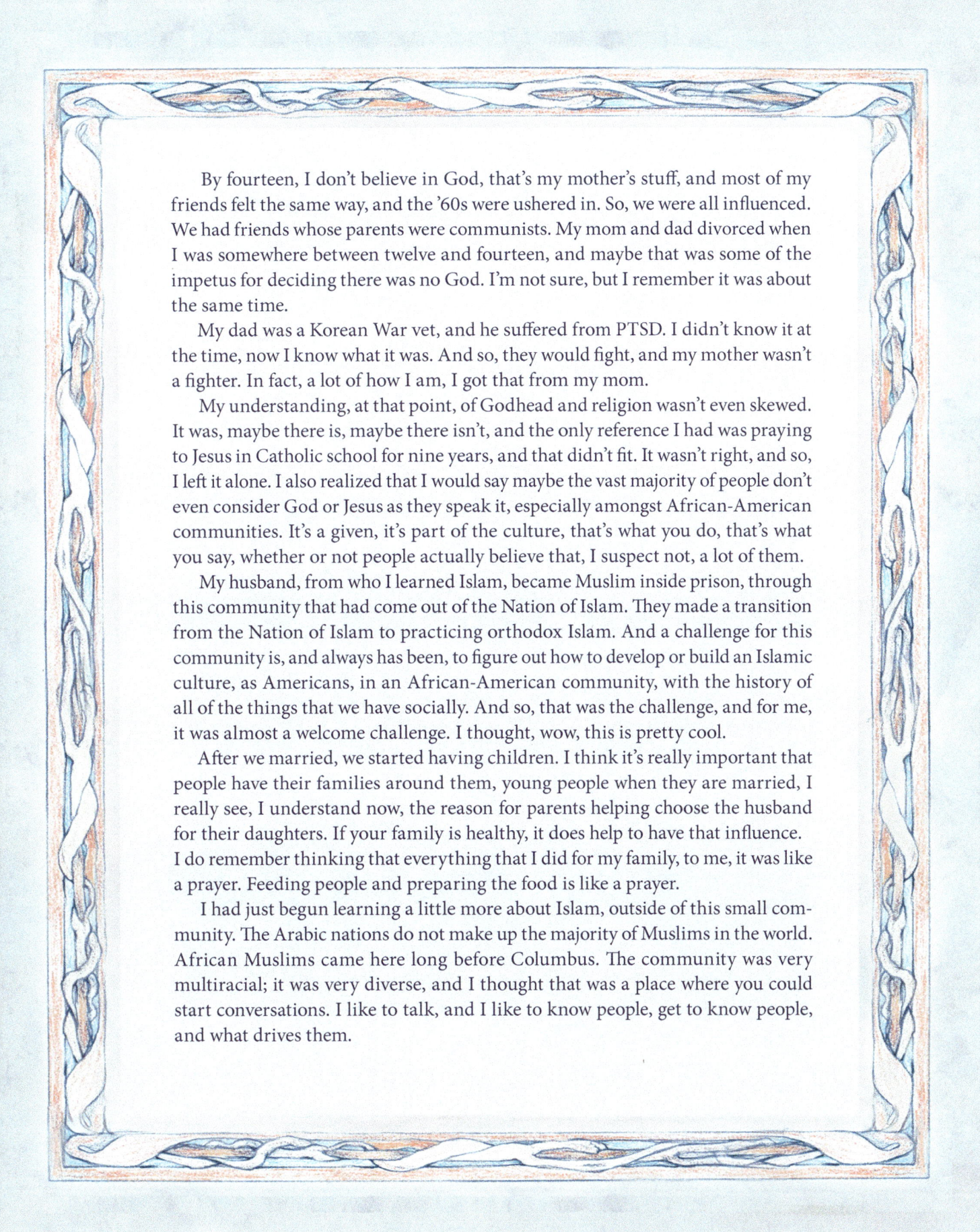

By fourteen, I don't believe in God, that's my mother's stuff, and most of my friends felt the same way, and the '60s were ushered in. So, we were all influenced. We had friends whose parents were communists. My mom and dad divorced when I was somewhere between twelve and fourteen, and maybe that was some of the impetus for deciding there was no God. I'm not sure, but I remember it was about the same time.

My dad was a Korean War vet, and he suffered from PTSD. I didn't know it at the time, now I know what it was. And so, they would fight, and my mother wasn't a fighter. In fact, a lot of how I am, I got that from my mom.

My understanding, at that point, of Godhead and religion wasn't even skewed. It was, maybe there is, maybe there isn't, and the only reference I had was praying to Jesus in Catholic school for nine years, and that didn't fit. It wasn't right, and so, I left it alone. I also realized that I would say maybe the vast majority of people don't even consider God or Jesus as they speak it, especially amongst African-American communities. It's a given, it's part of the culture, that's what you do, that's what you say, whether or not people actually believe that, I suspect not, a lot of them.

My husband, from who I learned Islam, became Muslim inside prison, through this community that had come out of the Nation of Islam. They made a transition from the Nation of Islam to practicing orthodox Islam. And a challenge for this community is, and always has been, to figure out how to develop or build an Islamic culture, as Americans, in an African-American community, with the history of all of the things that we have socially. And so, that was the challenge, and for me, it was almost a welcome challenge. I thought, wow, this is pretty cool.

After we married, we started having children. I think it's really important that people have their families around them, young people when they are married, I really see, I understand now, the reason for parents helping choose the husband for their daughters. If your family is healthy, it does help to have that influence. I do remember thinking that everything that I did for my family, to me, it was like a prayer. Feeding people and preparing the food is like a prayer.

I had just begun learning a little more about Islam, outside of this small community. The Arabic nations do not make up the majority of Muslims in the world. African Muslims came here long before Columbus. The community was very multiracial; it was very diverse, and I thought that was a place where you could start conversations. I like to talk, and I like to know people, get to know people, and what drives them.

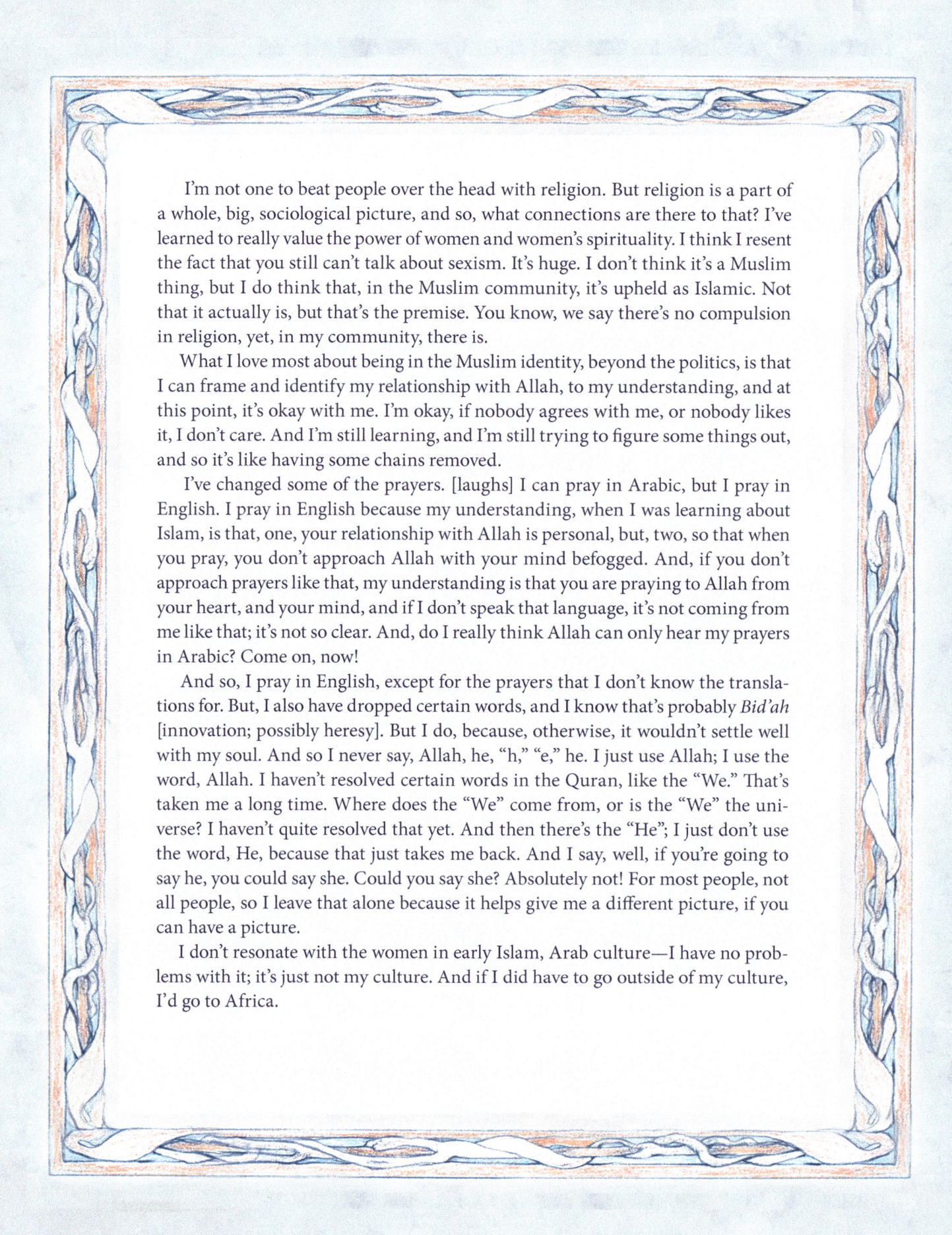

I'm not one to beat people over the head with religion. But religion is a part of a whole, big, sociological picture, and so, what connections are there to that? I've learned to really value the power of women and women's spirituality. I think I resent the fact that you still can't talk about sexism. It's huge. I don't think it's a Muslim thing, but I do think that, in the Muslim community, it's upheld as Islamic. Not that it actually is, but that's the premise. You know, we say there's no compulsion in religion, yet, in my community, there is.

What I love most about being in the Muslim identity, beyond the politics, is that I can frame and identify my relationship with Allah, to my understanding, and at this point, it's okay with me. I'm okay, if nobody agrees with me, or nobody likes it, I don't care. And I'm still learning, and I'm still trying to figure some things out, and so it's like having some chains removed.

I've changed some of the prayers. [laughs] I can pray in Arabic, but I pray in English. I pray in English because my understanding, when I was learning about Islam, is that, one, your relationship with Allah is personal, but, two, so that when you pray, you don't approach Allah with your mind befogged. And, if you don't approach prayers like that, my understanding is that you are praying to Allah from your heart, and your mind, and if I don't speak that language, it's not coming from me like that; it's not so clear. And, do I really think Allah can only hear my prayers in Arabic? Come on, now!

And so, I pray in English, except for the prayers that I don't know the translations for. But, I also have dropped certain words, and I know that's probably *Bid'ah* [innovation; possibly heresy]. But I do, because, otherwise, it wouldn't settle well with my soul. And so I never say, Allah, he, "h," "e," he. I just use Allah; I use the word, Allah. I haven't resolved certain words in the Quran, like the "We." That's taken me a long time. Where does the "We" come from, or is the "We" the universe? I haven't quite resolved that yet. And then there's the "He"; I just don't use the word, He, because that just takes me back. And I say, well, if you're going to say he, you could say she. Could you say she? Absolutely not! For most people, not all people, so I leave that alone because it helps give me a different picture, if you can have a picture.

I don't resonate with the women in early Islam, Arab culture—I have no problems with it; it's just not my culture. And if I did have to go outside of my culture, I'd go to Africa.

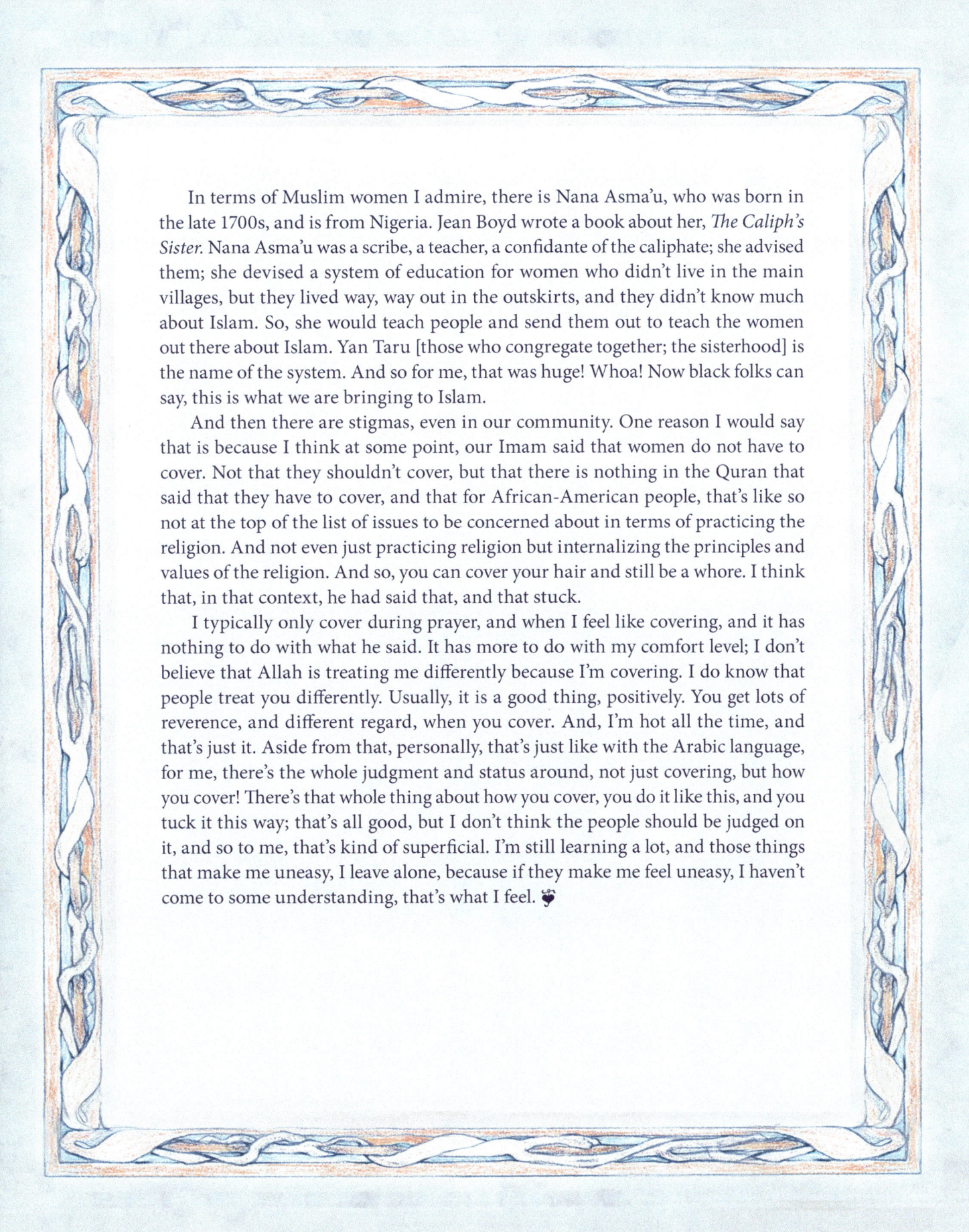

In terms of Muslim women I admire, there is Nana Asma'u, who was born in the late 1700s, and is from Nigeria. Jean Boyd wrote a book about her, *The Caliph's Sister*. Nana Asma'u was a scribe, a teacher, a confidante of the caliphate; she advised them; she devised a system of education for women who didn't live in the main villages, but they lived way, way out in the outskirts, and they didn't know much about Islam. So, she would teach people and send them out to teach the women out there about Islam. Yan Taru [those who congregate together; the sisterhood] is the name of the system. And so for me, that was huge! Whoa! Now black folks can say, this is what we are bringing to Islam.

And then there are stigmas, even in our community. One reason I would say that is because I think at some point, our Imam said that women do not have to cover. Not that they shouldn't cover, but that there is nothing in the Quran that said that they have to cover, and that for African-American people, that's like so not at the top of the list of issues to be concerned about in terms of practicing the religion. And not even just practicing religion but internalizing the principles and values of the religion. And so, you can cover your hair and still be a whore. I think that, in that context, he had said that, and that stuck.

I typically only cover during prayer, and when I feel like covering, and it has nothing to do with what he said. It has more to do with my comfort level; I don't believe that Allah is treating me differently because I'm covering. I do know that people treat you differently. Usually, it is a good thing, positively. You get lots of reverence, and different regard, when you cover. And, I'm hot all the time, and that's just it. Aside from that, personally, that's just like with the Arabic language, for me, there's the whole judgment and status around, not just covering, but how you cover! There's that whole thing about how you cover, you do it like this, and you tuck it this way; that's all good, but I don't think the people should be judged on it, and so to me, that's kind of superficial. I'm still learning a lot, and those things that make me uneasy, I leave alone, because if they make me feel uneasy, I haven't come to some understanding, that's what I feel. ♥

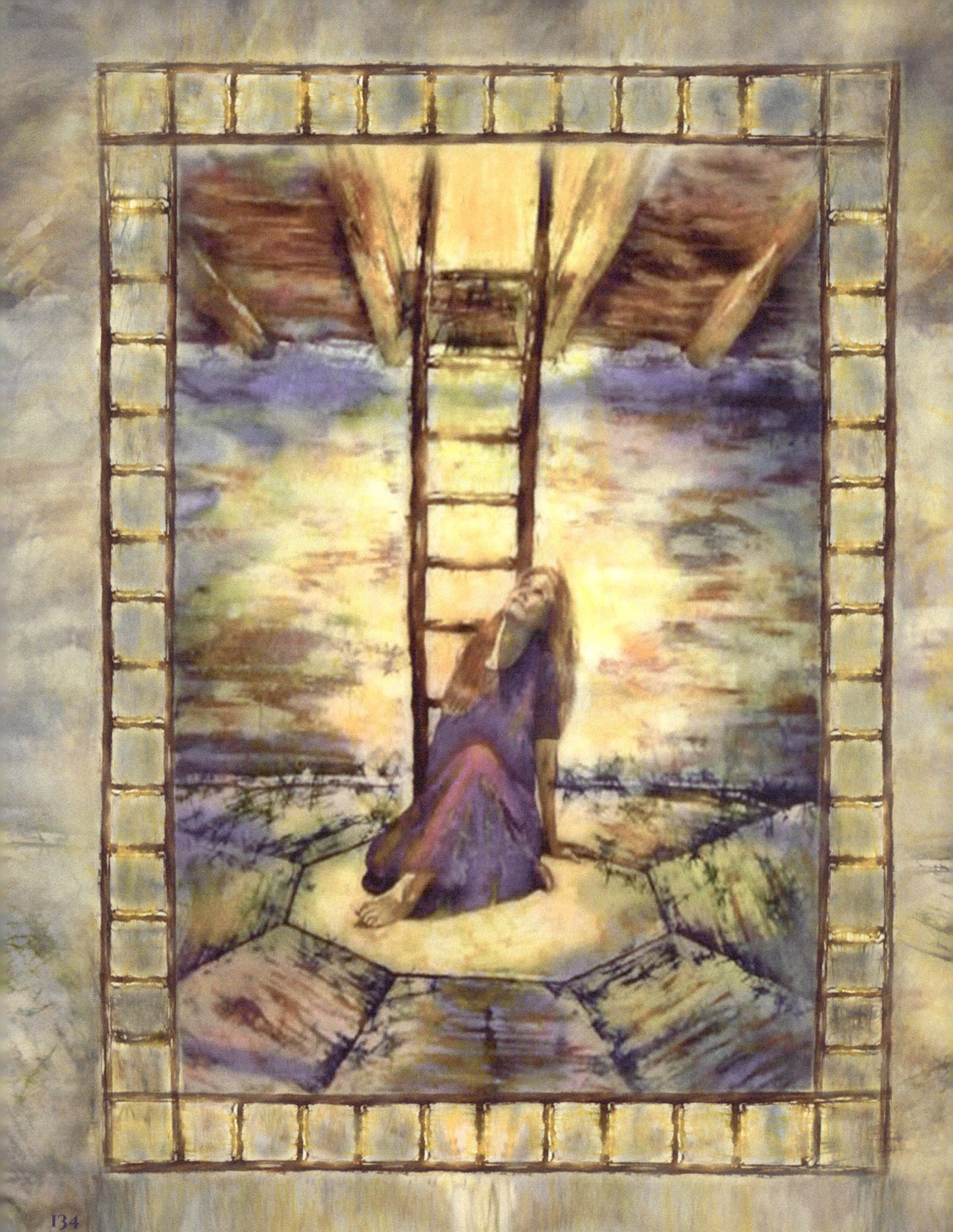

Creating Heart Space
Recipes for the Sacred

Beauty and Harmony are evident in a life lived with intention. Moments of presence exude imminent harmony. Even our human foibles, our *nafs*, can be viewed through the lens of this refinement when we develop the state of the objective observer, pausing and noticing, then looking within to discover motivation or false beliefs that may have run their course.

As we accept those aspects that we previously found unlovable, we allow this beauty and harmony to permeate our being. The grace of this presence begins its steady work, creating a confidence with origins in the infinite, rather than a false sense of superiority born of propping up a fragile sense of self. This deeper confidence brings forth profound compassion for self and others, as well as patience for our human state. This naturally results in a deep, emanating beauty, as we invite all of our attributes into the circle of the Beloved, the home of our higher selves. By turning attention to the needs of others and to our authentic selves, we bring ourselves more fully into each moment.

Wazifa—Ya Sami

Divine Archetype—The All-Hearing One

The wise say that those who listen deeply and hear Divine Truth, or *Haqq*, are blessed with grace. We live in a culture where listening and deeply hearing are becoming lost arts, as our senses are bombarded with stimulus. Human relationships suffer if we are unable to give full attention and listen to the story of another. The ideal in Islam is to give one's full attention to listen and hear the voice of the Beloved, the voice of Allah, the voice of the Spirit of Guidance.

Standing Practice

In a standing position, place the hands behind the ears, palms facing forward, as if cupping the hands to listen. Allow the upper torso and the space around the breastbone to be open, head uplifted and slightly back, face pointing towards the heavens. Intone the Seed sound, Ya Sami. Do this eleven times. Then, remaining in this posture, be silent and still. Listen. Contemplate the possibility that with each breath God is whispering to us, Compassion, Mercy, *ar-rahim, ar-rahman*, and that this is our human inheritance.

Walking Practice
Reversal of Attention

Go to a natural setting and focus on the breath, on the deeper hearing, *Ya Sami*, the all-hearing aspect of the self. Then, walk slowly, and feel the great luminosity emanating from the pulsing, humming life abounding in the natural world. Synchronize the breath with the steps. Become deeply aware of the footfalls upon the earth and with the inner voice repeat a sacred phrase that feels comfortable. With practice, the supportive love of the natural environment can be experienced any time we turn our attention to it.

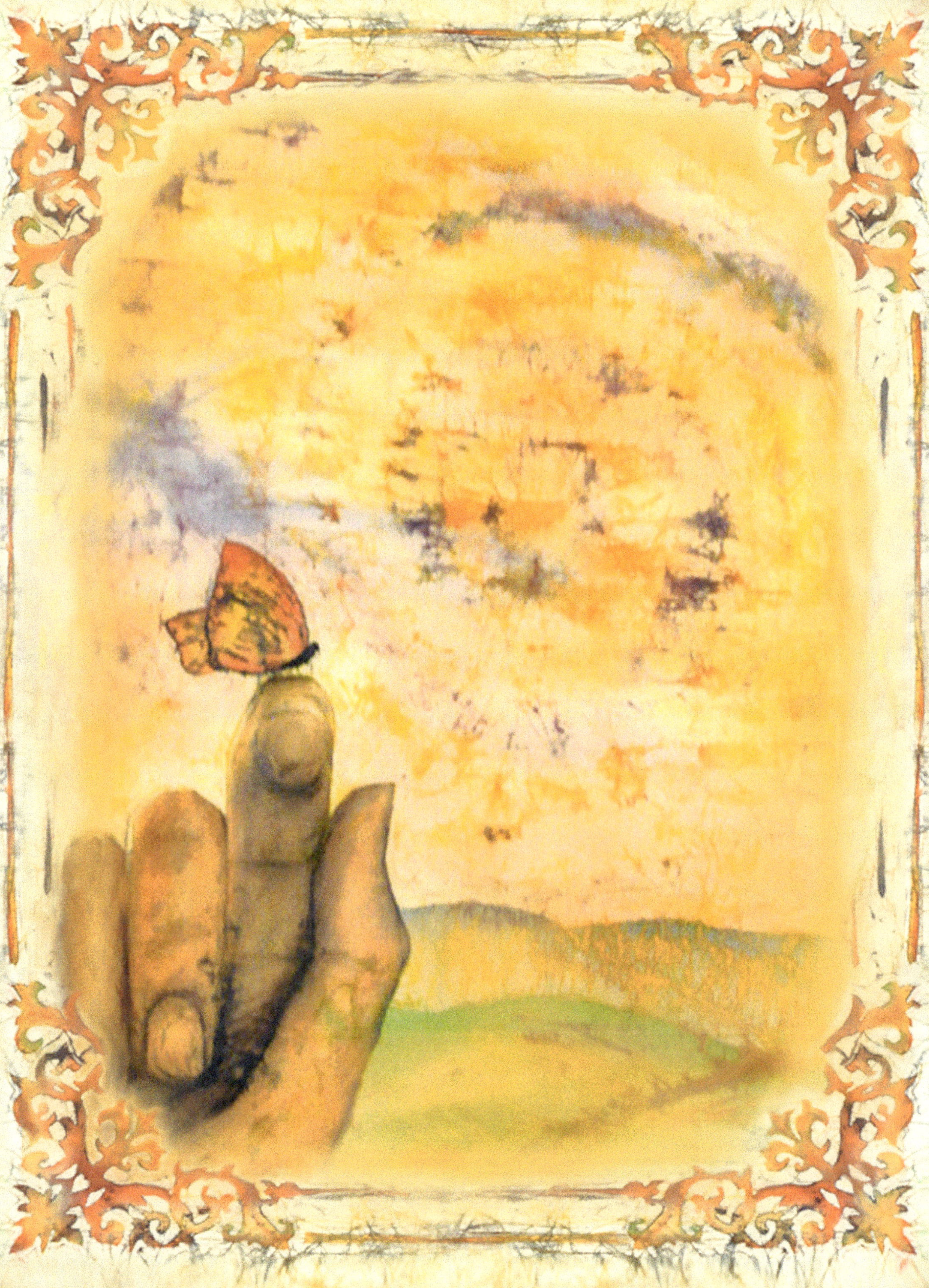

BEING HUMAN
6

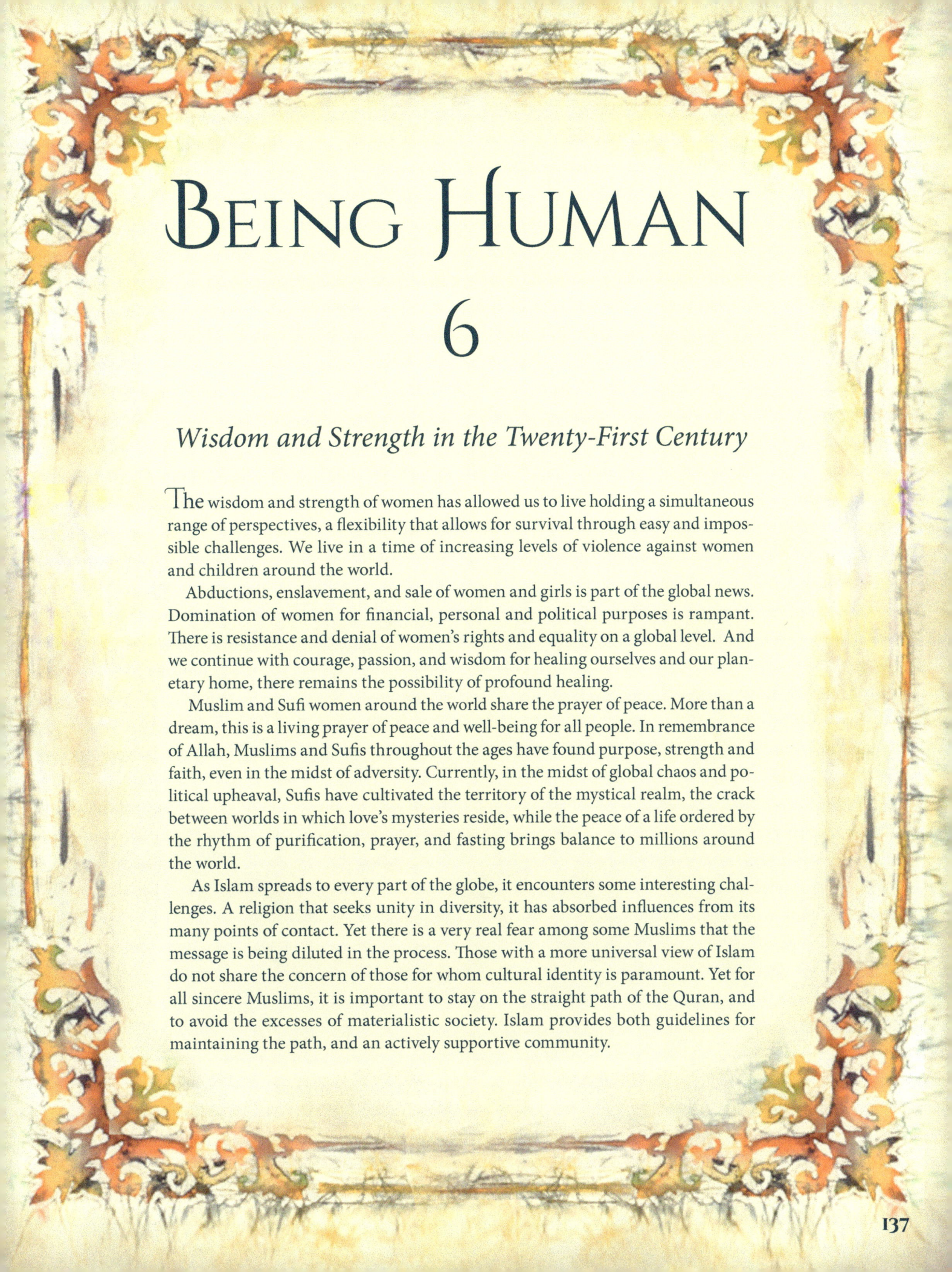

Wisdom and Strength in the Twenty-First Century

The wisdom and strength of women has allowed us to live holding a simultaneous range of perspectives, a flexibility that allows for survival through easy and impossible challenges. We live in a time of increasing levels of violence against women and children around the world.

Abductions, enslavement, and sale of women and girls is part of the global news. Domination of women for financial, personal and political purposes is rampant. There is resistance and denial of women's rights and equality on a global level. And we continue with courage, passion, and wisdom for healing ourselves and our planetary home, there remains the possibility of profound healing.

Muslim and Sufi women around the world share the prayer of peace. More than a dream, this is a living prayer of peace and well-being for all people. In remembrance of Allah, Muslims and Sufis throughout the ages have found purpose, strength and faith, even in the midst of adversity. Currently, in the midst of global chaos and political upheaval, Sufis have cultivated the territory of the mystical realm, the crack between worlds in which love's mysteries reside, while the peace of a life ordered by the rhythm of purification, prayer, and fasting brings balance to millions around the world.

As Islam spreads to every part of the globe, it encounters some interesting challenges. A religion that seeks unity in diversity, it has absorbed influences from its many points of contact. Yet there is a very real fear among some Muslims that the message is being diluted in the process. Those with a more universal view of Islam do not share the concern of those for whom cultural identity is paramount. Yet for all sincere Muslims, it is important to stay on the straight path of the Quran, and to avoid the excesses of materialistic society. Islam provides both guidelines for maintaining the path, and an actively supportive community.

Dream Sequence

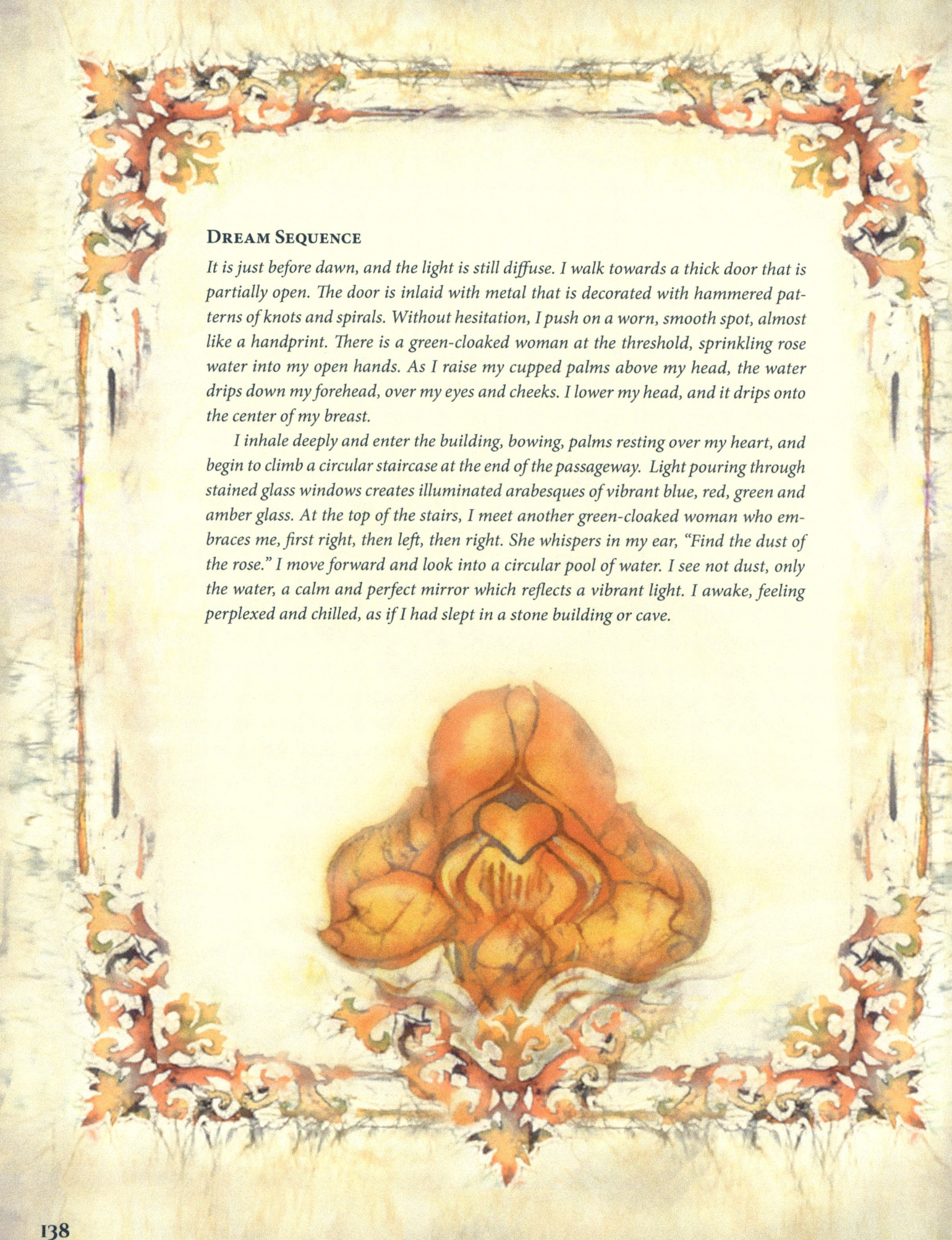

It is just before dawn, and the light is still diffuse. I walk towards a thick door that is partially open. The door is inlaid with metal that is decorated with hammered patterns of knots and spirals. Without hesitation, I push on a worn, smooth spot, almost like a handprint. There is a green-cloaked woman at the threshold, sprinkling rose water into my open hands. As I raise my cupped palms above my head, the water drips down my forehead, over my eyes and cheeks. I lower my head, and it drips onto the center of my breast.

I inhale deeply and enter the building, bowing, palms resting over my heart, and begin to climb a circular staircase at the end of the passageway. Light pouring through stained glass windows creates illuminated arabesques of vibrant blue, red, green and amber glass. At the top of the stairs, I meet another green-cloaked woman who embraces me, first right, then left, then right. She whispers in my ear, "Find the dust of the rose." I move forward and look into a circular pool of water. I see not dust, only the water, a calm and perfect mirror which reflects a vibrant light. I awake, feeling perplexed and chilled, as if I had slept in a stone building or cave.

Women in Islamic Societies

Many feminists question the status of women within Islam. And it is quite true that within some Muslim societies, women are denied basic human rights. This is unfortunate as it was clearly not the message or way of the Prophet Muhammad. Yet, it is also true that liberation will look different within an Islamic society than it does in Western society. How can women of strong faith achieve rights while maintaining the traditional structure of family, home, and community that is the fabric of an Islamic society? To understand and support this, one must consider the context in which most Muslim women live. Liberation does not mean adopting a Western way of life. Rather, it means the freedom to choose, to be able to express their faith without enduring discrimination from non-Muslims or oppression within the Islamic community.

Muslim women often face discrimination in public life. Still, voices of Muslim women are increasingly being raised and heard. Resistance to this awakened female leadership is often supported by selective quotes carefully chosen from Hadith to diminish the emerging power and leadership of women. Quotes such as, "Those who entrust their affairs to a woman will never know prosperity," are being questioned by Islamic feminist scholars, as they seek to preserve the beauty of the original message of the Quran, and allow women their rightful place in society.

After the death of Muhammad, certain elite male followers decided what was essential to preserve in Islam, based on their own interests. Infighting during that era led to divisive tactics and to the assassination of several successive leaders.

Modern Muslim women reexamine the interpretations of their holy texts. There is no sanction in the Quran for such action as stoning women accused of dishonoring their family. This practice originated in tribal society and has been falsely associated with Islam. The careful analysis and rigorous scholarship of current engagement of women studying the Quran and Hadith is bringing new insight and understanding to Islam and to the message of Prophet Muhammad, which includes deep respect for women.

This respect is actually a common theme in the Quran. Verses strongly condemn the preference for male babies that was the norm at the time of Khadijah and Muhammad's marriage. The extreme practice of female infanticide was contrary to the message of Muhammad. Education for girls was encouraged. Although inheritance was traditionally passed down through the male lines in Arab lands and in other parts of the world, the Quran stresses the rights of women to inherit property. Practical matters of concern for equality within society are often addressed within the Quran. Heroic accounts of women pursuing learning in an environment where it is strongly discouraged are not uncommon, and they are profound, such as the story of young Pakistani woman, Malala Yousafzai, who survived being shot by the Taliban.

Risking punishment and imprisonment, these brave women continue to read, write, study, and engage in other academic pursuits, following the advice of the Prophet Muhammad, who stressed the importance of knowledge and of generosity in sharing ideas and increasing literacy for both men and women.

140

Islam in the West

The twentieth century brought new interpretations of Islam as it continued spreading across the globe. In some places, desperation has led to narrow, radical, or militant views. In North America, Islam was slow to take root. Until recently, most people knew more about religions such as Buddhism, than Islam, even though the latter is a continuation of the Judeo-Christian tradition, as Jesus and Abraham are cited in the Quran.

By 1910 various Sufi orders had found their way to parts of the United States. Sufi practices and meditations led to an awareness of their foundation within Islam, although the path of the mystic is also seen to be universal. Now there is an ever-growing interest in translations of the mystical poetry of Rumi, Rabia, Hafiz and others.

The first official mosque in North America was built in Cedar Rapids, Iowa, in 1934. However, such religious centers were rare, and seen as exotic in the United States until much later in the twentieth century.

In the late 1950s, African Americans began to hear about Islam through Elijah Muhammad. Many Muslims feel Elijah Muhammad's interpretation is a distortion of the faith, primarily because of the role he established for himself as supreme leader. While controversy surrounds his leadership, the Nation of Islam has had a profound influence in America, helping to bring stability into impoverished African American communities. The focus on family and living clean, free of drugs and alcohol, continues to change the lives of people who found themselves in moral despair in the midst of an unjust and racist society.

One of the most famous converts to The Nation of Islam was Malcolm X, known by his Muslim name el-Hajj Malik el-Shabazz. He was one of the first of a generation of African-Americans who traveled to Africa and the Middle East seeking a lost identity. When he made the Hajj (Pilgrimage to Mecca), Malcolm X found in Mecca spiritual affinity and moved to an acceptance of original Islamic teachings. In time, other Black Muslims have turned to the broader faith that is rooted in Quran and the teachings of Muhammad and the Prophets of Allah.

In the twenty-first century, we see women in the West drawn to Islam for some of the same reasons that many African Americans have embraced this religion. As the foundations of society are destabilized by increasing materialism, and increased objectification and denigration of women, they are questioning these cultural norms and turning instead to the way of the Prophet Muhammad and the ideals of Islam.

In essence, Muhammad advocated a natural hierarchy of intelligence that we are just beginning to comprehend. It is a hierarchy that is neither imposed nor artificial. Respect for the voice of every person, young or old, regardless of gender, background, physical appearance, or other considerations, is true submission to the will of Allah. This profound kindness and compassion is the essence which brings peace.

Islam affirms the universality of God and the unity of the prophets. The Quran directs the believer to acknowledge the validity of other religions. Although tolerance is not always practiced, it is the ideal.

The Prophet Muhammad, as a humble servant of God, did not wish for followers to idealize him. It is of psychological interest to notice the repetitive tendency on the part of human beings to ignore the teachings of the prophets while attempting to super-humanize them. By idealizing, rather than honoring, the prophets, we limit the possibility of believing in their humanity, and hence limit our own ability to follow and understand their guidance.

The message of compassion and mercy is beyond and within all time, space and dimensionality. This birthright from a loving Creator and Sustainer is the message of the Prophet Muhammad. Praise and remembrance of the Supreme Being, profound Unity—Allah—is the primary purpose of a Muslim's life. Reality is composed of the seen and the unseen; the simultaneous realms of existence of every day human life, the angelic and invisible worlds, and the divine world.

The Mystic Tradition

As the human race faces increasing challenges, the esoteric role of the mystic within society becomes increasingly important. The Sufi or dervish works with the unseen realm to release forces for the benefit of all. As an individual becomes ever more awake, this presence touches all they come in contact with, and thus helps humanity. Some Sufis follow the rhythm and order of a traditional Islamic life, and some vary their practices, but the deep dedication to awakening presence and invoking the healing power of profound universal love is at the core of Sufism. This healing power is beyond description and so most easily referred to in poetry, song, or silence.

The Believers, men and women, are protectors, one of another. They enjoin what is just and forbid what is evil, they observe regular prayers, practice regular charity, and obey Allah and His Messenger. On them will Allah pour Mercy, for Allah is Exalted in Power and Wise.
—Quran, Sura 9: 71

143

Interview With Lobna (Luby) Ismail

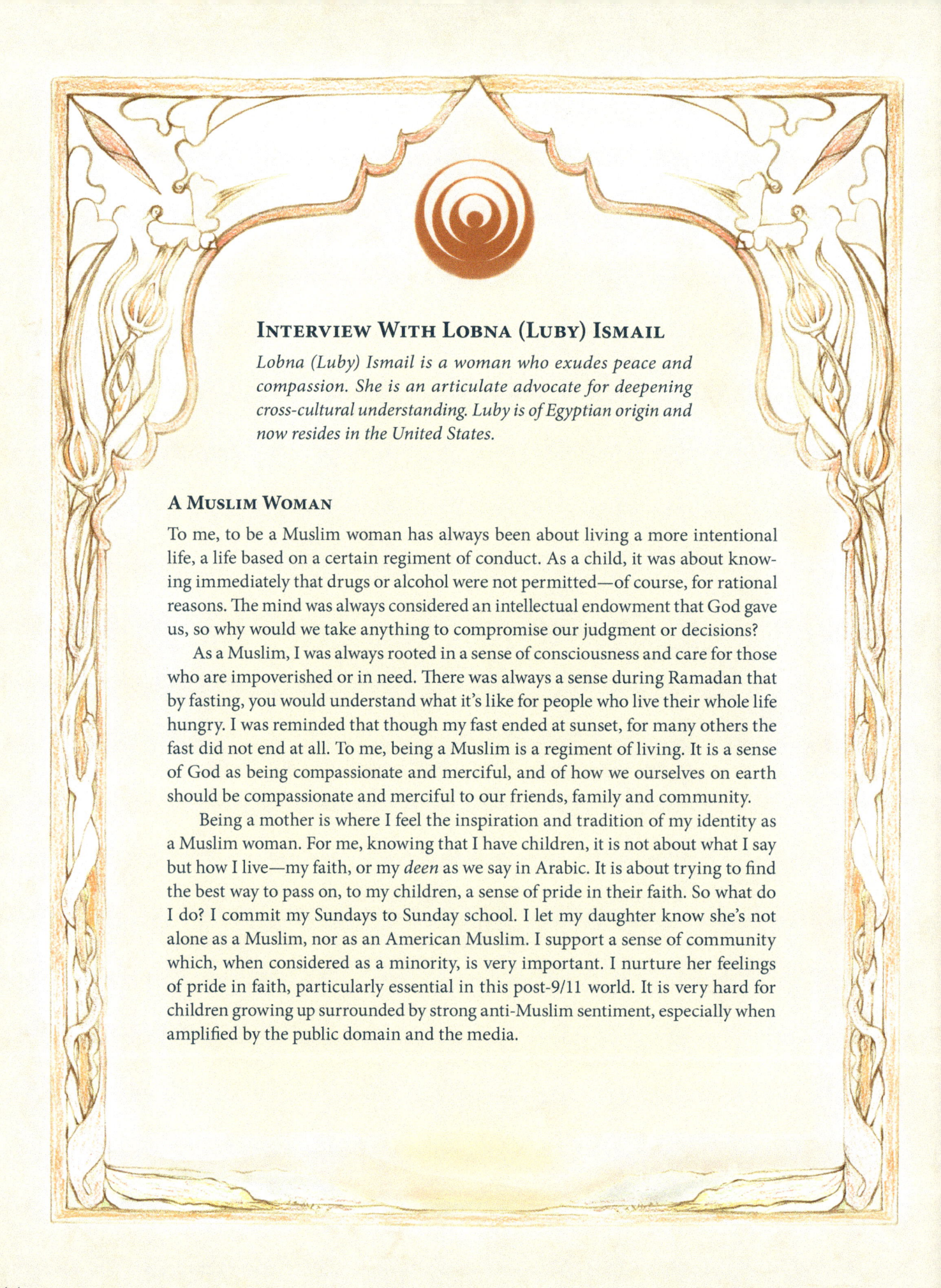

Lobna (Luby) Ismail is a woman who exudes peace and compassion. She is an articulate advocate for deepening cross-cultural understanding. Luby is of Egyptian origin and now resides in the United States.

A Muslim Woman

To me, to be a Muslim woman has always been about living a more intentional life, a life based on a certain regiment of conduct. As a child, it was about knowing immediately that drugs or alcohol were not permitted—of course, for rational reasons. The mind was always considered an intellectual endowment that God gave us, so why would we take anything to compromise our judgment or decisions?

As a Muslim, I was always rooted in a sense of consciousness and care for those who are impoverished or in need. There was always a sense during Ramadan that by fasting, you would understand what it's like for people who live their whole life hungry. I was reminded that though my fast ended at sunset, for many others the fast did not end at all. To me, being a Muslim is a regiment of living. It is a sense of God as being compassionate and merciful, and of how we ourselves on earth should be compassionate and merciful to our friends, family and community.

Being a mother is where I feel the inspiration and tradition of my identity as a Muslim woman. For me, knowing that I have children, it is not about what I say but how I live—my faith, or my *deen* as we say in Arabic. It is about trying to find the best way to pass on, to my children, a sense of pride in their faith. So what do I do? I commit my Sundays to Sunday school. I let my daughter know she's not alone as a Muslim, nor as an American Muslim. I support a sense of community which, when considered as a minority, is very important. I nurture her feelings of pride in faith, particularly essential in this post-9/11 world. It is very hard for children growing up surrounded by strong anti-Muslim sentiment, especially when amplified by the public domain and the media.

Formative Years

I grew up amidst predominantly conservative Christians. I actually connected closely with the evangelical community because their youth groups had the same values as myself, in terms of abstaining from what's considered "teenage mischief." They also shared a love of God and a love of doing good. They were my community and I wanted to be in their youth group. We got together in the band room; they brought their Bibles, and I brought my Quran. We read from scripture, respected and loved one another, because we knew each other as fellow peers, friends and neighbors—not by a label.

Who I am today stems out of this. There was a wonderful sense of our family having been adopted. My parents, who were new immigrants and the only Egyptians in the community, felt it most at our first Christmas. Our mailman, Mr. Adams, brought us our first Christmas tree. My parents couldn't reject this sincere extension of neighborly welcome, symbolic of how they wanted us to be a part of their town and country's most festive time. I remember a local publication, the *Winter Haven News*, doing a story on us—about our Christmas tree and lights. Though it is not common amongst Muslims to celebrate Christmas, we felt we weren't causing any offense—and we weren't being caused any offense based on faith. We love Jesus. We believe in Jesus, in his miracles, in the virgin birth and in the second coming of Christ. We shared so much; why not share in the celebration?

As my husband says, do not strive more to do your prayers, strive more to live your life as a prayer. Prayer is really for you to stop, pause, reflect, and remember your blessings. It reminds you of the daily doings, and lets you reflect on how you are living your life. In what way are you part of your society?

Faith

I have always been about the spirit of the faith. In Ramadan, fasting always reminds us to be thankful. At the same time, due to my condition with multiple sclerosis, I am required to take meds and am often distracted from how I want to live my faith. I know my children live in a non-Muslim majority country, where they have soccer matches or wrestling meets, making focus on the faith more difficult. We remember that in the Quran, if you don't fast, you can always make it up later, or feed the poor. We've found local soup kitchens and food banks, and always made contributions—not just of our time, but of donations as well. We always pay the *zakat* [alms for the poor], not only remembering to help strangers, but our family and friends also.

We always strive to live our life in spirit of the faith. Can we do better? Yes, but every day is a new day.

As a Muslim, I always try to remember the blessings of what my family and I have, not taking essentials like food, water and shelter for granted. Being mindful, in Islam, is born out of a sense of care for the orphans—because Muhammed himself was an orphan. There is a sense that I have not only a duty to myself, but to my society at large and to my earth. It is not about being arrogant, selfish or filled with greed, but about remembrance of blessings. There's a *hadith* that says, "I will not feed myself until I know that my neighbor is fed."

Islamic dress is diverse based on a range of reasons: family, community, national and personal preferences. Interpretation of dressing modestly varies. Modest dress originally comes out of Judaic-Christian teachings; Orthodox Jewish, Catholic and Orthodox Christians and other Christians (Amish, Mennonite) may wear modest dresses or skirts, cover their hair, and otherwise be modest in their dress. Today, depending on where you are in world, dress can be based on traditional or political respects, typically, with women being told what they can or can't wear.

What Women Wear

I respect the question regarding women's dress in Islam, but also resent it. There is too much talk of what is on a woman's head, rather than what is in a woman's head. For both Muslims and non-Muslims, there's an idea that because a woman covers her hair, she is more religious, pious, or a better Muslim. The faith is much deeper than a piece of cloth on your head as a measure of one's piety or religious devotion.

In my own family, the interpretation of modesty varies. Some may cover their hair, but wear tight jeans. Some don't cover their hair but won't wear tight clothing. Some in the younger generation cover their hair, but as a fashion statement, reflected in elaborate scarves and outfits.

This question poses a desire to better understand Muslim women, yet perpetuates the idea that Muslim woman come in two forms: covered or not. In America, they say it is a triumph when woman in Afghanistan can remove the *burqa* [head to foot covering]. This may be one symbolic advancement—but women in Muslim-majority countries have said that access to education, health care, politics, and other equal opportunities is far more important than how they are dressed.

Marriage

Marriage, in Islam, is actually a contract between a man and a woman. Under Islamic law, women have the right to choose, agree on, and determine stipulations in a marriage—often contrary to public thought. The best example is Prophet Muhammad. He not only worked for Khadija, but she was older than him—and she asked him to marry.

Marriage, to me, has always been an equitable partnership. Fortunately, my husband and I have been married for over 25 years. We've strived to know how to best support one another in our desires and ambitions. At the same time, we raise our children in a home where we have shared values: we don't drink alcohol and we prescribe to modesty—not only dress, but in how we behave. Laila, our seven-year-old, came home one day saying her school was having a dance, at a high school. My husband said: there are no dances in first grade. As open and tolerant as we are, we felt it was just too young to acculturate a child to the presumed normalcy of a dance.

Divorce is permitted in Islam, but it is important to separate what may be cultural norms—which may predate Islam—that aren't necessarily Islamic, or under *Shariah*, [Koranic canonical law] (for example, arranged marriages). A woman have the right to divorce, the right to approve of whom she marries, and the right for her financial earnings or inheritances to be solely for herself.

Hajj

I have never been to *Hajj*, but I've done *umrah* [pilgrimage to Mecca at any time of year]. I did it first just after I was diagnosed with multiple sclerosis, and was able to walk. More recently I did it in 2009, using my scooter. As my daughter Laila says, "Mommy, you can't walk with your legs but you walk with your heart." I have a neurological condition, multiple sclerosis, which makes walking challenging.

Iblis—The Devil

I always think of *Iblis* not as a person or figure with horns, but as the daily temptations that can sway you from being grateful—instead leaving you stuck in negativity, or in a mode of complaining and constant criticism. Every day is a battle, or a *jihad* [struggle] to stay straight, to remain in a state of peace. That is the daily struggle. I believe in sin as a force, which sways you off from a place of peace and gratitude, trying to lure you from the intention to be and do good and be the best person within oneself.

Islam—Sufism

I consider myself on the path of both Islam and Sufism. Growing up a mainstream Muslim with parents from Egypt, I do believe in a sense of duty to follow the five pillars of Islam and to be more exact in my observance of the faith. Yet, more recently, I've been introduced to the Sufi path, which emphasizes remembrance. ❦

Modern Women Mystics and Scholars

Irena Tweedy
1907—1999

Irina Tweedy was a British Sufi mystic of the Naqshbandi order who became the first Western woman trained in this branch of Sufism. Born in Russia, she studied in Vienna and Paris, and married after World War II. Her husband died in 1954 and Tweedy turned to the spiritual path, the mystical journey of the soul. Her quest led her to Northwest India where she met, Radha Mohan Lal, a Sufi Sheikh from the Naqshbandi Order, whom she called Bhai Sahib (Elder Brother).

Tweedy created a written record of her spiritual journey, recording the struggles, challenges, difficulties and doubts, as well as the high points of realization and transcendence. This diary eventually became the book—*Daughter of Fire: A Diary of Spiritual Training with a Sufi Master.*

In the book, Tweedy offers a first-hand view of the annihilation of the ego and the discovery, beneath the surface of the personality, of the mystery of *Ishq*—a love which has no opposite, a love which is the Mystery of Creation. She began working with groups in the late 1960s. This form of Naqshbandi Sufism spread throughout Europe, Australia, North America and around the world.

Professor Annemarie Schimmel
1922–2003

Professor Schimmel was a voice that provided insight into the spiritual reality and dimensions of Islam. She was one of the greatest scholars of Islam and Sufism of the twentieth century. Fluent in many languages, including German, English, French, Arabic, Persian, Turkish, Urdu, Sindhi, Punjabi, and Pushto, she began her academic career at age twenty-three. She served as Professor of Indo-Muslim Culture at Harvard.

There is a story that on one of her travels in Konya, Turkey, she placed her fountain pen on Rumi's tomb praying for inspiration and wisdom.

Thirst

"Make thirsty me, O friend, give me no water!
Let me so love that sleep flees from my door!"
    Yes, sleep flees, if he sees the burning eyelids,
    He would be drowned if he would
    Cross the sea of tears;
    He would be poisoned if he should dare to drink
    That potent wine which you
    Poured in the goblet of my eyes:
    Those eyes which once beheld your radiant face
    And try to mirror it on every tear...
    ...Those eyes which are a veil.
Make me more thirsty, friend, give me no water—
My thirst is proof that you are thirsty, too.

        —Annemarie Schimmel

Murshida Vera Corda
1913-2002

Murshida Vera was born shortly before the United States entered into the First World War. From her first memories, she experienced mystical states within nature, and, as a child, dreamed of the great Sufi master, Hazrat Inayat Khan, long before meeting him in the body. She was a successful graphic artist and educator. Sufi disciple for over fifty years, she was given the title of Murshida, or spiritual teacher, when she began guiding other disciples in the Sufi tradition.

In the early 1970s, she founded the New Age Seed Schools in the San Francisco Bay Area, based on the mystical teachings of Hazrat Inayat Khan, and developed a complete curriculum from infancy through elementary school, training teachers and parents in the spiritual, intellectual, social, physical, and moral development of children. The school was based on the mystical principles of Sufism, and incorporated music, dance and art into the curriculum.

Murshida Vera Corda took to heart the profound relationship of teacher and student, guide and *mureed* (initiate). Hazrat Inayat Khan says the hardest thing in the world is to learn to be a student. Murshida Vera was an inspiring teacher and student until her passage into the unseen at the age of eighty-nine. She died at home in the consciousness of the angels, and her nearest Friend, Allah.

She was exceptional in her concentration as a student and a teacher, *mureed* and guide, generously focusing on the *mureeds* in her neighborhood and at a distance. She sent a monthly report to her two living teachers, Pir Vilayat and Pir Moineddin, between the new moon and the full moon, until the end of her life.

Before sending this report on her spiritual state, she told the author she sometimes devoted three days to preparation, introspection and purification, before feeling she could write accurately. She requested the same commitment from her mureeds. She generously focused her loving attention on each mureed at a distance, particularly attuning to the state of the "smiling forehead" (the ideal of balance, as described by Hazrat Inayat Khan). Included also in her attention were the mureed's partners, children, and parents in this healing focus.

Murshida Vera lived fully and generously the message of Love, Harmony and Beauty at the forefront of her life, with every breath.

PRAYER FOR GUIDES OF CHILDREN

Beloved One,
Almighty God,
Through the chain of all Masters,
Through the Guides of all angels and children,
Place our feet firmly on the path of light,
Illuminate our minds,
Purify our hearts, And fill us with joy,
That we may be clear channels to our children.
      Amen

                —Murshida Vera

INTERVIEW WITH NOOR-MALIKA CHISTI

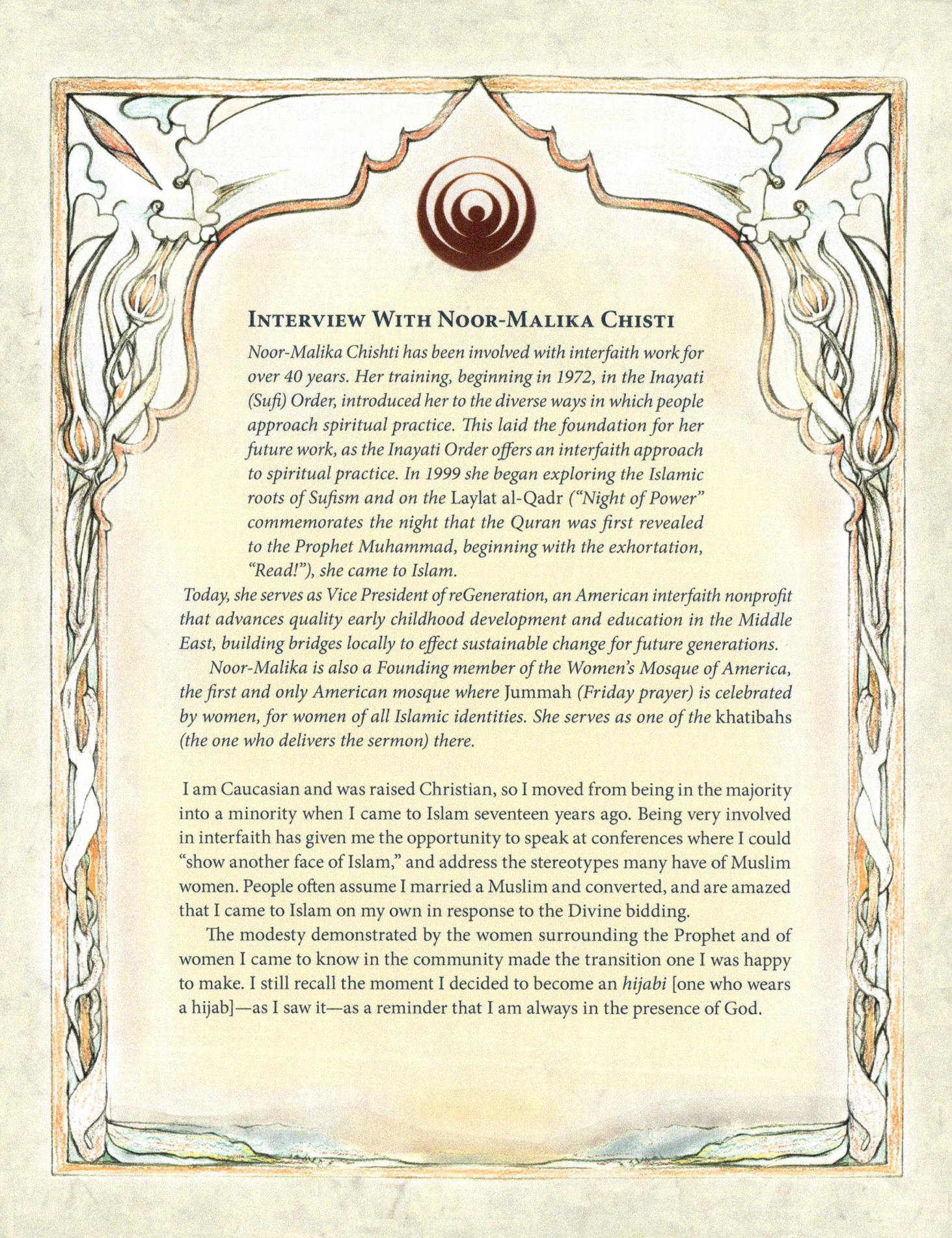

Noor-Malika Chishti has been involved with interfaith work for over 40 years. Her training, beginning in 1972, in the Inayati (Sufi) Order, introduced her to the diverse ways in which people approach spiritual practice. This laid the foundation for her future work, as the Inayati Order offers an interfaith approach to spiritual practice. In 1999 she began exploring the Islamic roots of Sufism and on the Laylat al-Qadr *("Night of Power" commemorates the night that the Quran was first revealed to the Prophet Muhammad, beginning with the exhortation, "Read!"), she came to Islam.*

Today, she serves as Vice President of reGeneration, an American interfaith nonprofit that advances quality early childhood development and education in the Middle East, building bridges locally to effect sustainable change for future generations.

Noor-Malika is also a Founding member of the Women's Mosque of America, the first and only American mosque where Jummah *(Friday prayer) is celebrated by women, for women of all Islamic identities. She serves as one of the* khatibahs *(the one who delivers the sermon) there.*

I am Caucasian and was raised Christian, so I moved from being in the majority into a minority when I came to Islam seventeen years ago. Being very involved in interfaith has given me the opportunity to speak at conferences where I could "show another face of Islam," and address the stereotypes many have of Muslim women. People often assume I married a Muslim and converted, and are amazed that I came to Islam on my own in response to the Divine bidding.

The modesty demonstrated by the women surrounding the Prophet and of women I came to know in the community made the transition one I was happy to make. I still recall the moment I decided to become an *hijabi* [one who wears a hijab]—as I saw it—as a reminder that I am always in the presence of God.

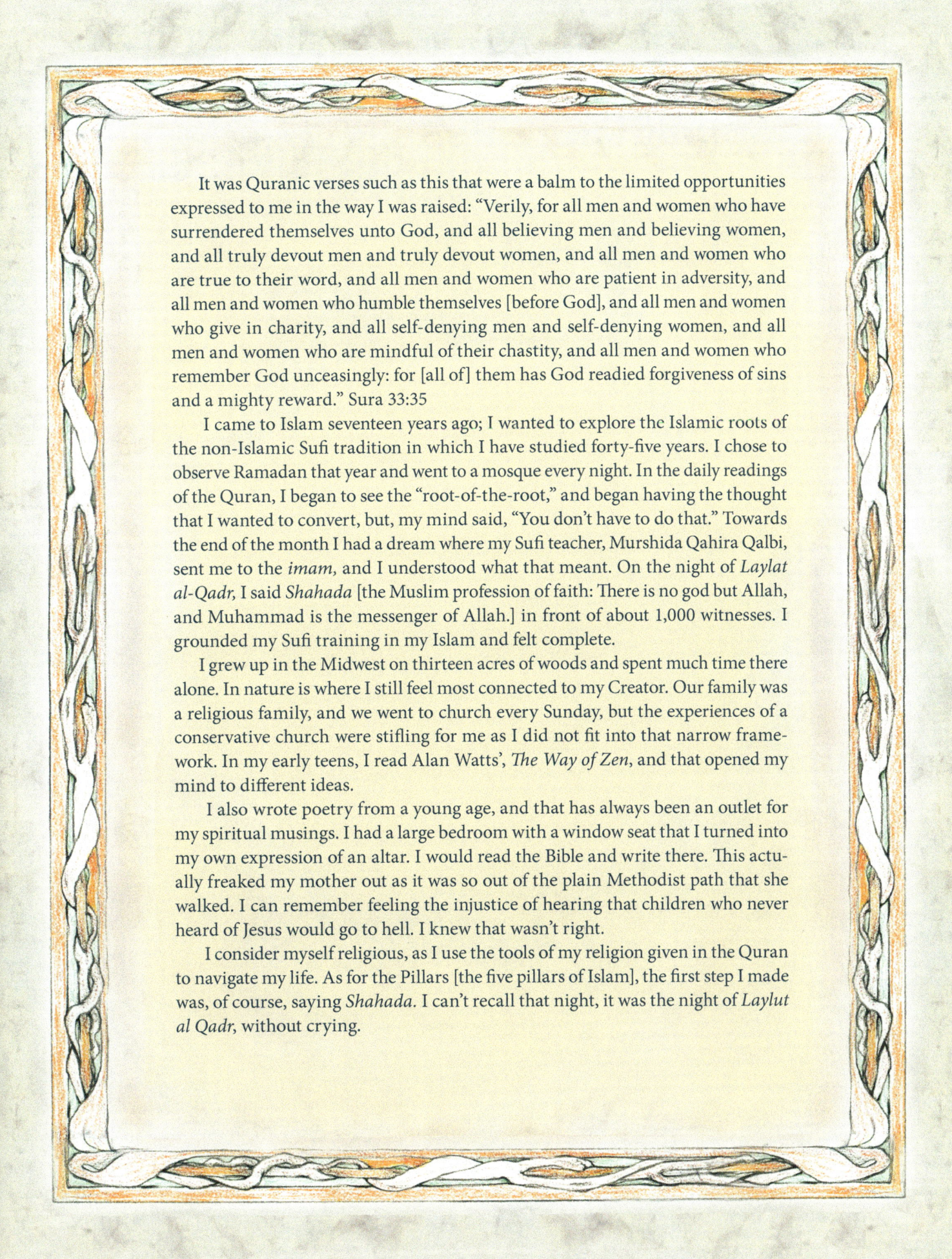

It was Quranic verses such as this that were a balm to the limited opportunities expressed to me in the way I was raised: "Verily, for all men and women who have surrendered themselves unto God, and all believing men and believing women, and all truly devout men and truly devout women, and all men and women who are true to their word, and all men and women who are patient in adversity, and all men and women who humble themselves [before God], and all men and women who give in charity, and all self-denying men and self-denying women, and all men and women who are mindful of their chastity, and all men and women who remember God unceasingly: for [all of] them has God readied forgiveness of sins and a mighty reward." Sura 33:35

I came to Islam seventeen years ago; I wanted to explore the Islamic roots of the non-Islamic Sufi tradition in which I have studied forty-five years. I chose to observe Ramadan that year and went to a mosque every night. In the daily readings of the Quran, I began to see the "root-of-the-root," and began having the thought that I wanted to convert, but, my mind said, "You don't have to do that." Towards the end of the month I had a dream where my Sufi teacher, Murshida Qahira Qalbi, sent me to the *imam,* and I understood what that meant. On the night of *Laylat al-Qadr,* I said *Shahada* [the Muslim profession of faith: There is no god but Allah, and Muhammad is the messenger of Allah.] in front of about 1,000 witnesses. I grounded my Sufi training in my Islam and felt complete.

I grew up in the Midwest on thirteen acres of woods and spent much time there alone. In nature is where I still feel most connected to my Creator. Our family was a religious family, and we went to church every Sunday, but the experiences of a conservative church were stifling for me as I did not fit into that narrow framework. In my early teens, I read Alan Watts', *The Way of Zen,* and that opened my mind to different ideas.

I also wrote poetry from a young age, and that has always been an outlet for my spiritual musings. I had a large bedroom with a window seat that I turned into my own expression of an altar. I would read the Bible and write there. This actually freaked my mother out as it was so out of the plain Methodist path that she walked. I can remember feeling the injustice of hearing that children who never heard of Jesus would go to hell. I knew that wasn't right.

I consider myself religious, as I use the tools of my religion given in the Quran to navigate my life. As for the Pillars [the five pillars of Islam], the first step I made was, of course, saying *Shahada*. I can't recall that night, it was the night of *Laylut al Qadr*, without crying.

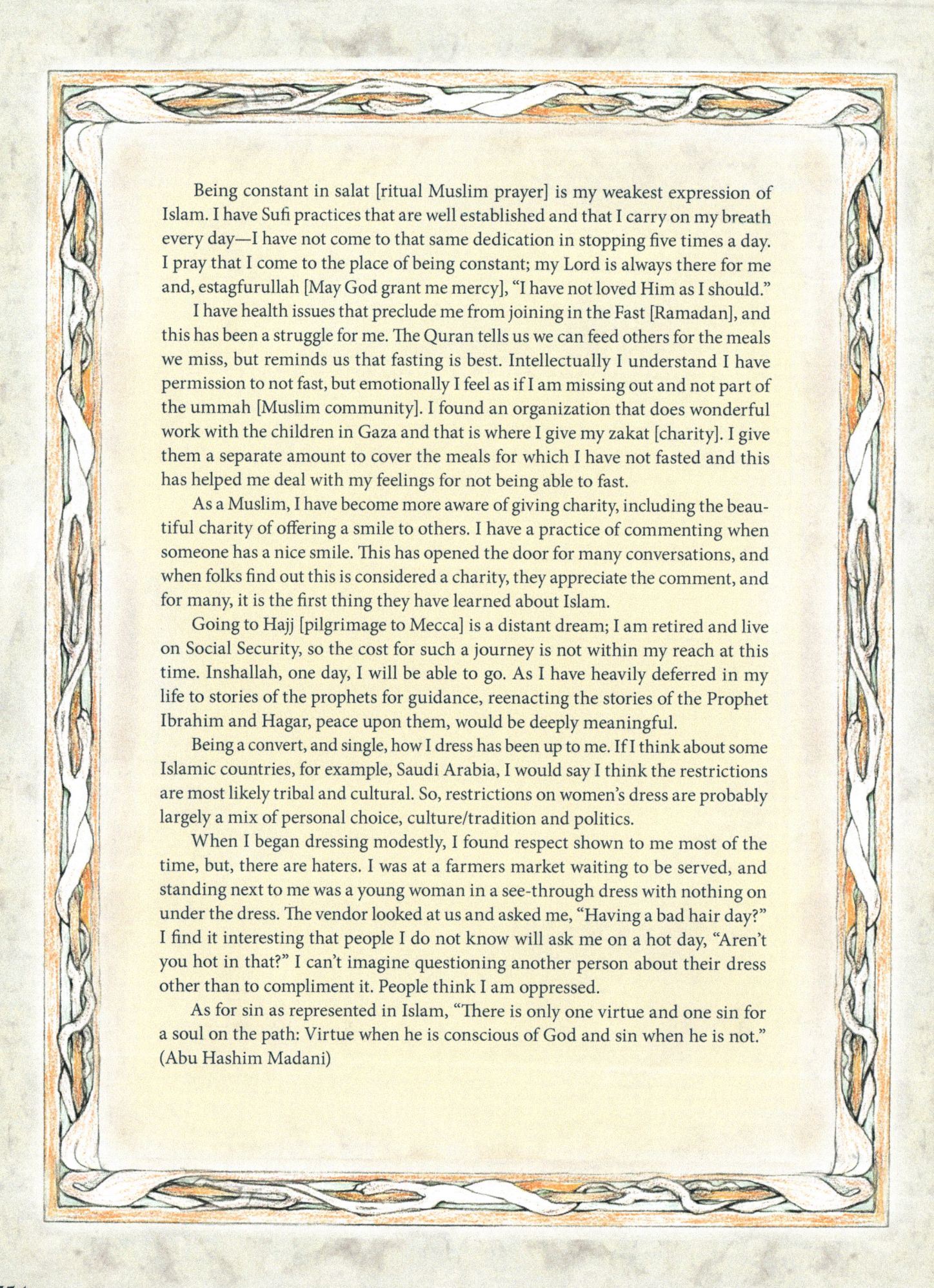

Being constant in salat [ritual Muslim prayer] is my weakest expression of Islam. I have Sufi practices that are well established and that I carry on my breath every day—I have not come to that same dedication in stopping five times a day. I pray that I come to the place of being constant; my Lord is always there for me and, estagfurullah [May God grant me mercy], "I have not loved Him as I should."

I have health issues that preclude me from joining in the Fast [Ramadan], and this has been a struggle for me. The Quran tells us we can feed others for the meals we miss, but reminds us that fasting is best. Intellectually I understand I have permission to not fast, but emotionally I feel as if I am missing out and not part of the ummah [Muslim community]. I found an organization that does wonderful work with the children in Gaza and that is where I give my zakat [charity]. I give them a separate amount to cover the meals for which I have not fasted and this has helped me deal with my feelings for not being able to fast.

As a Muslim, I have become more aware of giving charity, including the beautiful charity of offering a smile to others. I have a practice of commenting when someone has a nice smile. This has opened the door for many conversations, and when folks find out this is considered a charity, they appreciate the comment, and for many, it is the first thing they have learned about Islam.

Going to Hajj [pilgrimage to Mecca] is a distant dream; I am retired and live on Social Security, so the cost for such a journey is not within my reach at this time. Inshallah, one day, I will be able to go. As I have heavily deferred in my life to stories of the prophets for guidance, reenacting the stories of the Prophet Ibrahim and Hagar, peace upon them, would be deeply meaningful.

Being a convert, and single, how I dress has been up to me. If I think about some Islamic countries, for example, Saudi Arabia, I would say I think the restrictions are most likely tribal and cultural. So, restrictions on women's dress are probably largely a mix of personal choice, culture/tradition and politics.

When I began dressing modestly, I found respect shown to me most of the time, but, there are haters. I was at a farmers market waiting to be served, and standing next to me was a young woman in a see-through dress with nothing on under the dress. The vendor looked at us and asked me, "Having a bad hair day?" I find it interesting that people I do not know will ask me on a hot day, "Aren't you hot in that?" I can't imagine questioning another person about their dress other than to compliment it. People think I am oppressed.

As for sin as represented in Islam, "There is only one virtue and one sin for a soul on the path: Virtue when he is conscious of God and sin when he is not." (Abu Hashim Madani)

In *Sunan al-Tirmidhi* [a collection of *hadiths*], a *hadith*, is narrated: Allah's apostle said, "Every son of Adam sins, the best of the sinners are those who repent." — *Sunan al-Tirmidhi*, hadith 2499.

Both of these references shine a light for me in the practice of *Muhasibi* [introspection], which I have done for many years. It has helped me to catch myself in a thought, word or deed and self-correct in the moment.

I have found Islam grounded my Sufi training. I have tools that I do not think I would have learned if I had not had a Sufi background. In Islam, I have had the honor of studying with the late Dr. Maher Hathout, one of the founders of the Muslim Public Affairs Council, and Dr. Jihad Turk, president, Byan Claremont Islamic Graduate School, and former Director of Religious Affairs at the Islamic Center of Southern California. It is the oldest and largest mosque in the Los Angeles area, which Dr. Hathout helped establish.

Imam Jihad was also the Muslim leader of the 2013 reGeneration's Interfaith Pilgrimage to the Holy Land. We had a Christian and Jewish leader as well, and visited sacred sites for all three religions. I serve as vice president of reGeneration, "which promotes social change in the Middle East through supporting the innovation of quality early childhood development and education for Jewish, Christian and Muslim children, so that together they can imagine and create a better future for themselves and the world."

I am big on stories that show examples of Islamic values. Of course, studying what I can about [the Prophet's wives] Khadijah (R.A.) and Aisha (R.A.) are inspiring. [R.A., Radihiallhu Anhu, is used when referring to close companions of the Prophet. It translates into: "May Allah be pleased with him or her."]

I love the work of Tamam Khan (*White Shade Cloud Overhead at Noon*), as being an example of bringing these women into my life. I wish I could find something on the life of Hagar but the only thing I found was the work of a Jewish Scholar, the late Savina Teuval (*Hagar the Egyptian: The Lost Tradition of the Matriarchs*) and the midrash, by Rabbi Phyllis Berman, which can be found on the Seven Pillars House of Wisdom website.

One story in particular that inspires me is when the Prophet *Ibrahim* left Hagar and baby Ishmael in the desert. She asked if it was his idea to leave her there or if he was guided by God. When she was told that it was the guidance from Allah, she accepted her situation. I have had times where I felt that I was being left in the desert and this story gave me a way to look at it.

Noor-un-Nisa Inayat Khan is a woman in the history of Islam who particularly inspires me. She was the daughter of Hazrat Inayat Khan, founder of the Inayati Sufi Order. The family lived in Suresnes, France, when WWII broke out. Noor was trained as a radio operative in England, and air-dropped outside of Paris.

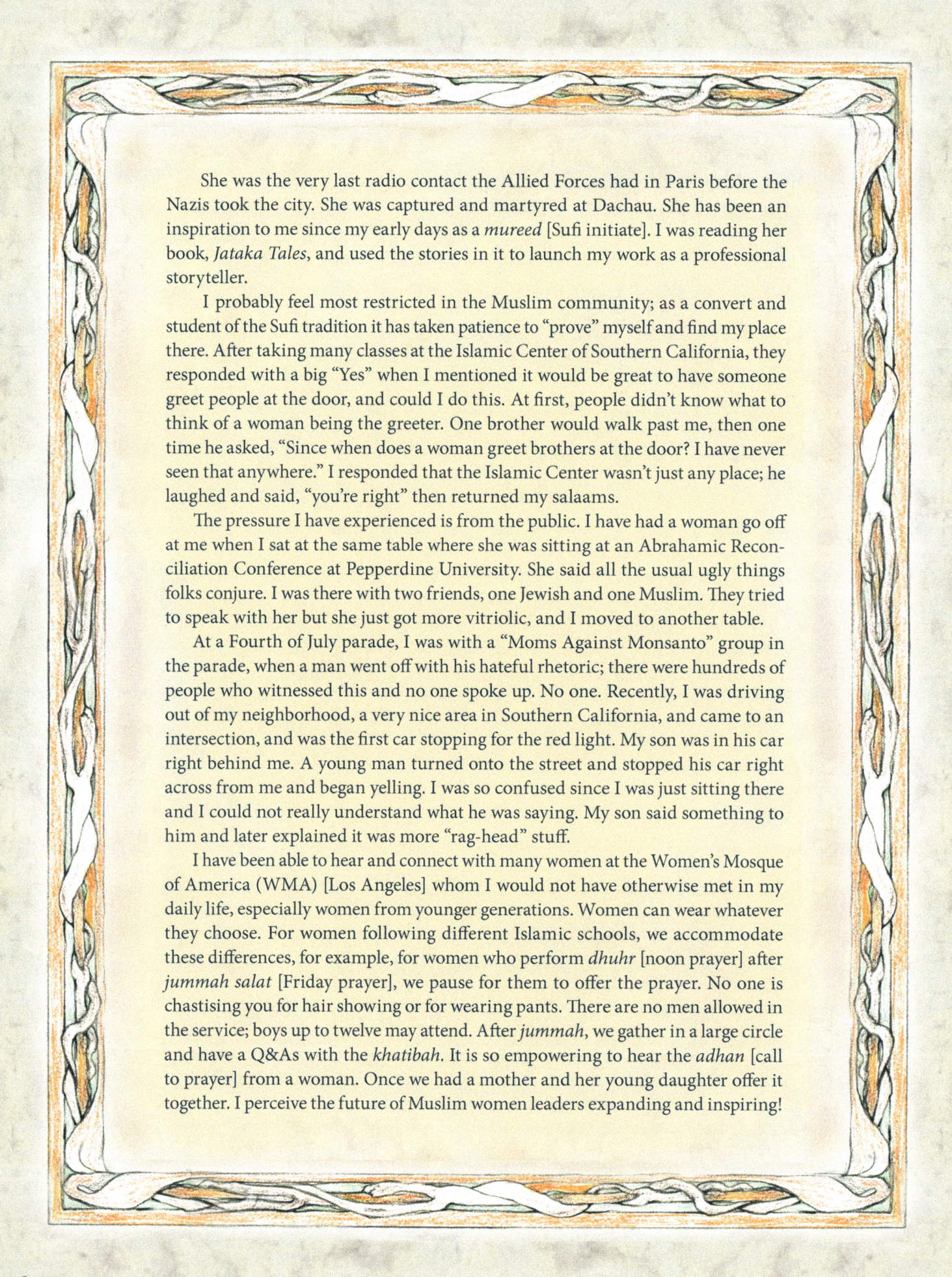

She was the very last radio contact the Allied Forces had in Paris before the Nazis took the city. She was captured and martyred at Dachau. She has been an inspiration to me since my early days as a *mureed* [Sufi initiate]. I was reading her book, *Jataka Tales*, and used the stories in it to launch my work as a professional storyteller.

I probably feel most restricted in the Muslim community; as a convert and student of the Sufi tradition it has taken patience to "prove" myself and find my place there. After taking many classes at the Islamic Center of Southern California, they responded with a big "Yes" when I mentioned it would be great to have someone greet people at the door, and could I do this. At first, people didn't know what to think of a woman being the greeter. One brother would walk past me, then one time he asked, "Since when does a woman greet brothers at the door? I have never seen that anywhere." I responded that the Islamic Center wasn't just any place; he laughed and said, "you're right" then returned my salaams.

The pressure I have experienced is from the public. I have had a woman go off at me when I sat at the same table where she was sitting at an Abrahamic Reconciliation Conference at Pepperdine University. She said all the usual ugly things folks conjure. I was there with two friends, one Jewish and one Muslim. They tried to speak with her but she just got more vitriolic, and I moved to another table.

At a Fourth of July parade, I was with a "Moms Against Monsanto" group in the parade, when a man went off with his hateful rhetoric; there were hundreds of people who witnessed this and no one spoke up. No one. Recently, I was driving out of my neighborhood, a very nice area in Southern California, and came to an intersection, and was the first car stopping for the red light. My son was in his car right behind me. A young man turned onto the street and stopped his car right across from me and began yelling. I was so confused since I was just sitting there and I could not really understand what he was saying. My son said something to him and later explained it was more "rag-head" stuff.

I have been able to hear and connect with many women at the Women's Mosque of America (WMA) [Los Angeles] whom I would not have otherwise met in my daily life, especially women from younger generations. Women can wear whatever they choose. For women following different Islamic schools, we accommodate these differences, for example, for women who perform *dhuhr* [noon prayer] after *jummah salat* [Friday prayer], we pause for them to offer the prayer. No one is chastising you for hair showing or for wearing pants. There are no men allowed in the service; boys up to twelve may attend. After *jummah*, we gather in a large circle and have a Q&As with the *khatibah*. It is so empowering to hear the *adhan* [call to prayer] from a woman. Once we had a mother and her young daughter offer it together. I perceive the future of Muslim women leaders expanding and inspiring!

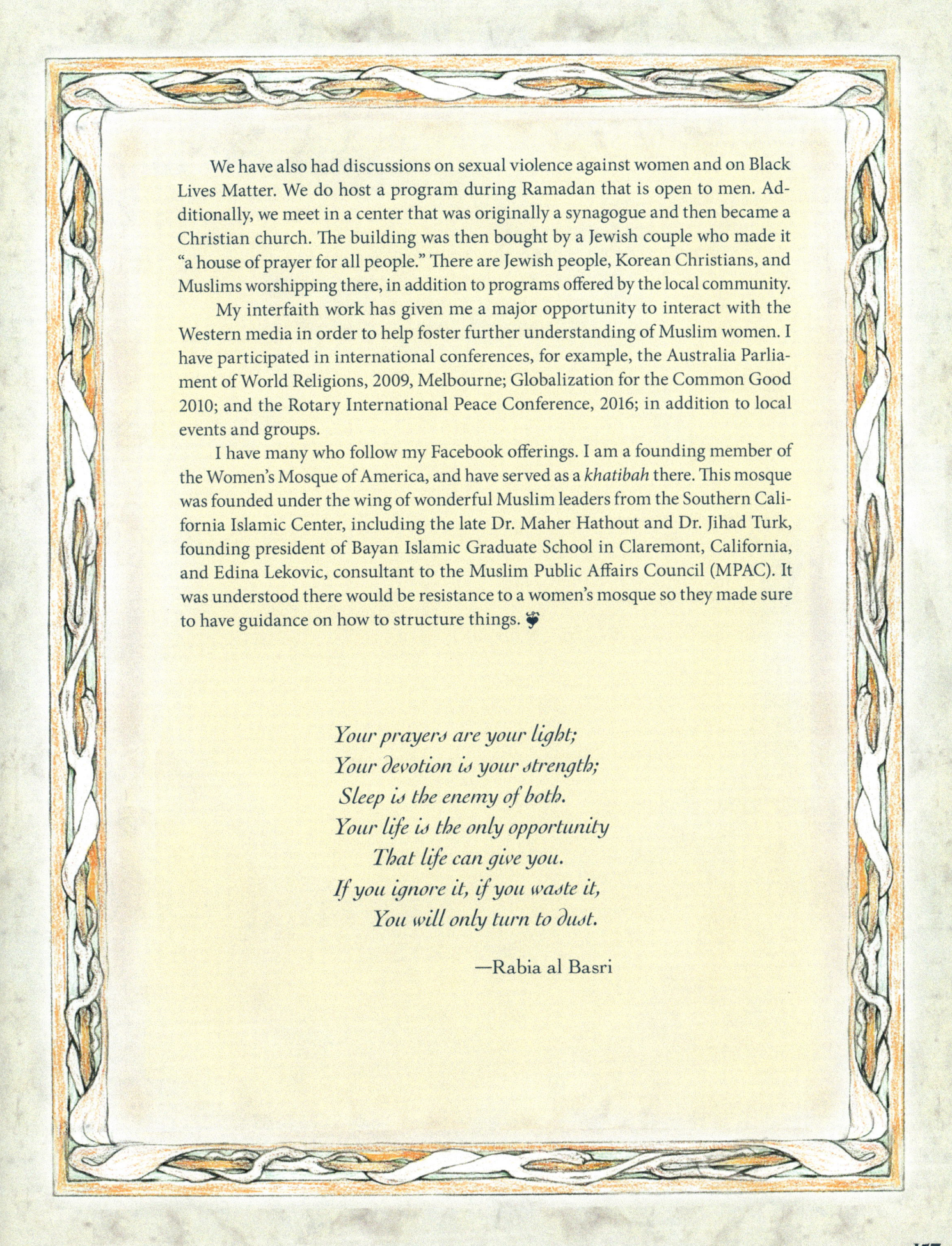

We have also had discussions on sexual violence against women and on Black Lives Matter. We do host a program during Ramadan that is open to men. Additionally, we meet in a center that was originally a synagogue and then became a Christian church. The building was then bought by a Jewish couple who made it "a house of prayer for all people." There are Jewish people, Korean Christians, and Muslims worshipping there, in addition to programs offered by the local community.

My interfaith work has given me a major opportunity to interact with the Western media in order to help foster further understanding of Muslim women. I have participated in international conferences, for example, the Australia Parliament of World Religions, 2009, Melbourne; Globalization for the Common Good 2010; and the Rotary International Peace Conference, 2016; in addition to local events and groups.

I have many who follow my Facebook offerings. I am a founding member of the Women's Mosque of America, and have served as a *khatibah* there. This mosque was founded under the wing of wonderful Muslim leaders from the Southern California Islamic Center, including the late Dr. Maher Hathout and Dr. Jihad Turk, founding president of Bayan Islamic Graduate School in Claremont, California, and Edina Lekovic, consultant to the Muslim Public Affairs Council (MPAC). It was understood there would be resistance to a women's mosque so they made sure to have guidance on how to structure things.

Your prayers are your light;
Your devotion is your strength;
Sleep is the enemy of both.
Your life is the only opportunity
That life can give you.
If you ignore it, if you waste it,
You will only turn to dust.

—Rabia al Basri

Noor-un Nisa Inayat Khan
Twentieth-Century Sufi Saint
1913—1944

Noor-un Nisa Inayat Khan is a woman of great spiritual strength who was also a French spy in World War II. She was the daughter of Hazrat Inayat Khan, the Indian Sufi mystic, and Ora Ray Baker, an American mystic, relative of Mary Baker Eddy, who founded of the Church of Christian Science.

As a girl growing up in France in the 1930s, Noor-un Nisa helped her mother and father with the care of her younger siblings. Raised in a family of musicians and mystics, she had a refined appreciation of beauty and wisdom, and wrote delightful fairy tales. The best-known story is a version of The Jataka Tales, the lives of the Buddha in animal nature.

When World War II broke out, this courageous and beautiful young woman volunteered to work behind enemy lines in France as an SOE (Special Operative Executive) for the British. With her multilingual background, she was a great asset to the resistance, and her kind-hearted nature motivated her to risk her life to protect the innocent victims of Nazism and the war. She risked her life for freedom of religion and the Sufi ideals of Love, Harmony and Beauty.

As a spy, Noor-un Nisa was successful in gleaning and communicating important information to British intelligence from behind enemy lines. Unfortunately, she was eventually betrayed and turned over to the Germans. This valiant young woman was tortured and forced to remain in a crouching chained position for months. It is said she never gave way to self-pity or to hatred for her captors, nor did she reveal her mission or the intelligence information that she possessed. She told her jailers, "The day will come when you will see the truth."

Officer Nora Inayat Khan was eventually taken to the crematorium at Dachau and shot. This inspiring saint left the earth September 12, 1944. She posthumously received the British George Cross and the French "Croix de Guerre with Gold Star." In 2012 a statue was unveiled of Noor-un Nisa in Gordon Square, London. Several books and films based on her life have been produced in the last decade.

Whoever works righteousness, man or woman, and has Faith,
   Verily, to him will We give a new Life,
A life that is good and pure,
   And We will bestow on such their reward
     According to the best of their actions.

                    —Quran, Sura 16: 97

159

Nana Asma'u
1793—1864

Nana Asma'u, a Nigerian Qadiri Sufi, lived through decades of civil war and was a leader for reconciliation and peace. She was vigilant in highlighting and incorporating a Muslim moral code that included education and training in independence and personal mastery. This important leader is known as something of a superwoman who influenced society and propeled significant change as an educator, mother and scholar. She is remembered for her life story of persistence and success, and for the beauty of her songs and poems, which reflect the way of Peace, the way of Islam.

Dr. Saadia Khawar Khan Chishti

Dr. Saadia is a devout Muslim scholar who served as a member of the Higher Education Commission of Pakistan, as an advisor to the Government of Azad Kashmir for Curriculum Development from the point of view of Islam, and as a Harvard fellow. She is a contributor to *Islam and Ecology: A Bestowed Trust* (Religions of the World and Ecology), considered one of the best books of 2017.

An academic leader for many years, she teaches and exemplifies the enlightened perspective of female spirituality in Islam and Sufism. She is also a dedicated student of the twentieth-century American Sufi saint Sufi Ahmed Murad Chishti, Samuel Lewis, known as Murshid SAM. She has dedicated her life to following in the footsteps of those who live the ideal of abd'allah, service to God.

Dr. Saadia writes:

> *One must consider the spiritual life of the great female saints, from those who belonged to the household of the Prophet, to saintly women who have adorned every century of Islamic history to this day. One must also study the spiritual aspect of those everyday roles of women, which are sacralized by virtue of being lived and practiced according to the Shari'ah, and therefore in conformity with God's will. Likewise, one must delve into Sufi teachings and practices as they apply to women and as they provide concrete paths for spiritual realization. Finally, it is necessary to recall the feminine aspect of Islamic spirituality as such, as reflected in the doctrines concerning the nature of God, the wedding of the soul and spirit, and feminine symbolism employed in discussing the nature of the Divine Essence and the being's quest for the Divine Beloved.*

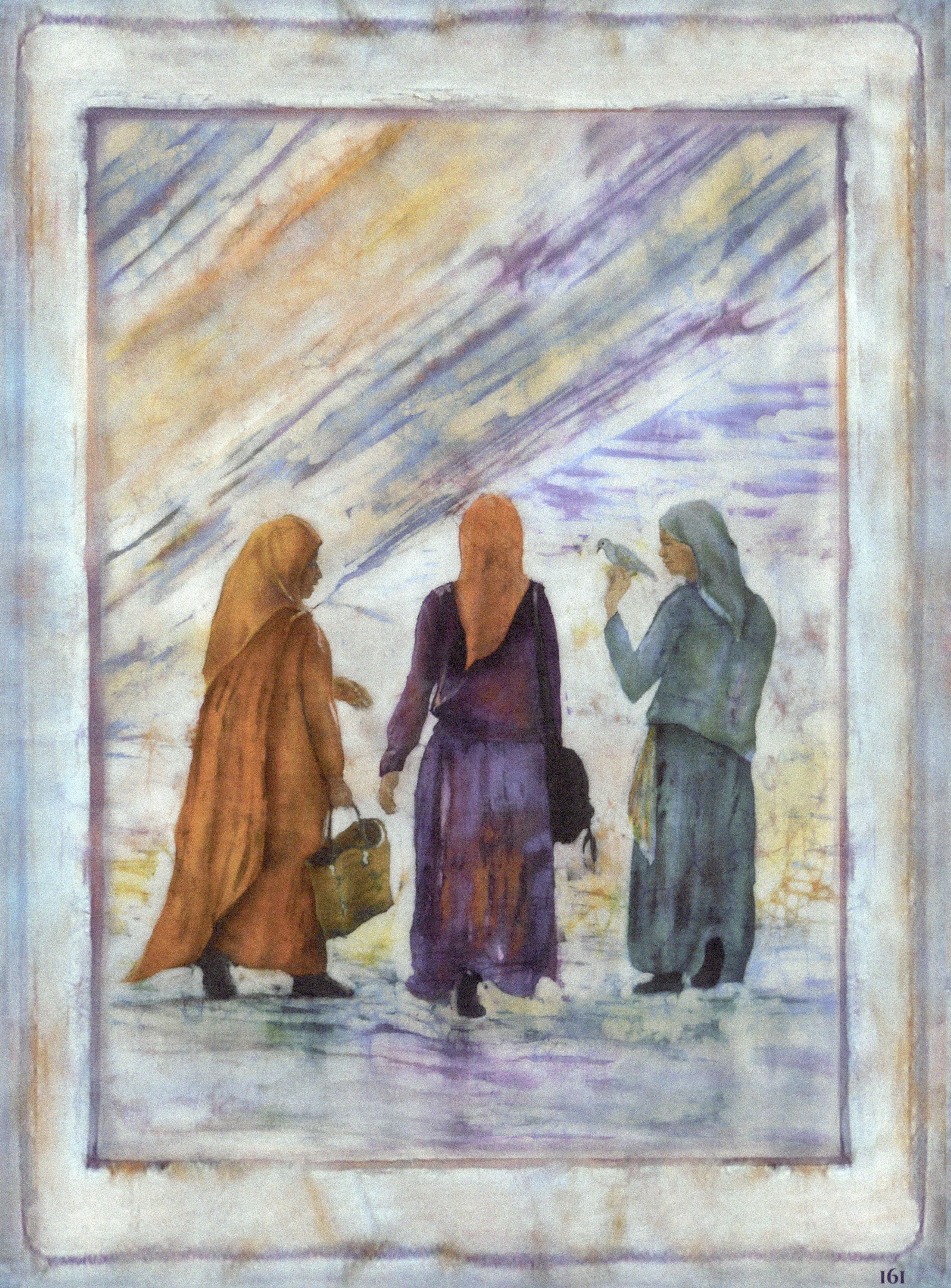

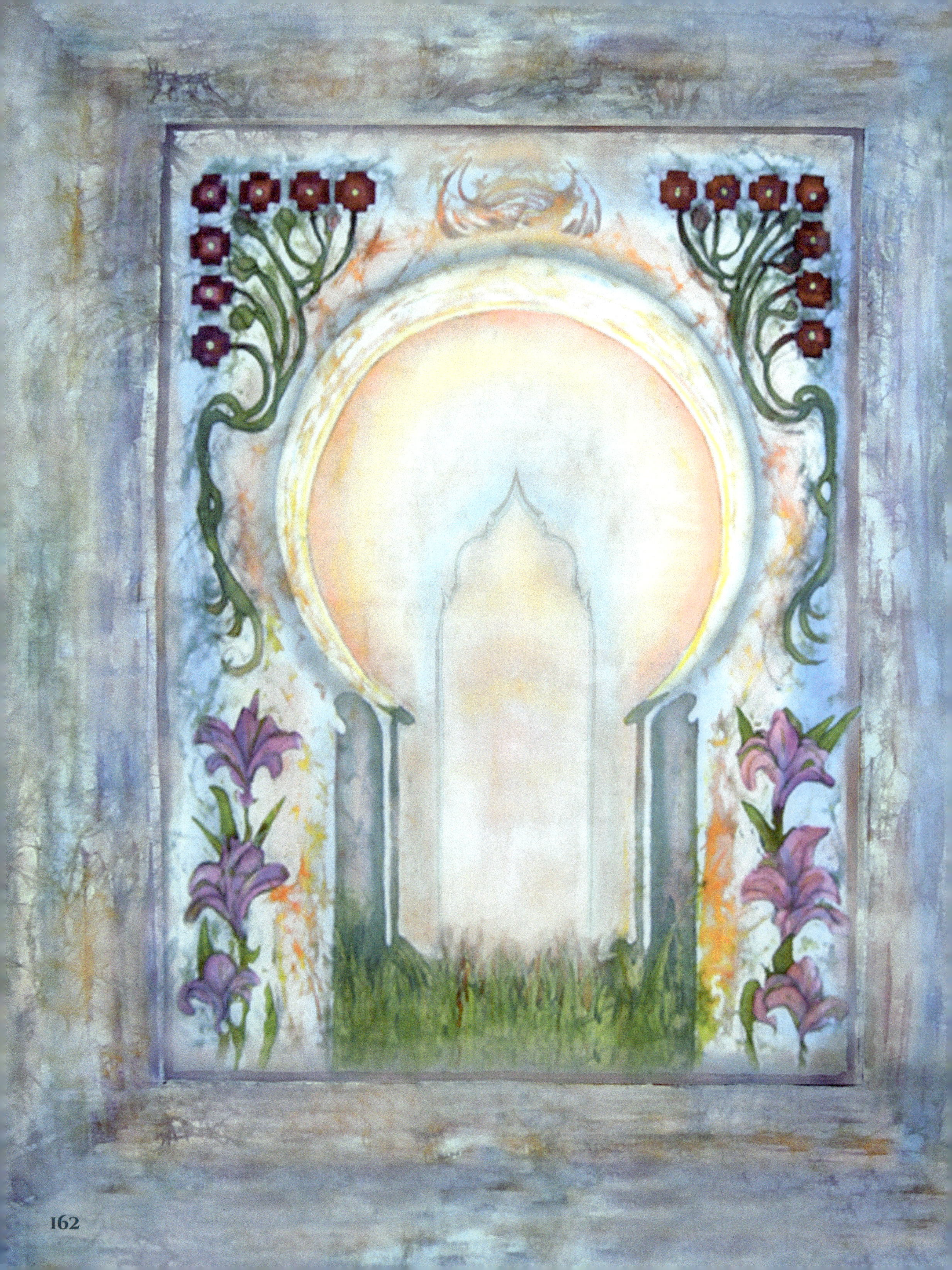

Creating Heart Space
Recipes for the Sacred

The ninety-nine names or attributes of Allah represent all of the manifestations of the created universe. Allah encompasses them all. Reciting these names is saying Yes to existence and the interplay of opposites, saying Yes to Being.

Wazifa—*Ya Hadi*
Divine Archetype—the Guide, the Leader

God in infinite mercy and compassion guides all creatures to the right path that is their destiny. Repeating this sacred name invokes the divine guidance within—opening the inner ear to intuition and guidance in all aspects of life.

Walking Meditation

Begin to walk in a counterclockwise circle, being conscious of posture; feet upon the earth, imagining a chord extending from the base of the spine up through the crown, extending to heaven, as the feet caress the earth with each grounding step. Feel yourself as an extension of the infinite. Take a moment to release tension in neck and shoulders, feel your presence within your physical body, acknowledging alignment where it is felt as breath brings more and more present awareness into consciousness.

Inhale Ya Hadi—Exhale Ya Hadi

Open the left palm and extend the arm perpendicular from the waist at the elbow in front of you. Consider that you are symbolically holding Truth in this palm. Raise the right arm and extend it. Closing the palm of the hand, as if holding something precious, and point the index finger toward the sky. Continue walking, inhaling, Ya Hadi, exhaling, Ya Hadi.

Sitting Meditation

Find a comfortable seated position, using a pillow on the floor under the tailbone, or sit in a chair in a manner that allows the back to be erect. Take a moment to become comfortable and release physical tension in the neck and shoulders. Let the head come down toward the earth in prostration. Slowly raise the head, and establish meditation posture. Begin to intone on one note the sound, Ya Hadi. Extend the vowel sounds, ah and ee. Repeat for three minutes. Sit in silence. Contemplate the Guide who has led you to this moment in time and space. Be thankful and open.

Recipes to Nourish Body and Soul

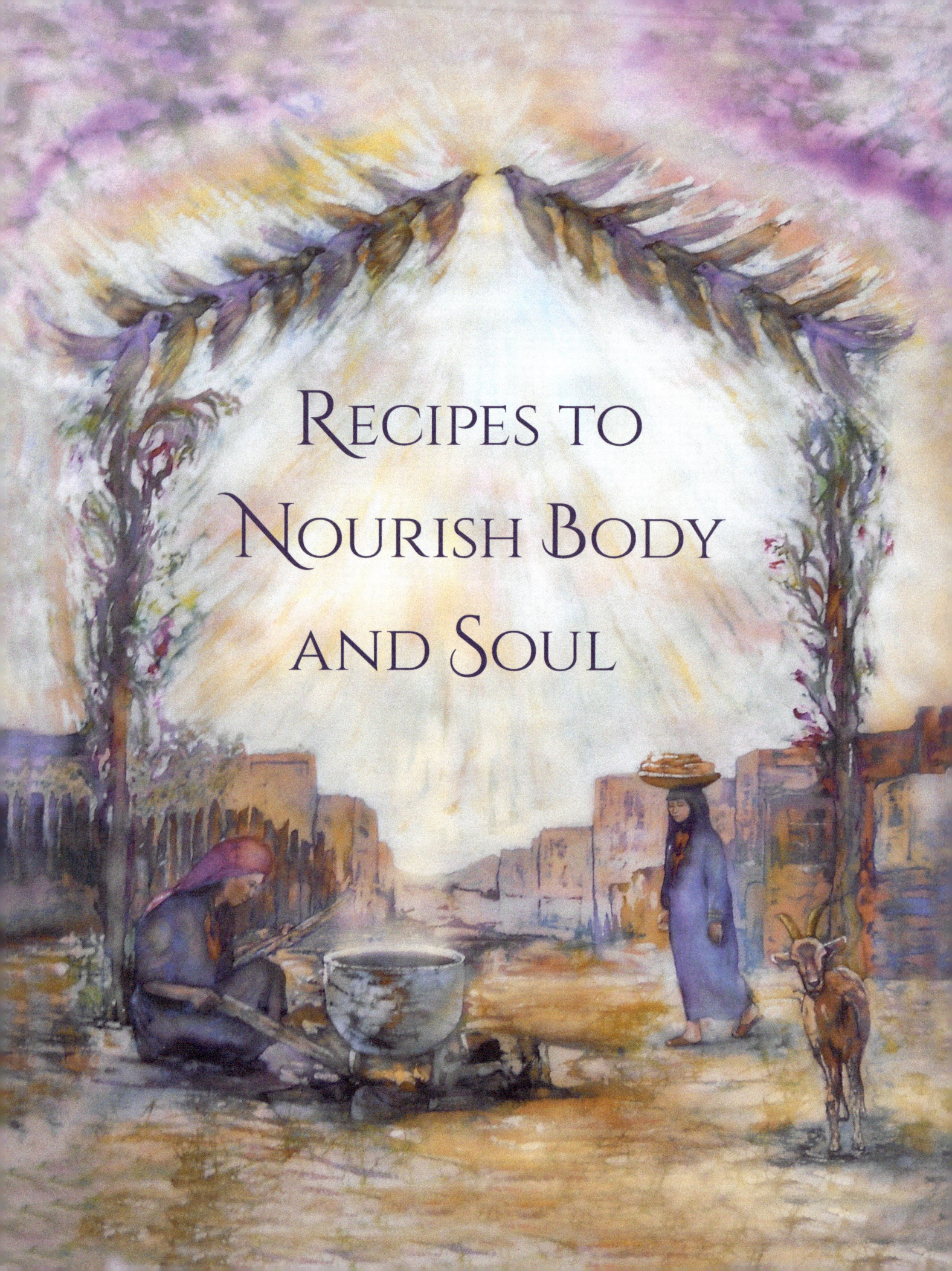

The Prayer of Sharing Food

Throughout history women have gathered to prepare food, to share recipes and stories, and to support each other through the creative act of cooking together. The action of sharing food provides the opportunity to delight in mixes of scents, textures, colors and tastes and to experience that delight with others.

The following pages offer a sampling of recipes from women whose stories are found in this book. The act of being the host is an opportunity to demonstrate reverence for another; to embody the aspect of deep respect and to provide nourishment for the guest.

The high art of hospitality is the common thread that unites women and men across traditions. We celebrate that unifying principle while offering tasty variety in these pages. Take a deep breath to inhale the subtle aromas…and enjoy!

Source of Nourishment

My joy, my hunger, my shelter, my friend,
My food for the journey, my journey's end.
You are my breath, my hope, my companion,
My craving, my abundant wealth.
Without you, my Life, my Love,
I would never have wandered across these endless countries.
You have poured out so much grace for me,
Done me so many favors, given me so many gifts—
I look everywhere for Your love,
Then suddenly I am filled with it.
O Captain of my Heart,
Radiant Eye of Yearning in my breast.
I will never be free from you as long as I live.
Be satisfied with me, Love, and I am satisfied.

—Rabia al-Adawiyya

Chickpea and Potato Salad
Chana Bateta
By Surya

Ingredients:
2 cans organic chickpeas
¾ pound boiled potatoes, cut into ½-inch cubes
2 cups tamarind sauce, available at Asian markets
1 cup water
2 teaspoons canola oil
½ teaspoon black mustard seeds
1 green chili, seeded and chopped
¼ teaspoon turmeric
½ teaspoon salt
¼ teaspoon cayenne
2 teaspoons sugar
1 tablespoon fresh lemon juice
¼ cup cilantro, finely chopped

Directions:
In a large pan, heat oil and add mustard seeds until the seeds begin to sputter.
Add green chilies, turmeric and salt, and stir.
Add tamarind sauce, chickpeas, chili powder and sugar, and mix.
Add water and bring to boil.
Reduce heat; simmer covered for 10 minutes.
Add potato cubes, stir, cover and cook for 10 more minutes.
Add lemon juice and cilantro and serve.
Serve hot or cold with or without a simple salad of finely chopped sweet onion and cucumber, as a snack or a side dish.

Quick and Easy Chutneys

Cilantro Chutney—Blend 1 cup tightly packed cilantro, a seeded, chopped green chili, a pinch of salt and ½ a cup of lemon juice.

Mint Chutney—Substitute 1 cup tightly packed mint instead of cilantro; add the rest of the ingredients as above, and a teaspoon of sugar. Blend.

Cilantro-Mint Chutney—Use ½ cup of mint and ½ cup cilantro. Prepare as above.

Yogurt Chutney—Blend cilantro, or cilantro and mint, green chili, and salt to taste, into a smooth paste; add 1 cup yogurt, mix and chill. Garnish with ½ teaspoon ground black pepper and freshly ground slightly roasted cumin seeds.

Tamarind Chutney—1 cup Tamarind Paste, 3 cups water, ½ cup chopped cilantro, 1 seeded green chili, ½ teaspoon cayenne, 1 teaspoon slightly roasted cumin, ¼ teaspoon salt, 1 tablespoon brown sugar or maple syrup. Blend all ingredients, chill and serve.

Tamarind, Yogurt, Mint Cilantro Chutney— Stir together a combination of above chutneys to your taste. Chill, serve and enjoy!

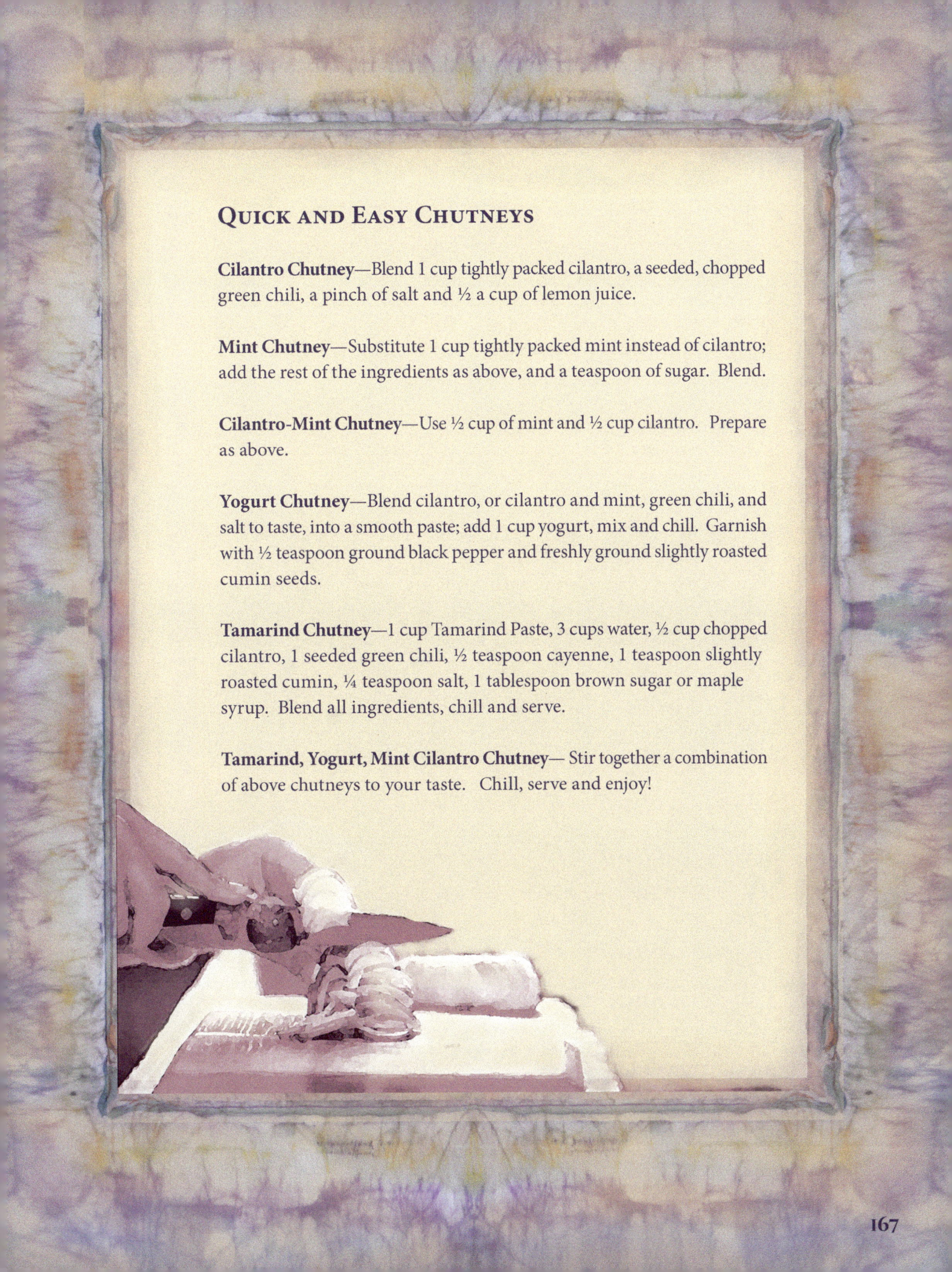

Coconut Sauce—Master Recipe
By Surya

Indgredients:
1 (14-15 ounce) can unsweetened coconut milk
1 small shallot or yellow onion, finely chopped
¼ (scant) teaspoon turmeric
1 red chili salt, deseeding optional
Salt to taste
¼ cup chopped tomato
1 clove garlic, chopped
½ teaspoon cumin powder
Fresh lemon juice to taste
2 tablespoons chopped cilantro (to sprinkle on the finished dish)

Directions:
Puree the tomato, garlic and red chili; add the turmeric, cumin and salt to the puree.
Heat a thick-bottomed pan and dry-fry the shallot on medium heat until aromatic.
Add a tablespoon of coconut milk and stir until the coconut scorches slightly.
Stir in the tomato mixture and bring to a simmer.
Add the rest of the coconut milk, and cook on medium heat, stirring frequently.
Simmer for 10 to 15 minutes.

Variations:
Add a can of organic beans of your choice—pinto, kidney, whatever you have in your pantry. Simmer a little longer.
Cook any greens—spinach, kale, Swiss chard—add, and simmer a little longer.
A mixture of beans and greens works well.
Steamed frozen corn added, with or without beans, is delicious.
Roast chicken, skin removed, and cut into pieces. Add to the sauce to make a quick main dish when there are unexpected guests.
Cooked, peeled, green banana, with or without cooked meat or leftover chicken.
Canned tuna or salmon, drained.
Cooked shrimp.
Boiled eggs, halved—lower gently into the sauce and simmer for 5 minutes.
Tofu.

After adding the food of your choice to the master mix, gently simmer for 5 to 7 minutes. Add lemon juice to taste. Sprinkle with cilantro.

Serve with steamed rice or bread. Yummy with sweet rolls or Hawaiian bread; also great with polenta.

Sauce for Ethiopian Bread (Injera)
By Raaufa

Ingredients:
2 cups sour cream or yogurt, or combination, to taste
1-3 hot peppers, to taste
Salt, garlic, thyme, to taste
Injera bread*

Directions:
Place, in the blender, sour cream, yogurt, hot peppers, salt, garlic and thyme.
Add a small amount of water to the mixture to keep it to a thin texture.
Place a slice of Ethiopian bread on a large plate, and cover the surface with more of the mixture than is required, because the bread will quickly absorb it.
Place another layer of bread on top, and apply more of the sauce. The number of layers is optional, but usually, two is enough.
_____

* Injera, a sourdough-risen flatbread with a unique, slightly spongy texture, a national dish in Ethiopia and Eritrea available at Ethiopian grocery stores and online.

MEAT AND SPINACH CURRY
A MOROCCAN-INSPIRED MAIN DISH
By Amala

This is my version of a meal I was served at the home of a local Sufi sheikh. I was so impressed by the wonderful flavors of the meal and the gracious hospitality of my hosts that I have shared this meal at every opportunity. It is a quite filling dish and great for potlucks because of its short prep time. Total prep and cooking time: 30 minutes.

Ingredients:
2 pounds ground meat (beef, chicken, turkey or lamb)
32 ounces frozen spinach (thawed and drained)
1 yellow onion or 2 bunches of scallions (chopped)
1 - 2 red bell peppers (chopped)
2 10-ounce jars Patak's Mild or Hot Curry paste
8 ounces Basmati rice, cooked

Directions:
Brown the meat in a large skillet or Dutch oven.
Stir in 1 jar of curry paste.
Add spinach and other chopped ingredients.
Simmer mixture on low heat for about 10-12 minutes. (Do not drain.)
Season to taste: add more curry paste or other seasonings.
Serve over rice; serves many! (8-10)

Options:
Add butter, olive oil or scallions to rice while cooking.
Sauté bell peppers and scallions with meat before adding paste.

Hints:
For a soupier mixture, do not drain spinach.
For a thicker mixture, drain spinach or add more curry paste.
Extra curry paste can be stored in fridge for use in the next curry recipe.
Freezes well.

GREEN MASALA CHICKEN
OR: TOFU AND PEAS
By Surya

Ingredients:
2 cups cilantro leaves
1 cup mint leaves
1 jalapeno pepper, coarsely chopped
6 cloves garlic, crushed
¼ cup fresh lemon juice
½ cup water
1 tablespoon canola oil
1 onion, finely chopped
1-¾ pounds chicken breast, cut into 1" pieces
Or:
2 cups firm tofu cut into 1" pieces and 1 cup fresh or frozen peas
1-½ teaspoons turmeric
1-½ teaspoons garam masala*
1 cup coconut milk
Salt to taste

Directions:
Combine the cilantro, mint, jalapeno, garlic, lemon juice and water in a blender, and puree until smooth.
In a large, deep skillet—I use a karahi [Asian-style wok]—heat the oil.
Add the onion and cook until softened, about 5 minutes.
Add the chicken, or tofu and peas, and turmeric and cook over moderately high heat, stirring frequently, until golden in spots, about 7 minutes.
Add the garam masala and cook for one minute.
Add the cilantro puree and coconut milk, season with salt, and bring to boil. Simmer over low heat until the sauce is slightly reduced and the chicken is tender, about 10 to 15 minutes.
Serve with Basmati rice, sweet rolls or naan (Indian bread).

_____
**Garam Masala*, a spice combination used in many Indian dishes:
4 teaspoons cinnamon powder
2 teaspoons powdered cardamom seeds extracted from pods
2 teaspoons powdered cloves

LEMON ROASTED CHICKEN
By Habiba

Simple and delicious—Quantities can be varied.

Indgredients:
2 pounds chicken, skin on, cut up—use thighs or your favorite cut
2 lemons
Approximately ¾ cup chicken broth (low sodium)

Directions:
Preheat oven to 375°
Bakes approximately 1 hour

Wash and dry the chicken and place it in a baking pan so that the pieces don't touch. Pour the broth over the chicken so that it fills the baking pan to a depth of about ½".
Juice lemon and remove seeds.
Pour the lemon juice carefully over chicken pieces so that the pieces are coated, and place the dish in the oven.
After 40 - 45 minutes, when it is just starting to brown, baste the chicken. For a crispy crust, baste only once.
After an hour, when there is a golden brown crust on the chicken, remove the pan from the oven and let sit for a few minutes before serving.
Pour the sauce in the pan over rice or vegetables.

Variations:
A variety of vegetables can be cooked with the chicken: carrots, turnips, squash, parsnips (cut thin). Cut the vegetables in small pieces and place around the chicken.
Garlic or other seasonings can be added to the pan at the beginning.
1 tablespoon of honey can be added to the lemon juice.

Kofta Nazik
Delicate Meatballs
By Habiba

Indgredients:
1 pound lamb, ground (beef can be substituted)
3 eggs
3 tablespoon olive oil
1 small onion, chopped fine
1 tablespoon finely chopped parsley
1-2 tablespoons fresh dill, if available, or substitute 1 teaspoon dried dill
½ teaspoon cumin
1 teaspoon coriander
½ teaspoon salt and black pepper to taste
1 tablespoon quick cooking rice
Flour for coating
¾ to 1 cup broth or water

Directions:
Combine the onion, 2 eggs, and 1 teaspoon of oil in a food processor and liquefy.
Blend in the lamb, add the seasonings and rice. Knead to a smooth paste. (You can also put the meat through a meat grinder two times and mix the remaining ingredients in by hand).
Shape into walnut sized meatballs, rinsing the hands with water to keep the meat from sticking to them.
Arrange meatballs in a pan, pour the broth over and simmer gently, covered, for about 20 minutes, till the liquid is absorbed.
Drain and cool the meatballs.
Beat the remaining egg. Dip the meatballs in the beaten egg and roll them in the flour.
Heat the remaining oil in a frying pan. When it is hot, add the meatballs and fry them until crisp and golden brown all over.
Serve over rice with Yogurt Sauce (recipe follows), or another favorite sauce.

Yogurt Sauce

Ingredients:
1 cup yogurt
1 tablespoon lemon juice
1 tablespoon fresh mint leaves, chopped fine, if available,
Or 1 teaaspoon dried mint leaves
2 teaspoon honey or sugar
1 teaspoon toasted sesame oil
pinch salt

Combine all ingredients. Taste and adjust seasonings.
Enjoy!

Shirkhand
A Cooling Summer Dessert
By Surya

Ingredients:
2 cups sour cream or Greek yogurt
3 tablespoons sugar
¼ teaspoon ground cardamom
¼ teaspoon lemon juice
1 tablespoon chopped almonds and/or pistachios
6 to 8 strands of saffron

Directions:
Mix all ingredients except for nuts and saffron.
Pour into a bowl or individual serving bowls.
Sprinkle with nuts and saffron.

Rosewater Shortbread
Nan Berenji

By Asha

Ingredients:
1 pound unsalted butter—softened
5 cups rice flour
1 cup powdered sugar
2 tablespoons powdered sugar—for dusting
2 teaspoons ground cardamom
1 teaspoon baking powder
1 egg, well beaten
1 teaspoon chilled rosewater

Directions:
Preheat oven to 350°
Beat butter until it becomes creamy.
Gradually mix in flour.
Add 1 cup sugar and cardamom and beat for a few more minutes.
Mix in baking powder, egg and rosewater.
Make balls the size of small walnuts
Arrange 2 ½" apart on an ungreased cookie sheet, flatten slightly.
Bake cookies 15-20 minutes until they turn golden.
Remove gently with a spatula and allow to cool on wax paper or paper towel.
Dust with powdered sugar if desired

Wheat Free!

HEAVENLY DATE NUT CUSTARD

Ingredients:
¼ cup cornstarch
1 quart milk (can substitute almond milk, rice milk, etc.)
4 egg yolks
½ - ¾ cup sugar (to taste)
½ cup dates, chopped, plus 4 halves for garnish
¼ cup walnuts or pecans, plus 4 halves for garnish
1 teaspoon orange blossom water or rose water

Optional additions:
½ teaspoon cardamom
1 tablespoon orange zest
½ teaspoon vanilla extract
½ cup cream replacing ½ cup of the milk

Directions:
Dissolve the cornstarch in 1 cup of the milk, stirring briskly. Put the balance of the milk in a pan and simmer slowly over low heat.
Beat the egg yolks and sugar together until creamy. When the milk just begins to simmer, add the sugar mixture, stirring constantly, then the cornstarch milk.
Add the dates walnuts and orange or rose water. Simmer over low heat for 5 minutes.
Remove the custard from the heat and pour into 4 cups.
Garnish each cup with a date and walnut/pecan half. Refrigerate.

Eat and Enjoy!

CARDAMOM CAKE
By Surya

Ingredients:
4 eggs
3 cups flour
2 cups sugar
1 cup oil
1 cup plain yogurt
1 teaspoon baking powder
1 teaspoon baking soda
1 teaspoon cardamom powder
pinch of salt
1 cup raisins, optional
1 cup blanched almonds, walnuts or pecans, optional
¼ teaspoon saffron threads

Directions:
Preheat oven to 325°
Beat eggs, sugar, oil and yogurt together.
Sift dry ingredients and add to first mixture.
Line a 10" x 14" pan with foil, and grease.
Place in pan and bake for 35 minutes, testing for doneness.
Sprinkle with almonds and saffron.

Pineapple Bubble Cake
By Surya

Ingredients
1-½ cups all-purpose unbleached flour
1-½ teaspoons baking powder
¾–1 cup sugar
14-ounce can crushed pineapple
2 eggs, beaten

Directions:
Place all the ingredients in a bowl and mix well.
Pour into a 13" x 9" x 2" pan, or a pan of your choice, and bake in a pre-heated, 325° oven for 30–45 minutes, until the top is golden brown.

Topping Ingredients:
¾–1 cup sugar
½–¾ cup evaporated milk
1 stick butter
1 teaspoon vanilla essence
1 scant ½ teaspoon almond essence

Directions:
While the cake is baking, heat the sugar, evaporated milk and butter together in a microwave or on the stove top, until the butter is melted and the sugar dissolved. Turn off the heat and add vanilla and almond essences.

Let the cake cool for 10 minutes. Pour topping on the cake. Lift the edges of the cake to allow the topping to soak in. Sprinkle coconut or slivered toasted almonds on top.

Enjoy!

Turkish Delight with Almonds
Badam Halwa
By Surya

Ingredients:
1-¼ cups tapioca flour
2-½ cups water
½ pound slivered almonds
¼ cup pistachio pieces
2 cups sugar
½ teaspoon powdered yellow food color
1 teaspoon freshly ground cardamom seeds
¼ teaspoon saffron strands
¼ teaspoon lemon juice
¾ cup ghee (clarified butter)

Directions:
In a microwave-safe bowl, mix tapioca flour and water.
Add the rest of the ingredients except the ghee.
Add the ghee and mix well.
Cook in microwave at full strength for 10 minutes.*
Remove and stir well.
Reheat for 7 minutes and stir well.
Repeat this 3 to 4 times.
Halwa is ready when it is transparent and does not stick to the sides of the bowl.

Serve with coffee.   Delicious!

_____
*Cooking times may vary according to the voltage of the microwave. Recipe timed on 500 voltage.

Barfi
By Surya

Barfi is a dense, milk-based confectionery. Preparation time: 12 minutes.

Ingredients:
2 cups full cream milk powder
1-¼ cup double cream or heavy whipped cream
14-ounce can of condensed milk
½ cup finely chopped skinless pistachios

Directions:
Mix all the ingredients (except the nuts) in a rectangular, microwave-safe bowl and whisk till smooth.
Cook for 6 minutes on full voltage. Watch the dish carefully, and if the mixture looks like it might boil over, stop immediately and wait for 8-10 seconds. Start again and run for the 6 minutes, total.
Take the dish out of the microwave and stir well to break all lumps (lumps are the milk solids that are beginning to form due to the cooking).
Put the dish back in the microwave and set again on High for 6 minutes. Watch for the initial minute and then allow to continue cooking.
Remove from the microwave.
Sprinkle chopped nuts on the Barfi and let it rest for 10 minutes.
Cut into 2—2-1/2-inch **squares. Serve immediately or after cooling to room temperature.**

Recipe for Peace

Ya Salaam, the Source of Peace and Perfection,
The Bringer and Provider of Security and Well-Being.

Rising Beyond the Words
Language and Gender

All vibration carries power. The symbolism of language, the use of sound for specific meaning, has the effect of creating and defining our universal reality. We have lived under the accentuation of the patriarchal paradigm over the last several thousand years.

Language is power. It can be a source of enslavement; it can be a source of liberation. We affirm God as both male and female, mother and father, and beyond sexual definition and our limited understanding.

The continual repetition over millennia and through successive generations of God, defined as masculine only, delivers the hypnotic message that God is limited. These beliefs are established on a primal subconscious level, some suggest prior to birth, within the womb as the fetus develops, with other psychologists suggesting this imprinting begins with the first breath. Experiment with the remembrance of God the Mother and also God as Mystery, beyond any gender definition.

Freedom to Tell Our Stories

Let us live our essential story rather than our ideal story, a human story, releasing the idealized story that continues to enslave women and causes us to strive unrealistically. As we witness and learn one another's stories, we provide keys to unlocking ourselves from stereotypes that are used to control our behavior. The time is now, to engage actively in recovery of our stories from the ancient past, the now and the current future.

Peace in the Heart

Place yourself in a comfortable sitting position, spine erect, yet relaxed. If sitting on the floor, consider a pillow or blanket under the base of the spine, so the hips are slightly above the knees.

Breathe in Peace, Breathe out Peace.

Use the phrase, Ya Salaam, on the inhale, repeat the phrase on the exhale. The phrase can be audibly spoken, or spoken in the inner realm. When one is learning the practice, saying the phrase can help to cultivate focus of the mind on peace.

Salaam.

Let the rhythm of the inhalation be balanced with the exhalation. Count four as you inhale, count four on the exhale. Let the count be slow and even—peaceful.

Walk with attention, Breathe in Peace, Breathe out Peace.

Ya Salaam—inhale, *Ya Salaam*—exhale.

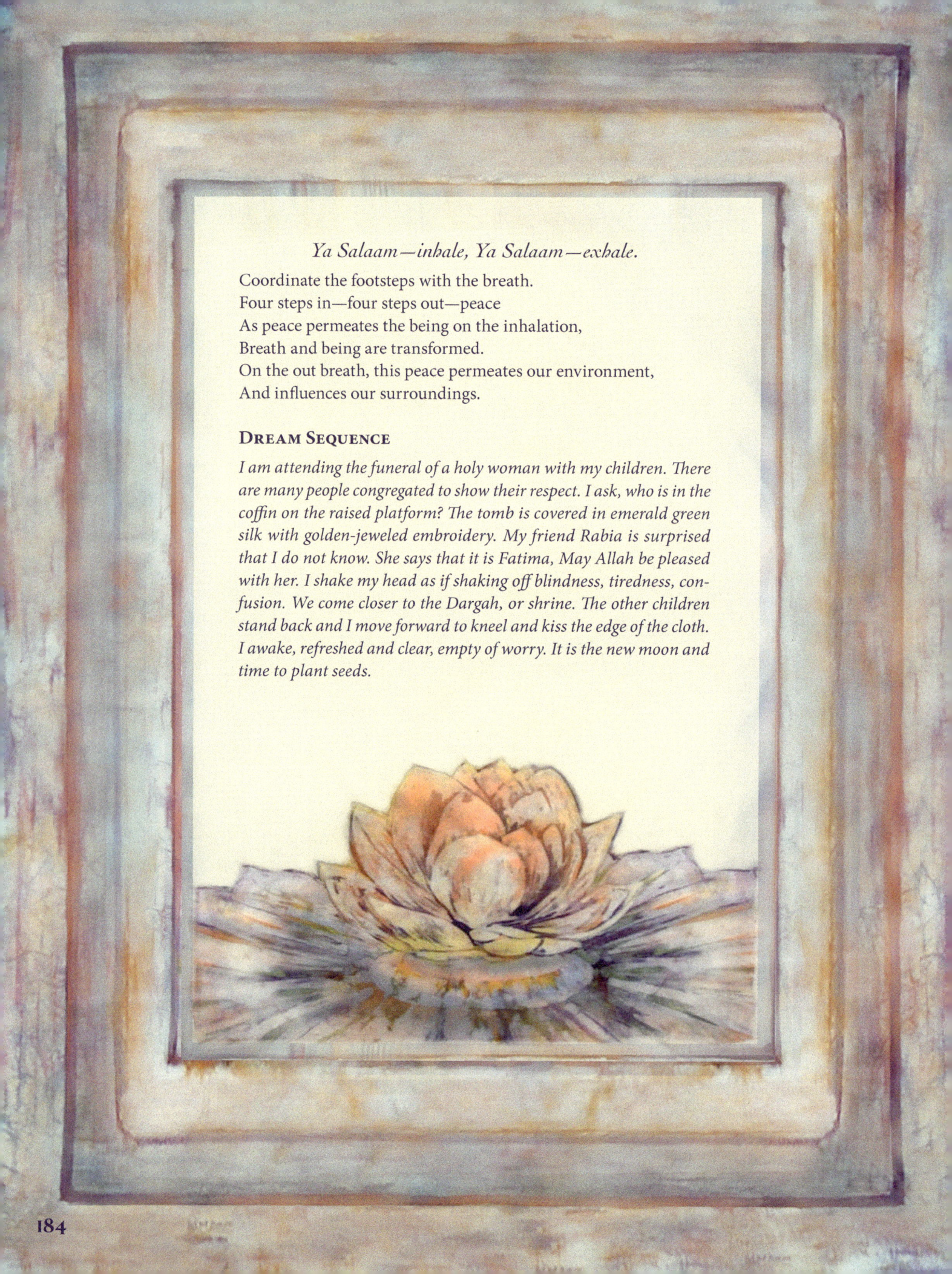

Coordinate the footsteps with the breath.
Four steps in—four steps out—peace
As peace permeates the being on the inhalation,
Breath and being are transformed.
On the out breath, this peace permeates our environment,
And influences our surroundings.

Dream Sequence

I am attending the funeral of a holy woman with my children. There are many people congregated to show their respect. I ask, who is in the coffin on the raised platform? The tomb is covered in emerald green silk with golden-jeweled embroidery. My friend Rabia is surprised that I do not know. She says that it is Fatima, May Allah be pleased with her. I shake my head as if shaking off blindness, tiredness, confusion. We come closer to the Dargah, or shrine. The other children stand back and I move forward to kneel and kiss the edge of the cloth. I awake, refreshed and clear, empty of worry. It is the new moon and time to plant seeds.

SPREADING PEACE

To the four directions—*Ya Salaam*

Peace to the East
Peace to the West
Peace to the South
Peace to the North

To the inner family—*Ya Salaam*

Peace to the female self
Peace to the male self
Peace to the inner child

To the natural world—*Ya Salaam*

Peace to the rocks
Peace to the vegetables, fruits and seeds
Peace to fish and birds and animals
Peace to humans
Peace to angels

Ya Salaam—peace, peace, peace

Walk with peace on the breath

As'Salaam Aleikhum—May peace be with you

Thoughts from the Illustrator

Illustrating *Sacred Voices* has been a journey on many levels, with all of the twists and turns of the sacred quest of mythology. Developing the imagery became an invitation to deepen my own spiritual practice and to consider the practices and lives of women from throughout the world. As the project has unfolded, I have felt a strengthening of my connection with the thread of wisdom that has connected those on the path of mysticism since time began, and a furthering of my understanding of the unique place that women have in the development of that path as expressed through Islam. These women's deep commitment to spiritual practice, and to living a life of service, expressing compassion for others, has been a profound inspiration in my own life.

The seed for this project was planted several years ago during a retreat led by Mariam Baker. During shared prayers and practices, I was surprised by a flash of insight; that Mariam and I were to work on a book project together. When we spoke later that day she told me about the *Sacred Voices* project. Since that first discussion, she and I have met at homes and retreat centers all over the country, and have developed a deep symbiotic creative collaboration as the project has continued to unfold.

Creating imagery to accompany Mariam's rich text has been a challenge and a gift. The physical expression of women from these traditions is as limitless as the women themselves, with far more variety than can be represented in these pages or illustrated with any image or group of images. These depictions are intended to symbolically represent all women. It is my hope that the reader's imagination will find the archetype of the Everywoman within these pages. My wish is that this artwork can speak, in some way, to that place of presence beyond language, and can touch that aspect of the human condition that is far beyond words and that cannot be illustrated by any single impression.

To create the artwork I have used primarily the ancient fiber art medium of batik wax resist applied to a pima cotton fabric, with additional drawings and digital applications. The process of working on *Sacred Voices* has pushed me to grow as both an artist and designer, and has opened my mind to the many possibilities of combining traditional media with digital applications. In that regard, the road of this journey continues to stretch far ahead into the distance, with many new possibilities revealed as each idea and creative experiment unfolds.

. In this unprecedented time upon our planet, I feel deeply inspired to work tirelessly for peace, both inner and outer, to discover what is unique and special in each of my fellow humans, and to focus on what can unite us within our variety of expression. This work for peace, in my understanding, must be carried out on many fronts; through the creation of artwork and the sharing of music; by teaching, and learning from, the generation that will follow; by deeply listening to views other than my own; or by simply sharing a meal or a smile with someone not yet known.

If each person acts as they are inspired to support unity and understanding, then there is potential for the planet to heal and for humanity to thrive. This is a lofty ideal, but one that brings joy to life, and is the guiding light behind these illustrations.

When Mariam and I originally set out on this journey we had no idea where we would go, as we ventured into the unknown territory that is inherent to the creative process. Bringing this phase of our pilgrimage to completion, I feel both humbled and inspired.

May the images in these pages be seeds of peace that flower and bloom far beyond what I can imagine and may the reader find those seeds within themselves.

Toward the One,
  Cynthia Dollard

Bibliography

Abu 'Abd ar-Rahman as-Sulami. *Early Sufi Women: Dhikr an-Niswa al-Muta 'abbidat as Sufiyyat.* Translated by Rkia E. Cornell. Louisville, KY: Fons Vitae, 1999.

Abu-Lughod, Lila. "A Tale of Two Pregnancies." In *Women Writing Culture.* Edited by Ruth Behar and Deborah A. Gordon. Berkeley: University of California Press, 1995.

Ahmed, Akbar S. *Islam Today: A Short Introduction to the Muslim World.* New York: I. B. Tauris, 1999.

Al-Ghazali, Abu Hamid Muhammad. *The Ninety-Nine Beautiful Names of God: Al-Maqsad Al-Asn Fi Sharh Asma Allah Al-Husna.* Translated by David B. Burrell and Nazih Daher. Cambridge The Islamic Texts Society, 1992.

Al-Hariri-Wendel, Tanja. *Symbols of Islam.* New York: Sterling, 2002.

Al-Shaykh, Hanan. *I Sweep the Sun off Rooftops.* Translated by Catherine Cobham. New York: Anchor, 1994.

———. *The Story of Zahra.* Translated by Peter Ford. New York: Anchor, 1994.

———. *Women of Sand and Myrrh.* Translated by Catherine Cobham. New York: Anchor, 1989.

Ali, Abdullah Yusuf, trans. *The Holy Qur'an.* Vols. I and II. A more accessible edition would be the 5th edition (all one vol.) from Wordsworth Editions, Hertfordshire, UK.

Almaas, A. H. *Diamond Heart: Elements of the Real in Man.* Berkeley: Diamond Books, 1987.

Armstrong, Karen. *Islam: A Short History.* New York: Chronicle Books, 2000.

———. *Muhammad: A Biography of the Prophet.* New York: Harper, 1992.

Asad, Muhammad, ed., trans. *The Message of The Quran.* Gibraltar: Dar Al-Andalus, 1980. Or: Watsonville, CA: The Book Foundation, 2008.

Attar, Farid Ud-din. *Conference of the Birds.* Translated by C.S. Nott. New York: Samuel Weiser, 1967.

Bakhtiar, Laleh. *Ramadan: Motivating Believers to Action: An Interfaith Perspective.* Chicago: Kazi Publications, 1995.

———. *Sufi: Expressions of the Mystic Quest.* New York: Tha—mes and Hudson, 1976.

———. *The Sublime Quran.* Chicago: Kazi Publishers, 1997.

Barks, Coleman. *The Essential Rumi*. San Francisco: Harper, 1995.

———, and Michael Green. *The Illuminated Prayer: The Five-Times Prayer of the Sufis*. New York: Ballantine Publishing Group, 2000.

Barlas, Asma. *Believing Women in Islam: Unreading Patriarchal Interpretations of the Qur'an*. Austin: University of Texas Press, 2002.

Brooks, Geraldine. *Nine Parts of Desire: The Hidden World of Islamic Women*. New York: Anchor Books, 1995.

Chebel, Malek. *Symbols of Islam*. New York: Assouline Publishing, 2000.

Chisti, Saadia Khawar Khan. "Female Spirituality in Islam" in *Islamic Spirituality*. Edited by Seyyed Hossein Nasr. New York: Crossroad, 1987.

Corbin, Henry. *Creative Imagination In The Sufism of Ibn 'Arabi*. Translated by Ralph Manheim. Princeton: Princeton University Press, 1969.

Douglas-Klotz, Neil. *Desert Wisdom: Sacred Middle Eastern Writings from the Goddess through the Sufis*. New York: Harpercollins, 1995.

El Saadawi, Nawal. *God Dies by the Nile*. Translated by Sherif Hetata. London: Zed Books, 1985.

———. *The Innocence of the Devil*, translated by Sherif Hetata. Berkeley: University of California Press, 1998.

———. *Walking through Fire:* A Life of Nawal El Saadawi, introduction by Sherif Hetata. London: Zed Books, 2002.

Fernea, Elizabeth Warnock. *Guests of the Sheik: An Ethnography of an Iraqi Village*. New York: Anchor Books, 1965.

———, and Basima Qattan Bezirgan. *Middle Eastern Muslim Women Speak*. Austin: University of Texas Press, 1977.

Frager, Robert. *The Wisdom of Islam: A Practical Guide to the Wisdom of Islamic Belief*. New York: Barrons, 2002.

Friedlander, Ira. *The Whirling Dervishes*. New York: Collier Books, 1975.

Friedlander, Shems, with al-Hajj Shaikh Muzaffereddin. *Ninety-Nine Names of Allah*. New York: Harper Colophon Books, 1978.

Fuller, Jean Overton. *Noor-un-nisa Inayat Khan*. Rotterdam: East-West Publications Fonds, N.V., 1971.

Goodwin, Jan. *Price of Honor: Muslim Women Lift the Veil of Silence on the Islamic World.* New York: Penguin, 1994.

Halaby, Laila. *West of the Jordan.* Boston: Beacon Press. 2003.

Hazleton, Lesley. *The first Muslim: The Story of Muhammad.* New York: Riverhead Books, 2013.

Helminski, Camille Adams, ed. *Women of Sufism: A Hidden Treasure, Writings and Stories of Mystic Poets, Scholars and Saints.* Boston: Shambala, 2003.

Hixon, Lex Nur Al Jerrahi. *Atom From The Sun Of Knowledge.* Westport, CT: Pir Publications, 1993.

Hirshfield, Jane, ed. *Women in Praise of the Sacred.* New York: Harper Perennial, 1995.

Khalidi, Tarif, trans. *The Muslim Jesus: Sayings and Stories in Islamic Literature.* Cambridge: Harvard University Press, 2001.

Khan, Dede. *Birth Stories of the Prophets.* London: East-West Publications, 1978.

Khan, Noor Inayat. *Twenty Jataka Tales.* The Hague: East-West Publications, 1975.

Kimball, Michelle R., and Barbara R. von Schlegell. *Muslim Women throughout the World: A Bibliography.* Boulder, CO: Lynne Rienner Publishers, 1997.

Kohl, James Vaughn, Robert T. Francoeur, and Marilyn A. Fithian. *The Scent of Eros: Mysteries of Odor in Human Sexuality.* New York: Continuum, 1995.

Lamb, Christina. *The Sewing Circles of Herat: A Personal Voyage through Afghanistan.* New York: Harper Collins, 2002.

Lewis, Bernard. *The World of Islam: Faith, People, Culture.* London: Thames and Hudson, 1976.

Lings, Martin. *Muhammad: His Life Based on the Earliest Sources.* Rochester, VT: Inner Traditions International, 1983.

Mernissi, Fatima. *Beyond the Veil: Male-Female Dynamics in a Modern Muslim Society.* Bloomington: Indiana University Press, 1987.

———. *The Veil and the Male Elite: A Feminist Interpretation of Women's Rights in Islam*, translated by Mary Jo Lakeland. Cambridge: Perseus Books, 1991.

Mijares, Sharon, Aliaa Rafea, and Nahid Angha, eds. *A Force Such As the World Has Never Known: Women Creating Change.* Toronto: Inanna Publications, 2013.

Miller, John, and Aaron Kenedi, eds. *Inside Islam: The Faith, the People and the Conflicts of the World's Fastest Growing Religion.* New York: Marlowe & Company, 2002.

Muhaiyaddeen, M. R. Bawa. *Asma'ul Husna—The Ninety Nine Beautiful Names of Allah.* Philadelphia: The Fellowship Press, 1979.

Muhammad, Hisham Kabbani, and Laleh Bakhtiar. Encyclopedia of Muhammad's Women Companions. Chicago: Gazi Publications, 1998.

Murata, Sachiko. *The Tao of Islam: A Sourcebook on Gender Relationships in Islamic Thought.* Albany: State University Press of New York, 1992.

Nafisi, Azar. *Reading Lolita in Tehran: A Memoir in Books.* New York: Random House, 2003.

Nasr, Seyyed Hossein. *Islamic Spirituality: Foundations.* New York: Crossroad, 1997.

———. *The Heart of Islam: Enduring Values for Humanity.* San Francisco: Harper, 2002.

Netton, Ian Richard. *A Popular Dictionary of Islam.* Chicago: NTC/ Contemporary Publishing Group, 1997.

Newby, Gordon D. *Concise Encyclopedia of Islam.* Oxford: Oneworld, 2002.

Nicholson, Reynold A., ed. and trans. *The Mathnawi of Jalalu'ddin Rumi.* Vols. 1-6. Cambridge: Gibb Memorial Trust, 1982.

———. *The Mystics of Islam (Arkana).* London: Penguin, 1975.

Noor, Queen. *Leap of Faith: Memoirs of an Unexpected Life.* New York: Miramax Books, 2003.

Nurbakhsh, Javad. *Sufi Women.* New York: Khaniqahi Nimatullahi Publications, 1983.

Nye, Shihab Naomi. *19 Varieties of Gazelle: Poems of the Middle East.* New York: Greenwillow Books, 2002.

Pickthall, Muhammad Marmaduke, trans. *The Glorious Qur'an.* New York: Tahrike Tarsile Qur'an, 2001.

Quasem, Muhammad Abul. *The Recitation and Interpretation of the Qur'an: Al-Ghazali's Theory.* London: Kegan Paul, 1982.

Rahnema, Zeinolabedin. *Payambar: The Messenger.* Translated from Persian by J. P. Elwell-Sutton. Lahore, Pakistan: Sh. Muhammad Ashraf, 1970.

Reinhertz, Shakina. *Women Called to the Path Of Rumi: The Way of the Whirling Dervishes.* Prescott, AZ: Hohm Press, 2001.

Sabbagh, Suha, ed. *Arab Women: Between Defiance and Restraint.* New York: Olive Branch Press, 1996.

Salahi, Adil. Muhammad, *Man and Prophet: A Complete Study of the Life of the Prophet of Islam.* Dorset: Element Books, 1995.

Seguy, Marie-Rose. *The Miraculous Journey of Mahomet: Miraj Nameh.* New York: Georges Braziller, 1977.

Smith, Margaret. *Rabi'a the Mystic A.D. 717-801 and Her Fellow Saints in Islam.* San Francisco: Rainbow Bridge, 1977.

Stowasser, Barbara Freyer. *Women in the Qur'an, Traditions, and Interpretation.* Oxford: Oxford University Press, 1994.

Turkmen, Erkan. *The Essence of Rumi's Masnevi: Including His Life and Works.* Konya, Turkey: Misket, 1992.

Tweedie, Irina. *Daughter of Fire: A Diary of a Spiritual Training with a Sufi Master.* Grass Valley CA: Blue Dolphin, 1986.

Upton, Charles, trans. *Doorkeeper of the Heart, Versions of Rabi'a.* Putney, VT: Threshold Books, 1988.

Van de Weyer, Robert. *366 Readings From Islam.* Cleveland: The Pilgrim Press, 2000.

Wadud, Amina. *Qur'an and Woman: Rereading the Sacred Text from a Woman's Perspective.* New York: Oxford University Press, 1999.

Yuksel, Edip, trans., with Layth Saleh al-Shaiban and Martha Schulte-Nafeh. *Quran: A Reformist Translation.* QRT 2010 edition Brainbow Press. (Non-sexist, non-sectarian version.)

JOURNALS AND OTHER INTERNET RESOURCES:
There are many excellent websites helpful to the study of Islam. Here are a few.

Angha, Seyedeh Nahid, founder. *Sufi Women Organization: International Humanitarian Organization Promoting Universal Human Rights.* http://sufiwomen.org

Cornell University. *Middle East & Islamic Studies Collection.* www.library.cornell.edu/colldev/mideast

Godlas, Alan. *Islam and Islamic Studies Resources: For Studying Islam and the Diverse Perspectives of Muslims.* http://islam.uga.edu

Hammoude, Noora and Safiya Godlas, founders. *IMAN: International Muslimah Artists Network.* www.imanworld.org

Helie-Lucas, Marieme, founder. *Women Living Under Muslim Laws.* http://www.wluml.org

Morgan, Robin, president. *The Sisterhood is Global Institute: The Think Tank of International Feminism.* http://sigi.org

Mujahid, Abdul Malik, president. *Sound Vision: Islamic Information and Products.* www.soundvision.com

Muslim Women's League. www.mwlusa.org

Nizami, Farhan Ahmad, ed. *Journal of Islamic Studies.* http://jis.oxfordjournals.org/

Rahman, Aisha, exec. director. *KARAMAH: Muslim Women Lawyers for Human Rights.* http://karamah.org

Taylor, Tayyibah, publisher and ed. *Azizah: A Magazine for Contemporary Muslim Women.* www.azizahmagazine.com

University of London School of Oriental and African Studies. *Centre of Islamic and Middle Eastern Law.* https://www.soas.ac.uk/cimel/

Films and Video:

Gardner, Rob, producer and director. *Enemy of the Reich: The Noor Inayat Khan Story*, Motion picture. United States: UPF (Unity Productions Foundation), 2014. www.enemyofthereich.com

Itier, Emmanuel, director, and Sharon Stone, producer. *Femme: The Movie.* United States: Vision Films, 2014. https://femmethemovie.com

Washburn, David, producer. *An American Mosque* [Motion picture]. United States: San Francisco Film Society, 2014. www.anamericanmosque.com

Glossary

Abd'Allah: Abd' is an Arabic word meaning slave or servant, and since surrender to Allah is central to Islam, many people are named Abd'Allah, (Abdullah) servant of God or slave of God.

al-Amin: The name of the 6th Abbasid Caliph who succeeded his father, Harun al-Rashid in the year 809 AD until he was deposed and killed by his brother al-Ma'mun. "Abbasid" refers to the dynasty descended from the Prophet's uncle al-Abbas, which ruled the Middle East from 750 AD until the Mongol Invasion of 1258.

Alhamdulillah: An Arabic expression meaning "Praise God," used in the same way as Hallelujah in English, or, "All praise and thanks to God."

Ansar: "Helpers." Refers to those citizens of Medina who helped the Prophet and his companions when they came to Medina from Mecca.

As-salaam Alaikum: A greeting —"Peace be with you." The response is "Wa alaikum as salaam," "And upon you be peace."

Baraka: Blessing, grace, Divine presence, a spiritual power which can be felt in the presence of certain spiritual teachers, objects and tombs of saints, which permeates the universe and draws people toward God.

Burqa: From a Persian word, purdah, meaning curtain and veil. A cloth which envelops the entire body and veils the face with a partly transparent rectangular piece of cloth.
In some styles the cloth is attached at one side so that the eyes can be seen.

Chador: In the Farsi language, chador means "tent," which describes the head to toe coverage of the chador garment worn by women of Iran. This is a large cloth, usually black or a drab color, which covers the body leaving only the face visible and sometimes covers part of the face. Women wear the chador to work or social gatherings. In some cities in Iran a lighter chador is worn, which is white with a colorful floral print.

Darga: Shrine built over the tomb of a Sufi saint or dervish.

al-Fatiha: The opening sura (chapter) of the Quran, recited all over the world as a prayer.

Fikr: Breathing rhythmically while concentrating on the zikr phrase, or one of the ninety- nine beautiful names of Allah, on each inhale or exhale.

ya Ghani: One of the ninety-nine beautiful names of Allah which means the One who is self-sufficient, who is satisfied and has no need of anything. It is a flowing forth of God's boundless treasure to all beings.

Ghusl: A full body washing required in Islam if an adult loses body cleanliness. This is done before the usual ritual ablutions before rituals and prayers, which is called wudu.

Hadith: A saying of the Prophet of Islam.

Hajj: The fifth Pillar of Islam is pilgrimage to Mecca at least once in one's life, to visit the house of God, called the Kaaba, in a ritual manner at a certain time of year. Completing the pilgrimage gives the pilgrim total forgiveness of sins.

Haqq: Truth; reality.

Haram: Forbidden, by Islamic law.

Hijab: Modest dress, such as the veil and headscarf, worn by Muslim women.

Iblis: In Islam the Devil is called Iblis or Shaitan, and described as a jinni (djinn) who was full of hubris and refused to bow to Adam.

Ibrahim: The Arabic name of Abraham in the Old Testament, who is regarded in Islam as a prophet and messenger of God.

Inshallah: If God wills.

Ishq: Love; passion.

Ismail: The Arabic name for the first son of Abraham in the Bible and Quran. Translated as "God has heard it," referring to Abraham and Sarah's desire to have a child. Ishmael (English) was born of Abraham's marriage to Sarah's handmaiden Hagar, and he became the patriarch of the Ishmaelites.

Jamatkhana: The name given to their mosque by followers of the Ismaili sect within Islam.

Jannah: An eternal paradise, the Garden.

ya Karim: The Generous, a name of God.

La ilaha illAllah: The Arabic phrase la ilaha illAllah is one of major pillars of the Muslim faith. This sacred phrase is a part of the basic Muslim statement of faith, it is a part of the call to prayer that echoes across the countryside five times a day throughout the Muslim world, and it is chanted at virtually every Sufi gathering. Translated as, "There is no god but God."

La Ilaha iIlallah Hu, Muhammadur Rasulullah: "Nothing exists except God"; God is within all things, omnipresent, and Muhammad is the Rasul (Prophet, Messenger) of God."

Maqluba: Literally, "upside down," a traditional dish of the Arabic Levant, of meat, rice, and vegetables. It usually is cooked in a pan with the tomatoes on the bottom, and flipped upside down before serving, so it is bright red on top from the tomatoes.

Mashallah: An Arabic phrase used to show appreciation, respect and sometimes translated loosely as "God willed it." Mashallah is used to express joy at good news.

Mihrab: Prayer niche.

Mu'min: An Arabic Islamic term which means "believer"; one whose faith and trust is firmly established in their heart, and submits to the will of Allah.

Mureed: Student on the path; "committed one."

Musa: The prophet Moses.

Nafs: The self, the soul or the ego.

Nifaas: Post-natal bleeding.

Niyyah: The intention that lies behind the act. One's intention is considered the most important part of performing ritual prayer.

Noor: Light.

Nuri: An Arabic female name meaning "shining."

Rasul: Messenger of God. Used to describe Muhammad and other prophets from the scriptures.

ya Rezaq: Sustainer, Provider, Giver of endless gifts of compassion and love, one of the names of God.

Ruh: Spirit or soul; the light ray of God which goes in and out with the breath, the part of us which does not die.

Ruh Allah: Spirit of God, a title used in the Quran when describing Jesus.

Salam u Salam: Peace. Salam is the preferred greeting when arriving and also when leaving. As-salaam Alaikum, "Peace be with you," is often said. Now often shortened to AsA or SMS by people texting.

Salat: The five times a day ritual prayers which are obligatory for Muslims, the second Pillar of Islam.

Sema: Ceremony of Listening; zikr of the Turn as performed by Mevlevi Sufis.

Semazen: One who participates (turns) in the Sema.

Shahada: Witness. The central Islamic testimony of truth: "There is no God but God and Muhammad is his prophet. The first Pillar of Islam.

Shebi Arus: The Wedding Night—the commemoration of Rumi's passing.

Sifat-i-Allah, Asma'ul Husna: Qualities or attributes of God, or The ninety-nine Beautiful names of God.

Sohbet: Company, conversation. In Sufism it is an intimate conversation between a teacher and students on spiritual topics.

Sunna: The traditional portion of Muslim law based on Muhammad's words or acts, accepted (together with the Koran) as authoritative by Muslims and followed particularly by Sunni Muslims.

Sura: A chapter or verse of the Quran.

Tahara: The concept of cleanliness. Muslims are required to maintain cleanliness of the body and clothes and surroundings and always perform wudu before prayers and also ghusl if necessary. Cleanliness also includes cleaning the teeth.

Tariqat: The Sufi doctrine or path of spiritual learning.

Tasbih: Prayer beads.

Tawhid: "Asserting Oneness" refers to the nature of God, that God is a unity not composed of parts, and a universal God, not a local or tribal God This monotheism is central to Islam. To Muslim scholars the science of Tawhid is a systematic theology about God, and in the terminology of mystics, the Sufis, Tawhid emphasizes that all is divine, and there is no absolute existence besides that of God, who can be reached through direct religious experience.

Tazkiah: Purification of the soul through self-discipline, to transform the nafs (ego).

Turbe: Tomb, specifically of Mevlana.

Urs: Wedding. The anniversary of the death of a Sufi saint, which the Sufis consider the return to union with God, the Beloved. In South Asia this anniversary is celebrated with religious music called qawwali.

ya Wahhab: The Bestower; the great Giver of gifts, a name of God.

Wazifa: A practice of evoking the qualities of the Divine by reciting one or more of the beautiful names of God.

Wudhu: Ritual ablutions before prayers.

Zakat: An obligatory alms tax, or annual donation of two-and-a-half percent of one's savings to the poor. This is the third Pillar of Islam, which is understood as purifying the soul of greed and selfishness.

Zikr: (dhikr) Remembrance of Allah: The practice of chanting the name of God or the zikr phrase, "La ilaha illallah."

The Journey Continues

Mariam Baker is a senior teacher of Sufi Ruhaniat International, a leader in the Dances of Universal Peace since 1974, and a senior teacher of the Mevlevi Order of America. She is the former director of Theater of Healing, and author of *Woman as Divine, Tales of the Goddess*, a book illuminating the divine feminine.

Mariam focuses on bringing to light the powerful and influential impact that women have had and continue to have in the world's religions and society. At this crucial time on our planet and in our human family, she emphasizes access to the *Womb-am Soul* for all of us, emphasizing the Heart of Compassion and Mercy for all Life.

Through her retreats and workshops across the globe, Mariam brings together community and students from a diverse range of ethnicities, nationalities and religions, honoring and exploring the uniqueness of each, while encouraging an emphasis on unity.

Mariam is the Executive Director of the SoulWork Foundation, a StarBirthing initiator, a passionate gardener, and a mother of five. She is a dedicated student of embodied spirituality, which she practices in her daily life. For more information, visit MariamBaker.org.
Photograph: Stephanie Mohan, *Creative Portraiture.*

Cynthia Dollard, **MFA**, is an artist, art professor, and community arts organizer. She works in a variety of media, both two- and three-dimensional, and actively seeks creative collaboration whenever possible. Cynthia has participated in the Sufi tradtiion most of her life. This practice has supported her ongoing work with people from a wide variety of backgrounds and beliefs, finding common ground through creative expression.

The artist first learned the medium of batik wax resist, used for the illustrations in this book, at the age of 12. Her painterly style of batik has remained a constant throughout her artistic life, and her work has been displayed at venues across the country.

Cynthia also teaches Qi Gong and Tai Chi. She believes that coordinating breath, body and intention is the key to successful creative endeavors, and she seeks to embody this belief in her daily life. She is the director of a community arts organization that hosts music festivals and other cutural events in her rural mountain community. "When people of all backgrounds find common ground with music, art, and story telling, the world can be transformed."

The belief in a shared humanity through creative expression is the common element that unifies all of Cynthia's activities, and is a primary inspiration for this project. To see more of the artist's work, visit: anytimearts.com.
Photograph: David Basse

CPSIA information can be obtained
at www.ICGtesting.com
Printed in the USA
LVHW071650170119
604287LV00020B/370/P

9 781457 554834